Crash Cultures

modernity, mediation and the material

Edited by Jane Arthurs and Iain Grant

intellect™
Bristol, UK
Portland, OR, USA

Reprinted in Hardback in Great Britain in 2003 by
Intellect Books, PO Box 862, Bristol BS99 1DE, UK

Published in Hardback in USA in 2003 by
Intellect Books, ISBS, 5824 N.E. Hassalo St, Portland, Oregon 97213-3644, USA

Consulting Editor:	Robin Beecroft
Copy Editor:	Peter Young
Cover Photography and Design:	Becky Goddard
Typesetting:	*Macstyle Ltd*, Scarborough, N. Yorkshire
Printing and Binding:	The Cromwell Press, Wiltshire

A catalogue record for this book is available from the British Library

ISBN 1-84150-071-2

Contents

Contributors

Carmen Alfonso, PhD student in the Department of Spanish, Birkbeck College, London.

Jane Arthurs, School of Cultural Studies, University of the West of England, Bristol.

Anne Beezer, School of Cultural Studies, University of the West of England, Bristol (retired).

Fred Botting, Department of English, Keele University.

Gerry Carlin, Department of English, University of Wolverhampton.

Iain Grant, School of Cultural Studies, University of the West of England, Bristol.

William Greenslade, School of Literary Studies, University of the West of England, Bristol..

Jean Grimshaw, School of Cultural Studies, University of the West of England, Bristol (retired).

Rebecca Goddard, School of Cultural Studies, University of the West of England, Bristol.

Michelle Henning, School of Cultural Studies, University of the West of England, Bristol.

Ben Highmore, School of Cultural Studies, University of the West of England, Bristol.

Harjit Kaur Khaira, Department of English in Education, University of Warwick.

Nils Lindahl-Elliot, School of Cultural Studies, University of the West of England, Bristol.

David Roden, School of Cultural Studies, University of the West of England, Bristol.

SHaH (Seminar for Hypertheory and Heterology) is based at the Institute for Cultural Research, University of Lancaster . Contributing members were Bruce Bennett, Fred Botting, Jonathan Munby, Paolo Palladino, Imogen Tyler, Scott Wilson.

Scott Wilson, Institute for Cultural Research, Lancaster University.

1 Introduction

Jane Arthurs and Iain Grant

At every moment of every day there is a crash event, affecting everything: transportation, economics, politics, computing, bodies, brains, cups and plates, birds, agriculture, chemistry, health, banking, manufacturing and so on, without end. Despite being insured, insulated by method, knowledge, prediction, risk analysis and technology against accidents, we are nevertheless permanently avoiding them. Every crash is followed by calls for legislation: 'it must never happen again' – and yet it always does. As roads and airways congest to the point of stagnation, we proclaim the miracle of modern safety regimes, while remaining haunted by the ghosts of disasters waiting to happen. As technologies advance, so catastrophe looms larger, threatening fiscal and economic, as well as physical systems. But the crash brings it all back home. From the crumpled remains of a Mercedes in Paris to the collapse of the World Trade Centre in New York; from Black Monday on the money markets to Chernobyl's meltdown; from *Crash* to *Titanic:* from James Dean and Jayne Mansfield to Warhol and Ballard – crashes are individuated, named, in order to prevent the sense that our history, far from being one of steady progress, is in fact an incremental accumulation of crashes. It preserves us from the fear of generalised catastrophe. All the better, therefore, should the victims be famous, and all the worse if, as when a Boeing hit an Amsterdam Tower block, effacing its illegal immigrant inhabitants, they remain anonymous. Every crash can be located on a scale in accordance with the celebrity or anonymity of its victims.

In analytic terms, every crash reminds us that we have stepped over the line separating the benignly abstract from the horribly concrete, from 'risk society' to crash cultures. How are we to study crashes, what method are we to use to ensure we absorb all their impact? Crashes take place where method goes awol and control fails (at least our control), where prediction runs up against its own inadequacies. Accident investigators, scouring fresh craters for oracular black boxes, regularly pale in the face of the profusion of fragmentary and merely suggestive evidence. The crash resists interpretation – not least because it is an event, with singular dates and places, shot through with time.

The taking place of events, their specificity, poses certain problems for their study. What might be the theoretical or practical value of conclusions reached on the basis of something so singular as an event? By definition, the conditions defining the event could not be repeated, revoking in advance the possibility of generalising from any such conclusions. Nor do events reach conclusions; they emerge and dissipate, ramify and connect, impact and explode. With events, the real does not wait to be prejudged or interpreted; rather it impacts on our senses, our emotions, our bodies – creating a material effect that only in time will be reduced and shaped by discourse. The use of the crash as a starting point in these essays is not as a scientific, forensic examination of their causes and effects. We approach the crash as a symbolic *and* material event that can produce insights about the experience of living in a modern, technologically saturated world. It is through these events that we can intimate the force of our conventionalised ways of seeing and being: the discursive management of the unruly materiality of everyday life. It also draws attention to the interrelations between inanimate machines and living bodies – the relations of dominance and submission in industrial societies, or the convergence between them that in cyberculture poses new challenges to the emancipatory politics of Marxism and feminism.

The essays collected here do not aim to provide a single perspective. Rather they are a convergence of disparate elements whose effect on the reader should be to open any number of connecting routes. Yet there are recurring foci of attention that are particular to the time and place of their production. In part, this is a matter of public history – we wrote in the aftermath of particular events in Britain – Princess Diana's car crash, the controversy over Cronenberg's film of Ballard's *Crash*, the disasters on the railways at Paddington and Hatfield, the millennium computer bug that threatened systems breakdown, but before the events of September 11th in New York. In part it is contingent on disciplinary discourses shaping our concerns – whether they be philosophical, cultural or film studies – but mediated through a series of discussions, convened by Ben Highmore at UWE in 1998, known as the 'Everyday Life' group (augmented later by other contributors who shared our interest in this project).

These discussions centred on a number of related theoretical questions, namely: how can we overcome the gap between the abstractions of theory and the lived experience of everyday life, between concepts and the materiality of the world of objects? In terms of culture, what relation do the aesthetic texts of the 20th century have to the historical conditions of modernity? Or philosophically, how can the relationship between representation and the real be conceptualised? And how do the entrenched dualities of Enlightenment thinking constrain both how we pose and answer these questions? Starting from de Certeau's *The Practices of Everyday Life* (1984), we drew on Benjamin and Barthes, Haraway and Baudrillard, Deleuze and De Landa, Freud and Lacan, Elias and Foucault, Adorno and Iragaray. We took as our object the collected fragments of a 'crash archive' in the spirit of an ethnographic method that eschewed totalizing ambitions. The crash offered a way to think through the problematic to the extent that it resists representation, being instead an experiential moment in history when time and space are collapsed and reconfigured. The crash seems knowable only through its anticipation and its effects, the time before and the time after.

The results are (inevitably) partial but, we hope, will provoke new thinking. Each essay has its own thesis, but first, here, we briefly explore some of the shared concerns.

The Oxford English Dictionary (OED) traces 'crash' as a word back to fifteenth century printing, linking it from the start to technologies of communication. Definitions range from noisy outbursts to overt destruction to information meltdown. Its onomatopoeic function means it is 'often impossible to separate the sound from the action', an inseparability of the material and its mediation that provides a structuring problematic of this collection. The crash is a 'noise' constantly in the background of the spread of communications, and reaching a crescendo from the mid-nineteenth century in discourses of commerce and mechanization. If noise it is, then the crash is also, in cybernetic terms, systemic noise that leads to collapse – the inseparable dereliction that accompanies all information, the cessation of exchange implicit in all trade, the broken transportation that is its animating possibility. The assumption that crashes are relatively rare, aberrant events, masks their ubiquity. The OED shows how the naming of the phenomenon proliferated into ever more explicit and elaborated fictional treatments of the crash as endemic to modern life.

Everyday life for the majority is hazardous and unpredictable. At its most extreme, we seem to be subjects of a system that is out of control, there being no human purpose behind the logic of capital accumulation and technological progress. In Marxist terms, the crash reveals the 'real relations' of capitalist production – the subjection of men to the inhuman machinery of industrialisation and technological rationalism, and the inherent irrationality of financial crises. Although the search for means to control these runaway tendencies is ongoing, we very readily wash our hands of the consequences when everything comes crashing down; it's just the market, or the inevitable unpredictability of so many forward technological leaps. Yet modernity is also fantasised as an untrammelled linear progress into a future in which the material world will be subject to the victorious human will alone. It is therefore accompanied by a horror of the prospect of an equal and opposite reversal, a cessation of evolutionary progress and regression towards devolutionary regress. As Grant explores in his essay, the cyclical time of pre-modern consciousness and rituals has been replaced by the metaphor of the open road on which we speed ever faster towards a utopian end. The crash insists on a failure of modernity's totalitarian ambitions, bringing us to an abrupt standstill.

These contradictory relations have become the focus of academic, as well as commercial, investigations of 'the risk society' (Beck 1992). Technoscience, Beck argues, which was once supposed to complete the project of rationalisation begun by the Enlightenment and banish terror, instead has provoked a new age of trans-spatial and trans-temporal hazards, as systems spread over the entire surface of the earth. Technological disasters are supposedly of a different scale of causes and consequences than hitherto. The singular, containable risks of the Wall Street Crash, WW1, and the sinking of the Titanic are less risky than a Chernobyl melt down. Yet what law necessitates that all risks concern the forward march of technology, rather than, as Greenslade's essay testifies with regard to the nineteenth century realist novel, the devolution of species? And in what sense is the actuality of the First World War measurable against the risk of the millennium bug that never happened? If the latter, not only no longer a potential risk but an not an actual one, counts nonetheless as an index of risk, then risk society remains too idealist a frame within which to analyse the materiality of the crash.

Central to a materialist account of the crash, is the relation between the imaging of crashes that proliferate across the mediascape and the phenomenology of everyday life. Our premise is that reproduced images cannot be separated from the world they represent; rather, they have a material existence that are constitutive of that world. As Highmore's essay points out, for a materialist semiotician like Barthes, images, rather than being a question of interpretation, are lived in our everyday routines and bodily reflexes. Speculation on the potential for a new form of photographic and technological consciousness became commonplace in the period between the two world wars. A modern form of photographic consciousness was developed that could protect and defend the self against the pain of catastrophe through self-objectification – producing the cold, rationalist worker/soldier of fascism whose fragile bodies and minds are armoured against the technological 'shocks' of the factory or the war zone. On the city streets, billboard images of speeding cars produce simultaneously both a phenomenal shock to the passer by and a semiotic screen for managing that shock.

This 'desensitizing' effect is often cited in contemporary debates about the 'scandal' of our voyeuristic enjoyment of screen death. Modern subjects have developed a protective shield, though 'the real' has ways of breaking back through. The heavily mediated experience of the celebrity car crash for example, in which the celebrity's body is immortalised through photography, signals in Grimshaw's essay both a defeat of the body and its victory over death. The brief release of death from its repression in modern culture, in which death and the body's decay has become a challenge to a technological society premised on the rational control of nature, is recovered for that project by its mediaization.

The important part played by convention, in protecting us from the material and sensual violence of modern existence is, however, matched by a 'hunger' to regain the intensity of experience that is lost as a consequence. The proliferation of crash scenes in the media of the twentieth century enables audiences to act out this oscillation, beginning with the short film *How It Feels to be Run Over* (1900), which puts the viewer in position to experience the effect of repeated virtual death. Littau's essay highlights the physiological pleasure, the stimulation of the senses that crash images provoke in cinema audiences in the early years of cinema, a pleasure that has been overlooked in the interpretative tradition of psychoanalytic criticism. SHaH, in their essay tracing the development of the mediated crash across the twentieth century, argue that these scenes both administer and then cushion the shock through repetition. But the degree to which we have become inured to the assault on our senses of the shocks of modern life is side-stepped, in their view, by immersive simulations in postmodern, virtual environments. They allow us to regain the intensity of an unmediated experience of the crash, just as cinema audiences responded to the first moving images at the turn of the last century.

This desire to imaginatively repeat the trauma of bodily destruction is not peculiar to modern or postmodern culture, though it is manifest in culturally specific ways. Several of the essays return to Freud's psychoanalytic account of the traumatised psyche to find an explanation. Freud's observation of the traumatic effects of modern technological warfare on the mind and body of the soldiers returning from the First World War was the impetus behind the publication of *Beyond the Pleasure Principle* in 1920. He wanted to explain the compulsion to repeat these painful experiences in the recurrent traumatic dreams suffered by these men. He compared it to the compulsive repetitions of the *fort/da* games of childhood, in which painful loss (of the mother) is symbolically re-experienced. Neither could be easily explained without some modification of his concept of the psyche as a homeostatic system regulated by the pursuit of pleasure and the avoidance of pain, qualified only by the restraints imposed by the reality principle. His solution was to posit the presence of an instinctual force, the 'death drive', which arises from the fact of sexual reproduction. The death drive works in opposition to the sex drive as a force of disintegration and entropy as matter regresses to the inorganic state from which we temporarily emerge as individuals. The death drive endlessly struggles, not with safety, but with aggressively inventive life.

In order to link this biologically grounded theory to the observed repetitions of the traumatised psyche, Freud speculated that the death drive is the effects produced in the psychic structure by the force of 'unbound' energy which the individual ego works to 'bind'. Trauma results when a massive influx of stimulus, from outside or inside the body, overwhelms the capacity to bind energy. The psyche is unprepared and therefore can't make any sense of the experience. It then has to be repeated in the imagination until the trauma is successfully bound to an idea to counteract the disintegrating force of the death drive. Once this has happened the painful tension created by the trauma can be discharged.

In Lacan's psychological account of the death drive the real remains a non-signifying but ever-present threat to the subject's 'bounded' integrity. If a shaming fascination with scenes of broken, fragmented, violated bodies nonetheless remains, this is not because such broken bodies in any sense enable the symbolisation of the real. Instead they constitute a necessarily repeated attempt to bind the disruption threatened by the real into social and representational convention thereby repairing the bounded self, as Arthurs demonstrates in her essay analysing the responses of the traumatised viewers of Cronenberg's *Crash*. The compulsion to repeat the traumatic event also points to the real which representations screen, thereby evoking the (impossible) satisfaction of the drives which could only be achieved through the disintegration of the individual ego. The planes crashing into the twin towers of the World Trade Centre were shown over and over again as television commentators struggled to find words for an event that ruptured the bounded image that Americans have of themselves. Yet Žižek, writing a few days later, points to the degree to which 'this threat was libidinally invested – just recall the series of movies from *Escape From New York* to *Independence Day*. The unthinkable, which happened, was thus the object of fantasy: in a way, America got what it fantasized about, and this was the greatest surprise' (Žižek 2001).

The saturation of modern cultures with technology produces both utopian and dystopian assessments of the human consequences of our convergence with the machine, a convergence that is figured in the conjunctions of flesh and metal that result from the crash. The emancipatory, humanist politics of Marxism and feminism have emphasised the use of machines by the ruling class to enhance their own dominance over their 'others', a dynamic in which those others become structured into a dualistic framework. In this dualism it is the body of the western white male that fuses with the machine, a fusion that provides transcendence over the body, and therefore over nature. As Khaira and Carlin demonstrate in their essay, while the black body disproportionately bears the wounds of the crash, it is excluded from sharing the white utopia of total mastery through convergence with the machine. Thus the fully technologised body as a fantasy of disembodiment, is freed not just from death but also from the restrictions and particularities of the local gendered or ethnic body – a fantasy that emerges most insistently in visual forms of narrative that provide a specular distance from the body. It is suggested by Beezer that this fantasy can be understood as a desire to totalise, to eradicate the other through the construction of a visual field of appearances, manufactured as objects for that subject, beyond which we may know nothing.

Using fragments, 'since the whole is untrue', a critical method based on Adorno's negative dialectics (1966), Beezer's essay works by juxtaposing fragments from disparate narratives to expose their inconsistencies and contradictions.

Narrative works to smooth over contradictions in an ideological unity of form that requires heroes and villains, causes and effects, beginnings and endings. Blame must be attributed – a primary focus of news stories. Investigators proliferate – loss adjusters, safety experts, journalists, police, biographers, detectives – all sifting through fragments of evidence to reconstruct the sequence leading up to the event. Claims and counterclaims are made as the fragments of evidence fail to add up to a watertight case. Thus in the aftermath of the crash, the ideological narratives of the culture can be subject to challenge in ways that reveal some hidden truths. Just as the crash rearranges the relation between objects, collage can be used as an aesthetic and analytic technique to reveal new relations. In Henning and Goddard's investigations of Amelia Earhart's disappearance, fragments of evidence and multiple stories are used to question the way we use evidence to construct meaning, thus working to undermine our faith in this process. The shrine to Diana at Kensington Palace is, in Lindahl-Elliot and Alfonso's essay, a bricolage of iconic fragments drawn from the dispersed times of her life and brought together in a popular alternative to 'official' narratives that worked to establish the meaning of her death. The shrines created an anachronistic 'heterotopia', a term used by Foucault to signify a space that, unlike utopias are real spaces that work to dismantle the established social and political hierarchies of modernity.

The disintegration of bounded entities and the mixing of disparate objects in the conjunction of human and machine has been claimed for an emancipatory politics through the figure of the cyborg. An amalgam of human, animal and machine, the cyborg in Haraway's *Manifesto* is re-imagined as offering a new relation between the (feminist) subject and the technologically saturated environment in which we live. 'The cyborg is our ontology; it gives us our politics' (Haraway 1991: 150). It exists across fictional and factual categories of experience, indeed its presence in science fiction works to blur the distinction between imagination and material reality. Haraway uses the figure of the cyborg to address the problems posed by the end of the traditional, humanist categories on which feminist epistemology and methodology have been based. Women can no longer be conceived as the nature over which men and their technology exert dominance. Whilst potentially both utopian and dystopian, there can be no possibility of retreat to an organic body to integrate our resistance. Subsequent writers have questioned whether an emancipatory politics can survive at all in a technoculture where human agency is in question as a result of the dismantling of the boundary between humans and their natural and technological environment. In Latour's 'actor network theory' humans don't have agency on their own but rather agency is acquired by a thing being a component of a larger system (a network), a network that crosses human/non-human boundaries. It is the network as a whole that effects and determines (Latour 1993). This dispenses with the binary between humans and machines which Marxist politics assumes.

Cyborg bodies and intelligent machines are hybrid identities produced from a concept of life based in DNA code that is continuous with cybernetic code. This means there is a physical continuity between nature, technology and culture. These exist in a non-linear network that constitutes a cybernetic system. Systems failure as a result of 'noise', does not end in collapse but rather gives rise to new and different orders in a self-organising way, as in the imperfectly copied genes of DNA that allows for evolutionary change. At the molecular level nature is a machine, the pre-personal material reality of body and world (Deleuze and Guattari 1984). This enables a concept of the drive that exists prior to any individuated organism, just as Freud conceived the death drive, thus decoupling reproduction from human sexual relations and allowing instead the replication of cyborgs. It is in this context that we might begin to understand Ballard's *Crash* (1973), in which the crash is figured as a 'fertilizing event'. In its repetitious and detailed descriptions of metal amalgamated with soft flesh, Roden's essay sees in *Crash* the construction of cyborg bodies that are not real unities (organisms), but drives. *Crash* is the metaphor of these drives, with the crash always an attempt to refashion the relation between organism and machine. While Botting and Wilson's essay argues that the libidinal economy of Cronenberg's *Crash* (1996), with its repetitious sequence of sex then crash then sex then crash, is the expression of a drive that is working towards the total consumption and consummation of all the energies stored in mechanical and biological apparatuses alike.

We invite you to explore in these essays the tangled wreckage of crashes and the traces of their impact in the lived materiality and mediated cultures of modernity – whether digital or cinematic, fictional or fiscal, virtual or actual, celebrated or anonymous, mass-produced or epoch making in their singularity.

The Essays

Bill Greenslade: Will it Smash?: Modernity and the Fear of Falling

By tracing the motif of the financial crash in the realist novels of Dickens and Trollope, Elliot, Meredith, Gissing and Hardy, the inherent irrationality of capitalist relations is revealed. By the end of the century the crash is figured as violent and unpredictable in its consequences, in a world devoid of moral certainty or just rewards for virtue. Failure or success becomes the only moral standard. Good is what survives. Modernity's 'other' erupts in the non-realist genres of the period, in horror, the supernatural or fantasy, where the crash encodes the ever-present fear of falling back and down into the primitive slime of homogeneity. Only through aspiring to an illusory, god-like power over the forces of capital could men hope to escape this fate. Thus a religious ethic is replaced by the 'will to power' of a punitive masculinity, manifest in the brutality of Wilcox in *Howard's End* or Jay Gatsby in *The Great Gatsby*. In these novels, the promise and adventure of 'being modern' is brutally rubbed out by the destructive forces that such power unleashes.

Seminar for Hypertheory and Heterology (SHaH): How it Feels

The effects on our consciousness of exposure to the shocks of modern life is mediated through the technologies of cinema, TV and computer simulations. Taking Freud's explanation of trauma management in *Beyond the Pleasure Principle*, these writers propose that the 'age of technology' has speeded up the oscillations of the *fort/da* process to the point that all feeling has been deadened. Only in the 'crash' can we find an approximation to 'the plenitude of barely imaginable intensity' which virtual death provides. Staged rail and car crashes were a popular spectacle in the cinema of the turn of the 19th century, allowing the audience safely to experience 'how it feels to be run over'. As we enter the 21st century, the speed of digital processing is made psychologically manageable through the mediating conventions of interactive digital games, saturated with the proximity of virtual death in increasingly 'realistic' scenarios. And theme park rides hurl us ever faster in emulation of the test pilot's 'out of body' experience in response to the G forces of his accelerating machine.

Karin Littau: Eye-Hunger: Physical Pleasure and Non-narrative Cinema

The story is often told of early cinema audiences fleeing auditoria as trains hurtled towards the camera. Such stories do not so much suggest that naive audiences mistook the screen image of the oncoming train for a real one, but that visual pleasure is a physical sensation. Rather than identifying psychologically with screen characters (contemporary film theory), audiences suffered eye-hunger, creeping through their 'flesh' and exciting their 'nerves' (early C20th film theory). If de-emphasising the psychological moment in cinema spectatorship allows us to re-establish the physiological underpinnings of the act of spectating, it also recontextualises cinema as one physical spectacular form amongst many: public executions in pre-enlightenment societies, or outings to the morgue at the turn of the twentieth century (and who would not be tempted to touch?). Drawing therefore on accounts of the physiology of cinematic spectatorship, this essay brings them to bear on a popular early twentieth century site of eye-hunger: crash-spectating.

Ben Highmore: Crashed Out: Laundry Vans, Photographs and a Question of Consciousness

Starting from the chance collision with a laundry van which killed Roland Barthes, Ben Highmore's essay demonstrates that there is more to connect semiotic analysis and traffic accidents, photography and the everyday experience of modernity than might at first be thought. He draws on key writers on modernity (Benjamin, Simmel, Marx and Junger) to argue that the binary distinctions commonly drawn between the real and the imaginary, the base and the superstructure, the material conditions of existence and their representation are simply untenable. Photographic representations are part of the phenomenological experience which produces our social being. They are in Simmel's words 'the sensory foundation of mental life' created out of socially produced memories which stretch back in history. Given that our experience of reality is inescapably semiotic, a refusal of cultural convention can lead either to an aberrant decoding or to being run over. In this view a billboard advert of a speeding car is of the same order as the speeding car itself in that we respond to both through a semiotic screen of cultural convention designed to manage the shock it produces. For a materialist semiotician, images are not simply a question of interpretation, they are lived in our everyday routines and body reflexes.

Jane Arthurs: Crash: Beyond the Boundaries of Sense

Audience research and Lacanian film theory are usually considered antithetical, the former producing historically and socially specific analysis of varied responses, the latter proposing a transcendent psychological positioning of the spectator. The essay argues that the reactions of audiences to *Crash* can be illuminated through a Lacanian interpretation of the death drive. Cronenberg's film is a deliberate assault on the 'screen' of visual conventions which serves to confirm our subjectivity, producing an experience in which the boundaries of the self are dissolved. This provides a perspective from which to explore the scandal that accompanied the film's exhibition in Britain, and the boredom, confusion, fascination and disturbance it produced in audiences. The trauma the movie provoked is taken as an index of its 'unbindability', and the scandalised responses it evoked as indices of the reconstitution of subjective boundaries. Drawing on audience research, this essay demonstrates these processes as people search for a workable discourse through which to make sense of the film. Whilst others, for whom *Crash* remained pointless or who turned away in disgust, quickly forgot the film in a process of abjection.

Fred Botting & Scott Wilson: Sexcrash

Set in a Canada that seems composed entirely of motorways and tower blocks, the opening sexual encounters in David Cronenberg's *Crash* present sex as a matter-of-fact, workaday activity: sex becomes the same, dull, daily grind as work, a banal, repetitive, mundane event absorbed in the pleasure principle of the productive and consumptive economy. The movie, with its insistent but climaxless repetition of sex scenes, surgery and crashes, demonstrates nothing but arbitrary and unmotivated repetition.

Everything is work: sex, entertainment, even death. In this sense, *Crash* is a film about the libidinal economy of labour. From this central insight, Botting & Wilson work outwards through the film as a generalised economy of automated sex, without desire to drive it or pleasure to end it. It is not the human characters who are the vehicles of sexual identity, nor are they the conduits of desire. Rather they suffer the effects of autosex, they become its victims and they eroticise themselves precisely as such in the form of their wounds and scars. The generalized lack at the core of this libidinal economy foregrounds sex as disaster. The crashes in *Crash* are not isolated events, but a chain reaction, a constant catastrophe that engulfs everything.

David Roden: Cyborg Ontology and the Autodestruction of Metaphor

Everywhere there are cyborgs: biological organisms become 'gene machines', DNA becomes code, organisms are homeostats; equally Schwarzenegger's Terminator, William Gibson's fictions, and sundry other cultural cyborgs populate the mediascape. Cultural critic Donna Haraway's 'Manifesto for Cyborgs' influentially celebrates cyborg politics. That is, where cultures tend to structure social relations in hierarchies, building origin myths into those structures, the cyborg establishes a metaphorical wealth of improper connectivity without origins: anything goes, in the promiscuous welding of flesh and technologies. However, this essay argues that Haraway's account of cyborghood is flawed: the technological avatar of difference, it turns out, defined as pure connection, effectively ceases to be a cyborg, since it becomes everything. Thus another welding ceremony is proposed: the abrupt collisions of flesh and metal, organic and machine parts, in J.G. Ballard's novel *Crash*, provide an account of cyborg existence that retains differentiation sufficiently to maintain the cyborg as a cyborg, rather than an all too human political dream.

Iain Grant: Spirit in Crashes: Fatalism, Number and Modernity

We are accustomed to viewing crashes as accidents. Yet the fundamental law of the crash is that it not remain an accident, but be explained through human or technological failure. For animists, crashes never were accidents, but made necessary by magic or the gods. Yet when technology goes out of our control, we invoke the sorcerer's apprentice: 'the car seemed to take on a life of its own'. In our struggle to maintain modernity's escape velocity from magic and the gods, we therefore invoke the ritual of explanation and the scapegoat of human failure; otherwise, therefore, our technology would be perfect. Thus, every crash occurs at a historical fork in the road: down fork one there lies the cyclical time of animistic magics; down fork two, endless advancement, infinite speed. Nineteenth and early twentieth century anthropological studies of 'primitive culture', describe the lengths to which it is possible to go in protecting cyclical time from running away into a linear sequence. Closed time is therefore a 'primitive' defense against a modernity that haunted it, just as the open road is modernity's defence against closed time. The crash returns. Was it an accident that the first vehicles in history were funeral chariots?

Harjit Kaur Khaira & Gerry Carlin: Racing Fatalities: White Highway, Black Wreckage

Progressive, linear time stretches into the future with the modern subject in the driving-seat in a relation of intimate convergence with the machine. But this highway is racially exclusive; it is a white highway in relation to which 'black mobility is often read as deviant and threatening by the white majority'. In colonial discourse the racially marked body is figured as always subject to or in violent collision with the technologies of white history. In the dominant, romantic myths of progress, the white body is able either to absorb or to transcend the multiple, violent shocks which new technologies give rise to, reaching an apotheosis in the figure of the cyborg – the fully technologised body immune to the reversals of death. The black body, in contrast, is subjected to their violence. These colonial discourses are traced across the visual field of representation, from the televised beatings of Rodney King to the death of the only black character in *Terminator 2*, from the sublime of European modernism in *Un Chien Andalou* to Frieda Kahlo's racially marked self-portraits of her technologically wounded body.

Anne Beezer: The Negative Dialectics of the Desert Crash in The English Patient

This essay uses the novel and the film of *The English Patient* to work through a critique of the poststructuralist economy of signification as a merely specular economy. In this reading, the crash into the desert of Amersy, the pilot in *The English Patient,* works as a symbolic expression of the totalitarian ambitions of a disembodied, white, masculine subjectivity to master the marked corporeality of others, to eradicate all distance and difference. The corporeality of things eludes the overseeing eye/I and its imaginary geographies. The other of the disembodied subject is precisely the embodied object, but not an object that exists as a mere conceptualisation or projection of otherness by that subject. In contrast to Amersy, the ethnically marked figure of Kip is used in the novel, but significantly not in the scopic regime of the film, to draw out a sensuous connection to his environment, entirely consequent upon corporeality. The conclusion draws out the importance of an ethics of alterity drawn from a mobilisation of corporeal feminism and Adorno's negative dialectics to argue against the self-sufficiency of the concept that subsumes the object.

Jean Grimshaw: The Iconic Body and the Crash

The cultural significance of Diana's iconic body produced the ritualised, collective response to her death. This could be compared to the sacrifices held in primitive cultures, but differs in important ways. The intensity of the response to the crash is relative to the more general absence of a collective ritualised response to death in modern cultures, diagnosed by both Elias and Baudrillard, a denial which returns as an equally ubiquitous fascination with 'virtual' death – a clean, non-tactile, disembodied, reversible death which saturates modern forms of visual culture, in films, games and popular television. Diana's death briefly reinstated the real body in the car crash. But the horror and collective grief this produced was not just a reminder of our own mortality but also an intimation of our collective responsibility, not just for this death, but for the mass destruction wrought by modern capitalism. That an individual driver was scapegoated cannot erase that moment when it seemed that Diana was killed by the profit to be made from her body as a commodified image. Nevertheless, it was her virtual embodiment as a photographic icon that allowed for the expression of the intimation of the eternal that lies beyond the modern, rational approach to death.

Nils Lindahl Elliot & Carmen Alfonso: Of Hallowed Spacings: Diana's Crash and Heterotopia

The rituals of mourning which Diana's death inspired produced an inversion of everyday relations and hierarchies, in Foucault's term, a heterotopia. Diana's ambiguous, liminal status at the time of her death, an outcast from the British establishment, becomes the occasion for a popular appropriation of the space-time of modernity. The media coverage produced, 'a sense of proximity where there is distance, sameness where there is alterity' that worked both to mask class difference while opening up a class critique. She stood in for the 'people' against the entrenched, uncaring emblems of class power, the Royal family. The everyday experience of time was also disrupted by the crash. The first shock brought it to an abrupt stop. There followed a concentration of biographical time in multiple, encapsulated narratives of Diana's life, embodied in the mementoes left at the Kensington Gardens shrine. Heterotopias create anachronisms by bringing together multiple times. The crash opened up a metaphysical moment, when the rituals of the shrine brought into play an earlier medieval consciousness. Yet these intimations of a 'beyond' remained firmly tied to a bricolage of found images of Diana's life in which her body is the focus, an image of perfection frozen in time.

Michelle Henning & Rebecca Goddard: Fuel, Metal, Air: The Appearance and Disappearance of Amelia Earhart

In 1937, the American aviatrix Amelia Earhart disappeared mid-flight. In three parallel but interlinked genres of 'fiction', this piece explores the immense ramifications of this disappearance. Theories abound: she was a spy; she crashed at sea; the Japanese captured her; she lived out her life on a desert island. But there is no certainty, and little evidence. By using overtly 'fictional' devices, however, this piece is able to explore the theories, the various interests and investments in those theories, and thus to reconstruct something of Earhart's moment, her histories and her significance. Meanwhile, Earhart re-emerges in her uncanny physical double (Goddard), giving rise to considerations of coincidence, events, encounters, doubles and disappearances. Finally, a series of false relics, in the form of digitally manipulated images apparently (though not very convincingly) represent the wreckage of Earhart's plane. Using biographical accounts of Earhart's flight interleaved with a fictional genre obsessed with 'clues' and reconstruction, poetic imaginings which take their cue from coincidences and deliberately faked pictures, the essay questions what constitutes evidence. In linking our present to Earhart's moment, they raise questions about what constitutes history and fiction.

References

Adorno, T. (1966) *Negative Dialectics* (tr. E.B. Ashton). London: Routledge

Ballard, J.G. (1973) *Crash*. London: Jonathan Cape.

Beck, U. (1986) *Risk Society: Towards a New Modernity* (tr. Mark Ritter). London: Sage.

Cronenberg, D. (1996) *Crash*. Miramax/Columbia Tristar.

De Certeau, M. (1984) *The Practice of Everyday Life* (tr. Steven Rendall). Berkeley, Los Angeles, London: University of California Press.

Deleuze, G. and F. Guattari (1972) *Anti-Oedipus: Capitalism and Schizophrenia* (tr. Robert Hurley, Mark Seem and Helen R. Lane). New York: Viking.

Freud, S. (1920) 'Beyond the Pleasure Principle', *Standard Edition of the Complete Psychological Works of Sigmund Freud 18*, 1–64.

Haraway, D. (1991) *A Cyborg Manifesto: Science, Technology and Socialist Feminism in the Late Twentieth Century*. In *Simions, Cyborgs and Women: The Reinvention of Nature*. New York: Routledge, 149–181.

Latour, B (1991) *We Have Never Been Modern* (tr. Catherine Porter). New York and London: Harvester Wheatsheaf.

Žižek, S. (2001) *Welcome to the Desert of the Real*. www.cms.mit.edu/zizek

2 'Will It Smash?': Modernity and the Fear of Falling

William Greenslade

'The first thing that strikes the moral enquirer into our social system is the respect in which wealth is held … with us, Money is the mightiest of deities', observed the writer Bulwer Lytton in 1833. (Smith 1968: 63) Like Lytton, nineteenth-century realist novelists found in the rise and fall of financiers and in the collusion between money and rank, fertile matter for their exploration of the moral bankruptcy of the age, particularly the exposure of hypocrisy and dishonesty in high places. Narratives of sharp practice and greed, and of gullible or clever speculation, in the distinctive circumstances of the period, couldn't fail to attract readers.

Commercial and banking crises had been an unstoppable feature of advanced capitalist society. In Britain, significant financial crises were registered at least once a decade from the 1820s to the 1860s, involving, variously, failing banks, bubble companies, credit companies and paper speculation. (Russell 1986, Baubles 2001: 262–3). Novelists who dealt with financial themes habitually as realist writers, set their fictions in precise, and so recognisable, moments of financial uncertainty.[1]

Both Charles Dickens's *Little Dorrit* and Anthony Trollope's *The Way We Live Now* are compendious studies of what Trollope himself called 'dishonesty magnificent in its proportions, and climbing into high places'. (Sutherland 1982: vii) These novelists investigate, with extraordinary comprehensiveness, systems and networks of patronage and corrupt influence. Dickens's fraudulent banker, Merdle, and Trollope's corrupt financier, Melmotte, are memorable figures. The scale of their towering personal ambition come to dominate, for a while, the lives of both the vulnerable and venial. The fall and suicide of each constitute a nemesis, long in the preparation. But as if the very grandeur of these emblems of systemic corruption have effaced the possibility of a competing angle of vision separate from that of the narrator, both novels lack a convincing, self-aware centre of critical consciousness through which the personal consequences of these individual, socio-economic and divine crashes is mediated.

George Eliot's *Daniel Deronda* marks a shift towards inaugurating such a consciousness. Here the crash-crisis positions the protagonist, Gwendolen Harleth, at the foothills of a protracted spiritual crisis, with 'the labyrinth of life before her and no clue' (Eliot 1876: 317). Gwendolen's prospects as the eldest daughter of a widow are totally changed by a bank failure, obliquely presented in the opening chapter. Mrs Davilow, her mother, loses her capital as 'Grapnell & Co.' fail 'for a million' (Eliot 1876, 1967: 43). The smash triggers Gwendolen's career of romance and forces her to seek a wealthy husband. She is fascinated not only by the predatory Henleigh Grandcourt, but by his wealth which will save her from the fate of becoming a governess. But Grandcourt's brutal destruction of her selfhood, delineated with compelling authority by Eliot, eventually prompts Gwendolen's refusal to rescue him from death by drowning.

The movement from Dickens and Trollope via the transitional Eliot to novelists of 1880s and 90s, such as Meredith, Gissing and Hardy, paralleled a paradigmatic shift in contemporary evolutionary thinking – from a gradualist, predominantly Lamarckian, model of evolutionary development to a more Darwinian paradigm, associated with the germ-plasm theory of the German biologist, August Weismann and the re-discovery of the work of Mendel at the turn of the century (Morton 1984: 165–70, Bowler 1984: 237–9). Whereas Lamarckian biology, promoted by the influential social theorist, Herbert Spencer, had stressed the organism's creative adaptation to the impact of change, in these later revisionary, neo-Darwinian accounts, development proceeded erratically, randomly, alarmingly. The organism now learnt nothing from experience but re-made itself on the sole basis of chance adaptation. Indeed the impress of the contingent and the haphazard threatened to obliterate memory, tradition and rationality. Transposed into the terms of the evolution of market-systems, the crash has violent and unpredictable consequences which allow the fictional protagonist less room to adapt by learning from the experience of disaster: the protagonist now suffers, in various ways, the personal consequences of the instability of the financial system, which is itself a symptom of a wider societal disintegration.

While Dickens and Trollope had few illusions about the damaging effects on the possessors of capital wrought by the activities of their corrupt financiers, each is placed by these writers as a symptom and symbol of moral infirmity. For all their grandeur, even their dignity, Merdle and Melmotte are bad men who have corruptly played an imperfect system which, in the end, proves too much for them: greater moral vigilance might have found them out. But in later nineteenth-century fiction moral culpability is increasingly beside the point since there are no moral fixes available. Both the agents of capital and its victims are beyond the formal control of the ideology of humanist even-handedness and instead are subjects of a massively and catastrophically adaptive market.

Writing at the turn of the century, as an appreciative critic of Dickens, George Gissing took the point.[2] For all his indictment of social evils in his fiction, Dickens, in Gissing's view, was hobbled by his ultimate aim: 'to amuse, to elevate, and finally to calm. When his evil-doers have been got rid of, he delights in apportioning quiet happiness to every character in the novel beloved by him and his readers' (Gissing 1924: 101–2). Gissing upheld the idea that Dickens's universe is a broadly providential one in which goodness finds its reward, and evil is punished, a 'final accounting'. By comparison, his own fictional world is (notoriously) unforgiving, as well as unrelenting. Whereas Dickens or Trollope, for all their anatomy of corruption in high places, leave a morally explicable universe largely in place, the same cannot be said for later post-Darwinian fictions, inflected by naturalism. For Gissing, Meredith and Hardy, the crash precipitates experience from which little can be learnt or recuperated; the violence and damage wrought by the initial disaster becomes a symptom of a whole life experience of unpredictability; the epistemology has shifted from an individual to a systemic basis to occlude the act of resistance, and to efface plots of recuperation and renovation.

In *The Whirlpool* (1897) Gissing, like Eliot, re-positions the crash by bringing it to the forefront of the narrative, making the crash the trigger for the major developments in the text. In chapter five of the novel, the banker, Bennet Frothingham, commits suicide, and within the hour the news spreads amongst its anxious investors. Frothingham's daughter, Alma, hoping to survive as a career singer, becomes involved in a shadowy world of sexual intrigue. Like Eliot's Gwendolen, she rescues herself from financial disaster through marriage, but the man in question, Harvey Rolfe, is half-committed to an ethic of marital independence. Through benign neglect Alma becomes the victim of sexual speculation by both male and female predators. While Rolfe is himself disenchanted with the system of finance which maintains his rather pointless existence, he becomes increasingly compromised by the forces against which (as the possessor of moral and financial capital) his wife has battled and against which, had he been a traditional Victorian gentleman, he would certainly have defended her.

The crash has moved centre stage. Its psychic and social meanings are now being investigated as symptoms as well as the causes of a far-reaching and immanent condition: in Gissing's text it finds representation in the figure of the 'whirlpool' of modernity. This is a condition of existence which afflicts each character in the novel who is made to manifest diverse symptoms of a pathology of modern living – indecision and anxiety, hysteria and mental breakdown, suicide and crime – which leaves nobody in the novel immune. No matter how hard Alma and Rolfe try to withstand it (by adopting, for example, a simple-life ethic, away from the metropolis) they fail. The point is that such a choice of life, in this novel, is exposed as illusory, since the condition to which Gissing's articulate and self-conscious protagonists are exposed is all-pervasive. *The Whirlpool* is a text whose diagnostic eloquence is precisely related to the sense of the embracing effect of modernity, in which, as Zygmunt Bauman puts it, 'human order is vulnerable, contingent and devoid of reliable foundations' (Bauman 1992: xi).

The irrationality of capital accumulation finds in Rolfe an answering ethic of *fin de siècle* social-Darwinist force. The bank crash is now naturalised as an 'explosion' in the system of capitalist relations which serves to demonstrate the necessity of prosecuting 'struggle' as the precondition for further economic progress. Rolfe's view is that such 'explosions' are necessary to cleanse the system: they 'promised to clear the air' – they are 'periodic, inevitable, wholesome. The Britannia Loan, &c, &c, &c, had run its pestilent course; exciting avarice, perturbing quiet industry with the passion of the gamester, inflating vulgar ambition, now at length scattering wreck and ruin. This is how mankind progresses' (Gissing 1897, 1997: 44). Social Darwinism naturalises ethics in a seductive but terrorist tautology: 'Good is nothing more than the conduct which is fittest to the circumstances of the moment.... Failure or success in the struggle for existence is the sole moral standard. Good is what survives.' is what the young (and callow) Somerset Maugham wrote in 1900 (Maugham 1967: 66). And of course such an ethic fed the cult of the machine in early-modernist European aesthetics (Kern 1983: 98–9).

The crash has become overlaid with a post-Darwinian obsession with decadence and degeneration. *Fin de siècle* typologies of the crash encoded the fear of descent: of a falling *back* and *down*; of reversion and retrogression back to primitive homogeneity. This process is figured in many of the period's non-realist fictions which are grounded in horror, the supernatural or fantasy (Hurley 1996), but even in the canonical children's novel of the period, Kenneth Grahame's *The Wind in the Willows* (1908). The anthropomorphic washerwoman/gentleman Toad reverts to animal type when, after his own latest 'crash' of a motor-car, he falls headlong from grace into the river from which he emerges, spluttering, to face the forgiving Rat. In Toad's downfall lies the possibility of redemption through renewed kinship with an animal community which instinctively knows its place and values it.

Toad's *hubris* is to embrace the destructive pleasures of modernity, untrammelled by habit or morality. His commandeering of the motor-car, as a contemporary symbol and type of destructive modernity, even makes him something of a proto-futurist. Marinetti's 'Founding Manifesto' of 1909 proclaimed that 'Time and Space died yesterday. We already live in the absolute, because we have created eternal omnipresent speed' (Kern 1983: 98). Yet Toad's comic seizure of the power by which to indulge the erotic pleasure of self-abandonment – 'the rush of air in his face, the hum of the engine, and the light jump of the car beneath him intoxicated his weak brain' (Grahame 1908, 1931: 258) – whatever its resemblance to the futurists' love of driving cars at speed and crashing them, is powered by Darwinian force where cunning is allied to recklessness in a spectacle of amoral assertion: 'I am the Toad, the motor-car snatcher, the prison-breaker, the Toad who always escapes ... you are in the hands of the famous, the skilful, the entirely fearless Toad' (Grahame 1908, 1931: 258). Earlier in the story it is a near-collision between the animal's canary-coloured cart and the speeding motor-car which prompts in Toad an ecstasy of conversion from horse power to the combustion-engine. *The Wind in the Willows* plays with the problematic and unstable relationship between the erect body of capital and its prone, reptilian, retrogressive (and decadent) 'other', now freighted by the imaginative hold of biological poetics.

Writers at the *fin de siècle* configured this instability at the powerfully beating heart of Empire. Within the city the circulation of money and power was increasingly subject to a dialectic of ostensible rationality and the uncontrollable forces of capital. The 'City of London' is now an inescapable determinant in how the city (of London) offers itself as a site for the struggle between risk and decadent stagnation. *Fin de siècle* writers explored a topography of instability by exploring the symbolic potential of the unwarranted fall to the ground. A key reference point was the famous opening chapter of Dickens' *Bleak House* (1853) with its 'dogs ... horses ... foot passengers' mired in the mud of London streets and presenting an antediluvian spectacle in which 'it would not be wonderful to meet a Megalosaurus ... waddling like an elephantine lizard up

Holborn Hill' (Dickens 1853: 49). The metaphors of collision and slippage on the streets drawn from this passage – 'foot passengers, jostling one another's umbrellas ... losing their foothold at street corners, where tens of thousands of other foot passengers have been slipping and sliding since day broke (if ever day broke)' (Dickens 1853: 49) – provided writers with insights into the social violence and psychic dysfunction which both sustains and is produced by the social order – now, at the end of the century, an unmistakably national and imperial one.

In the crash to earth of the millionaire Victor Radnor in the ironically-titled *One of Our Conquerors* (1892), George Meredith fuses, in a richly symbolic moment, a social and psychic collision: the site on which Radnor slips is proximate to the City of London where his wealth is produced. While 'crossing London Bridge at noon on a gusty April day', he hits his head on a pavement having become 'almost magically detached from his conflict with the gale by some sly strip of slipperiness, abounding in that conduit of the markets' (Meredith 1892, 1975: 1). Helped to his feet by a workman, whose dirty hands mark his hitherto spotless white waistcoat, Radnor utters a condescending remark which prompts a single retort from an anonymous passer-by 'and none of your dam punctilio'. The single word *punctilio* shoots 'a throb of pain to the spot where his mishap had rendered him susceptible' (Meredith 1892, 1975: 3). Radnor puts two fingers to the back of his head, and checked or stemmed the current of a fear' (Meredith 1892, 1975: 5); the action is proleptic of his later mental breakdown.

Meredith's streets are also Gissing's. The 'sly strip of slipperiness' in *One of Our Conquerors* is answered in the slippage of cab horses on the 'slimy crossings' of London streets and 'the collision of wheels' in *The Whirlpool* (Gissing 1897, 1997: 10). Such imagery encodes, in a very direct way, the hazardous texture of material life at the heart of the imperial state, the halting 'heart of Empire' at the end of the nineteenth century. This is, after all, a period marked by widespread joint-stock fraud and massive speculation in over-valued shares acquired by powerful new trust companies; Baring Brothers nearly went bust, as a result of such speculation and had to be rescued by the Bank of England in 1890 (Kynaston 1994: 422–37).

Fictional representations of the financial crash at the turn of the century are still invested with the fear of uncertainty, but now freighted with post-Darwinian sense of powerlessness in the face of the uncontrollable. John Galsworthy's *rentier* Forsytes for whom there was 'no dread in life like that of 3 per cent for their money' (Galsworthy 1906, 1951: 42), are still haunted by the fear of what Jeff Nunokawa calls 'the loss of property', characteristic of the 'nineteenth-century imagination' (Nunokawa 1994: 7). Galsworthy makes such fears lead to palpable states of depressing anomie and alienation. In *A Man of Property*, Old Jolyon, 'as lonely an old man as there was in London', sits 'in the gloomy comfort of the room, a puppet in the power of great forces that cared nothing for family or class or creed, but moved, machine-like, with dread processes to inscrutable ends' (Galsworthy 1906, 1951: 42). The material texture of everyday life seemed increasingly conditioned by such forces, articulated with ever more psychological clarity, even as they eluded control.

In the age of joint-stock banking and the increasingly centralised organisation of capital (Hobsbawm 1987, 1989: 43–4), there emerged a plutocracy, particularly in

America, which seemed to rival the system which it exploited. J.P. Morgan, Andrew Carnegie, John D. Rockefeller – these symbolised the glamour of fabulous wealth and the mystery of the economic system which had produced it. In Britain, Cecil Rhodes, a free-booting, charismatic figure of Empire with the King Midas touch, came to embody fantasies of aggrandisement in which he himself was caught up. As founder of the powerful British South Africa Company, his imperialist ambitions of the 1890s became, *de facto*, those of the British government itself. It was paradoxical, and in character, that he ruefully contemplated the globe, at the end of the nineteenth century, dominated by the exercise of British interest, as 'nearly all parcelled out ... divided up, conquered and colonised'. Now he reached to the stars: 'these vast worlds which we cannot reach. I would annex the planets if I could' (Clarke p. 95). The divine economy has turned to the production of financial gods.

Such fashioning of the overreaching self is an attribute of Scott Fitzgerald's pre-Crash, plutocrat, Jay Gatsby. From Gissing and Galsworthy to *The Great Gatsby* (1925) might be seen as a leap too far. But consider E.M. Forster's Condition of (Edwardian) England novel, *Howards End* (1910), as an intertext. Forster's plutocrat, Henry Wilcox, advises the lower-middle class clerk, Leonard Bast, (whom the early-Bloomsbury Schlegel sisters had taken up), to 'clear out of the Porphyrion Fire Insurance Company with all possible speed ... it'll be in the Receiver's hands before Christmas. It'll smash ... The Porphyrion's a bad, bad, concern – now, don't say I said so. It's outside the Tariff Ring' (Forster 1910, 1975: 139–140). Leonard takes the advice of Wilcox and quits his job; but the Porphyrion recovers and Leonard is unemployed. Margaret Schlegel tackles Wilcox: '"I think you told us that the Porphyrion was bad, and would smash before Christmas. "Did I?"' Wilcox replies. '"It was still outside the Tariff Ring, and had to taken rotten policies. Lately it came in – safe as houses now".' '"In other words, Mr Bast need never have left it",' Margaret observes (Forster 1910; 1975, 191). Wilcox then enters the justification that no one is 'to blame for this clerk's loss of salary' and that 'as civilization moves forward, the shoe is bound to pinch in places ...' (Forster 1910, 1975: 192).

Forster's narrator earlier refers to Wilcox's 'Olympian laugh' (Forster 1910, 1975: 140) and, indeed, Leonard has, unthinkingly, endowed Wilcox with the qualities of a charismatic Edwardian Croesus with godlike powers, which are exposed as mortal by the instability of the market over which he seeks to rule. Forster's plot will expose Leonard to the hegemony of punitive masculinity which ironically undercuts the Wilcox claim to omniscience. Leonard makes Helen Schlegel pregnant, and Wilcox, who has since married her elder sister Margaret, now has a vested interest in getting rid of him. The work is done by Charles, his shallow, motor-car driving son, but not before on his final walk along the country road, Leonard is passed by a 'motor'. In it is a 'type whom nature favours – the Imperial. Healthy, ever in motion, it hopes to inherit the earth' (Forster 1910, 1975: 314–5). In the novel these Toad-types have run over animals, smashed into other cars, and imposed their will on the highways, on which pedestrians, like Leonard, are of little account. Forster and Grahame have, albeit through differing literary modes, imaginatively anticipated, in the symbolism of the motor car, an embodiment of the 'juggernaut', the image with which Anthony Giddens has sought to characterise the phenomenology of modernity (Giddens 1990: 137–9). Leonard is, convincingly, its victim.

For Leonard Bast, read George Wilson, the garage-owner in 'the valley of ashes', located 'between West Egg and New York' in *The Great Gatsby*, whose wife, Myrtle, is killed by Jay Gatsby's motor-car (driven by Dolly Buchanan, who fails to stop after the collision). Wilson, like Leonard Bast, is a cog in the system. He literally oils the wheels of the motor-cars of the wealthy which figure the predatory and destructive power of capital (in Gatsby's case, acquired fraudulently), but softened – even disguised – by the glamour of conspicuous consumption. Like Leonard, Wilson takes a long walk to his death in the morning, but unlike Leonard, Wilson is set on revenge – he shoots Gatsby in his swimming-pool, before turning the gun on himself.

But of course, those who evade retribution are the Buchanans – Dolly, Myrtle's killer, and Tom, her lover. This morally disenchanted narrative allows for these types of the 'careless' to evade censure. For unlike the morally explicable world of Dickens and Trollope, Fitzgerald's vision of modernity offers the prospect of a moral chaos in which even the victim is caught up. Turning to Doctor Eckleburg's eyes, Wilson believes them to be those of God: '"God sees everything", repeated Wilson. "That's an advertisement," Michaelis assured him' (Fitzgerald 1925, 1950: 166). The face of capitalist production whose immanence springs from its particular prominence in a landscape, is devoid of order other than that which is symbolically ascribed to it: the 'one yard high' retinas, which 'brood on over the solemn dumping ground' have yellow spectacles drawn by 'some wild wag of an oculist' (Fitzgerald 1925, 1950: 29).

The phase of modernity marked by the impact of Darwinism and advanced capitalism has granted to the financial system the kind of role once accorded to the great maker: its huge socially constitutive and unregulatable power has reinstated the divinity which Darwinism sought to kill off. In the figuring of the crash by major fictions of this seventy year period we chart that transition between the individuated and the systemic crisis, between individual collapse and the recurrent apocalypse of the new divine order of capitalist production. The symbolic meanings of the crash have transmuted from the category of moral test to the spectacle of periodic disruption, even to intimations of ecological catastrophe. No longer are individuals called to final account. It not that Wilson has got the wrong man, but that getting the right man is not, any more, the point.

Notes

1. Mrs. Craik's *John Halifax, Gentleman* (1856) was set in the crisis of 1825, Charles Reade's *Hard Cash* (1863) dealt with events in 1847. Charles Dickens's *Little Dorrit* (1857) was influenced by a bank failure of 1856 (as was Anthony Trollope's *The Way We Live Now* (1875)), and by the crisis of the French *Crédit Mobilier* from 1857. Trollope's novel also recalled the Tipperary bank failure and subsequent suicide on Hampstead Heath of John Sadlier in 1856, as well as the failure of the railway speculator George 'King' Hudson in the railway 'mania' of the late 1840s. George Eliot's *Daniel Deronda* (1876) is, altogether more obliquely, set against the background of the failure of the Overend and Gurney bank in 1866 (Sutherland 1982: xxvii): the fictional time of the novel is set very precisely, in the years 1864–6.

2. Gissing wrote six introductions to a Rochester edition of Dickens's work, 1899–1901, which was discontinued by Methuen. These were collected together, twenty years after Gissing's death, as *Critical Studies of the Works of Charles Dickens* (1924).

References

Baubles Jr., Raymond L. (2001) 'The Bankruptcies of the Nation in Meredith's *One of Our Conquerors* and Gissing's *The Whirlpool*', in B.Postmus (ed) *A Garland for Gissing*. Amsterdam:Rodopi, pp. 261–70.

Bauman, Zygmunt (1991) *Modernity and Ambivalence*. Oxford: Polity Press.

—— (1992) *Intimations of Postmodernity*. London: Routledge.

Berman, Marshal (1982) *All That's Solid Melts Into Air*. New York: Simon and Schuster.

Bowler, Peter (1984) *Evolution: the History of an Idea*. Berkeley: University of California Press.

Clarke, I. F. (1966) *Voices Prophesying War 1763–1914*. London.

Dickens, Charles ([1853] 1971) *Bleak House*. Harmondsworth: Penguin.

—— ([1857] 1967) *Little Dorrit*. Harmondsworth: Penguin.

Eliot, George ([1876] 1967) *Daniel Deronda*. Harmondsworth: Penguin.

Fitzgerald, F. Scott ([1926] 1950) *The Great Gatsby*. Harmondsworth: Penguin.

Forster, E. M. ([1910] 1975) *Howards End*. Harmondsworth: Penguin.

Galsworthy, John ([1906] 1951) *The Man of Property*. Harmondsworth: Penguin.

Giddens, Anthony (1990) *The Consequences of Modernity*. Oxford: Blackwell.

Gissing, George ([1897] 1997) *The Whirlpool*. London: Dent.

Gissing, George (1924) *Critical Studies of the Works of Charles Dickens*. New York: Greenberg.

Grahame, Kenneth ([1908] 1931) *The Wind in the Willows*. London: Methuen.

Greenslade, William (1994) *Degeneration, Culture and the Novel 1880–1940*. Cambridge: Cambridge University Press.

Hobsbawm, Eric ([1987] 1989) *The Age of Empire 1875–1914*. London: Cardinal.

Hurley, Kelly (1996) *The Gothic Body: Sexuality, Materialism and Degeneration at the Fin de Siècle*. Cambridge: Cambridge University Press.

Kynaston, David (1994) *The City of London Vol. 1*. London: Chatto and Windus.

—— (1995) *The City of London Vol. 2*. London: Chatto and Windus.

Maugham, Somerset (1967) *Diary*. Harmondsworth: Penguin.

Meredith, George ([1891] 1975) *One of Our Conquerors*. St Lucia: University of Queensland Press.

Morton, Peter (1984) *The Vital Science: Biology and the Literary Imagination 1860–1900*. London: Allen and Unwin.

Nunokawa, Jeff (1994) *The Afterlife of Property: Domestic Security and the Victorian Novel*. Princeton; Princeton University Press.

Russell, Norman (1996) *The Novelist and Mammon*. Oxford: Clarendon Press.

Smith, Grahame (1968) *Dickens, Money and Society*. Berkeley: University of California Press.

Sutherland, John (1992) Introduction to Anthony Trollope, *The Way We Live Now*. Oxford: World's Classics.

Trollope, Anthony (1992) *The Way We Live Now*. Oxford: World's Classics.

3 How it Feels

SHaH*

> There came a day when a new and urgent need for stimuli was met by the film. In a film, perception in the form of shocks was established as a formal principle.
>
> Walter Benjamin

Collision Montage

How It Feels To Be Run Over (1900) is a 40–second film by the Hepworth Manufacturing Company. The film consists of a single shot of a tree-lined road receding towards the centre of the frame, where it vanishes around a bend. The static camera is positioned at waist height on the left-hand side of the road. The film opens with a horse and cart travelling teasingly towards the camera/audience, and then passing safely by, on the other side of the road, to move out of the right-hand edge of the frame. The road is momentarily obscured by the clouds of dust kicked up by the horse's hoofs, and, as it clears, a car can be seen approaching from a distance. Moving closer and travelling faster than the horse and cart, the driver and his two passengers notice the camera/audience and begin gesturing at it/us to move out of the way. The car veers across the road, towards the camera, and, just as it is about to collide with the camera, the entire frame filled by the coachwork of the car. There is a cut, and hand-written text is flashed very briefly on the screen:

?? / !!! / ! / Oh! Mother will be pleased.

How It Feels To Be Run Over identifies implicitly the characteristic pleasures of early cinema: the possibility offered by the new medium to allow the audience safely to experience 'how it feels' to crash. Early cinema may more accurately and productively be seen 'as less a seed-bed for later styles than a place of rupture, a period that showed more dissimilarity than continuity with later film style' (Gunning 1996: 71). 'Cinema of attractions' describes the aesthetic privileging of 'display' over 'story', suggesting that the gratification to be derived from early cinema was a 'pleasure of a particularly

---

* **Seminar for Hypertheory and Heterology** members who contributed to the production of this text were: Bruce Bennett, Fred Botting, Jonathan Munby, Paolo Palladino, Imogen Tyler, Scott Wilson. Special thanks to Karen Jürs-Munby for her translations of material and John Wilson for technical advice.

complicated sort' (Gunning 1989: 37). An analogy for the appeal of these films can be found in staged locomotive crashes, a popular spectacle at the turn of the century, or a Coney Island switchback ride called 'leapfrog', which sends two cars racing towards one another on an apparent collision course. The narrative, such as it is, consists of loosely linked or discrete shocks, violent events, intense moments, or surprising and disconcerting spectacles. It has been assumed that the prevalence of this violence was a consequence of the technical limitations of early film stock and the shooting speeds of early cameras, which prevented the production of shots lasting over a minute. It may be more productive, however, to think of early films not as constrained by limits of technology, but as a product of this technology, exploring its attractive or spectacular possibilities. In this respect *How It Feels To Be Run Over* may be read as an exploration of some of the formal possibilities of the medium, with what is possibly an ironic reference to the famous public screening of the Lumières' *L'Arrivée d'un Train* (1895), where the audience, apparently unfamiliar with any cinematographic conventions of spatial representation, reportedly ducked to avoid the oncoming locomotive. The status of the Lumières' film as the mythic, originary or primal scene of cinema is at once reaffirmed and problematised by *How It Feels To Be Run Over*. It resists a simple framing as a symptomatic re-playing of the traumatic primal scene of cinema and illustrates both the centrality of the crash in early cinema with its 'peculiarly modern obsession with violent and aggressive sensations (such as speed or the threat of injury)' (Gunning, 1996: 75) and the desire of cinema audiences to be moved without moving, *to feel*, via spectatorial positioning, that which ordinarily they would not feel: 'how it feels to be run over'. Collision montage.[1]

Cinema, then, crashes into the twentieth century. Or rather it simulates its technological impact *as* a crash. The simulated crash inaugurates a new aesthetic, a new mode of affect that reconfigures the human sensorium and subjects it to a new order of experience. The twentieth century *feels* differently. The stately horse-and-carriage narrative of modernity is superseded by the automotive impact of hypermodernity, which veers away from the steady pace of Enlightenment progress, accelerates, and smashes into the cinematic gaze of the future present. Retrospectively, and improperly, it is possible to allegorize *How It Feels To Be Run Over* as a machinic prophecy. But hypermodernity hits the gaze of the future present before it has a chance to blink, before it can recognise itself in any subject driving the machine; there is no time for a novelistic point of identification, the pupils of that gaze merely dilate and contract in a rapid, oscillating process of attraction and repulsion. Cerebral experiences supplant physical ones, as the desire to experience new and increased sensations increases. These experiences are both immediate and hyper-mediated through new media technologies, as everything is surveyed and felt through the lens of another.

In this essay we want to locate this crash at the imaginary juncture between two epochs: the Age of Technology emerges from the dust of the Age of Enlightenment and takes modernity in a different direction. This divergence is only visible, however, from the present, the point of impact that is already now another epoch in which crashing is a permanent condition. We have entered the Age of Information, where the very materiality of experience has been digitally reformatted.

The nineteenth century crashed into the twentieth century most spectacularly in World War One, when a nineteenth-century war machine of footsoldiers, horse-drawn artillery and mounted cavalry was hit by a wall of metal thrown up by automatic weapons, tanks and aircraft. It was in the context of this 'carnage incomparable' that Freud discussed the attraction-repulsion mechanics of human identification. Commenting on his grandson's behaviour, Freud noted, in *Beyond the Pleasure Principle,* how the child compensated for the loss of the maternal presence by acting out an aggressive game of departure and return in which the child activated an apparent 'instinct for mastery' by way of a symbol [object], a cotton reel or, more commonly these days, a toy car. In his reading of the 'fort/da' Freud proposes an 'economic motive', in which considerations of pleasure articulate the effects of trauma and their recurrence in play. Turning the child's 'distressing experience' into a game allows the child to deal with the shock of an unexpected loss by preparing the cathexis (in the form of anxiety) that restricts the impact of a shock: initially 'overpowered by the experience', the child, 'by repeating it, unpleasurable though it was, as a game … took an *active* part'; in the same way, dreams endeavour 'to master the stimulus retrospectively, by developing the anxiety whose omission is the cause of the traumatic neurosis' (Freud 1984: 285, 304). In other words, the child perversely replays 'how it feels' when he is 'abandoned' in order to more effectively 'manage' his anticipated shock at the mother's actual departure. Freud also noted how the child oedipalised the game, smashing his toys on the floor and exclaiming 'Go to the fwont!'. Freud also adds: 'he had heard at the time that his absent father was "at the front", and was far from regretting his absence; on the contrary he made it quite clear that he had no desire to be disturbed in his sole possession of his mother' (Freud 1984: 285).[2] 'Oh! Mother will be pleased'. The enigmatic coda to *How It Feels To Be Run Over* ironically anticipates, with pleasure, the displeasure of the mother, and in so doing acknowledges that the whole performance of the crash has been staged for an imagined maternal gaze.

A similar process to that outlined in *Beyond the Pleasure Principle* is at work in early cinema. The audience, overpowered by the shocks of urban and industrial life, are actively involved by the promoter's introduction and their own screams; with curiosity and anxiety aroused, they are partially prepared for the shocks that are to come and thus can easily transform the unpleasurable disturbance of psychic equilibrium into the fluctuation of pleasurable sensation. The oscillating movement away and back, the repeated movement of 'fort' and 'da', constitutes a subjective economy which, through aesthetic intervention, hotwires the shocks of modernity to the rhythmic pulses of systematic motion. As this process continues and escalates throughout the twentieth century, the famous cotton reel, the vehicle of self-identification, oedipal aggression and subjective experience, in its various guises of motorbike, car, ski jet or simply movie, TV or computer image, moves back and forward, faster and faster. Signifiers of identity become digitalized and absorbed into the general process of machinic functioning and vehicular flows. Individual machines simply become component parts of a networked mechanosphere, whose crashes seem to denote some 'other enjoyment' beyond the scope of human subjects. Faster and faster, fact and fiction, absence and presence, become indistinguishable in the hyper-real/reel. Ironically, the objects created by a human desire for increased sensation, be they films, games, computers, drugs, often leave the subject empty, bored, fatigued, suffering from sensory overload, numb, unable *to feel it* – and addicted, needing more. The fantasy experience of the present is the one that promises to be 'the real thing', slices of unmediated, raw, pure and uncut experience.

> This is not 'like TV only better'. This is life. It's a piece of somebody's life. It's pure and uncut, straight from the cerebral cortex. I mean you're there. You're doing it, you're seeing it, you're hearing it, you're *feeling* it.

This is the spiel used by Lenny Nero, central character of Kathryn Bigelow's film *Strange Days* (1995), to sell black market SQUID (Super-conducting Quantum Interference Device), 'clips' to a client. *Strange Days* is set at the other end of the century from *How It Feels To Be Run Over*, the story opening on 31st December 1999, but it displays a consistent ambiguous fascination with 'how it feels'. The first shot is an extreme close-up of a blinking eye, suggesting immediately a self-referential concern with spectatorship. 'You ready?', a disembodied voice asks on the soundtrack. 'Yeah, boot it', replies a second. There is a cut to a distorted, pixelated image accompanied by white noise and indistinct voices. The image resolves into a shot of the interior of a moving car. As with *How It Feels To Be Run Over*, the clip is a single 3-minute point-of-view shot filmed with an eye-level mobile camera and shows us the robbery of a restaurant from the disorientating subjective perspective of one of the thieves.

The shot ends with his/our death when he/we fall from the roof of a high building during a police chase and tumble down six storeys to the street. As with the 1900 film, the clip is cut short at the point of impact. The 'crash' cannot be incorporated into a narrative sequence but derails it. Just as he/we are about to hit the tarmac, there is a cut to a black screen followed by a few frames of colourful static patterns before Nero tears the SQUID rig from his head. He chastises his supplier, Tick, for not warning him this was a 'snuff' clip. 'You know I hate the zap when they die', he complains. 'It just brings down your whole day'.

Experiencing death, a moment that remains unrepresentable, is a disappointment. It is shown as both distressing and mildly depressing. It brings down your whole day, or rather returns you to yourself and the day you were having, one devoid of experience. It is as if SQUID offers the only means of genuine experience, an experience that, however mundane, is experienced by the Other. In Nero's words, 'One man's mundane and desperate existence is another man's Technicolor.' As technological development rapidly moves us towards the fantasy of total identification with the experience of another – total empathy, a generic index of humanity in science fiction – the imperative becomes to regain a sense of experience, to feel how it feels *to feel*.

'Feeling what the other feels' is not so far away from the voyeurism of the confessional media of the 1990s which dominate popular culture: Springer-style television shows, the rise of celebrity confession, group therapy. *Strange Days* envisages the fin-de-siècle culture as one obsessed with 'how it feels'. This returns us to the aesthetic of attractions we have identified as the beginning of cinema. Shock becomes not only the experience of technology or a way of coping with technology, the traumatic response, but its only purpose. There is no progression, no catharsis, no Enlightenment narrative, no deferment, only experience itself, the will-to-feel. 'Right here, right now'.

Nineteenth-century Nervous Breakdown

> 'The first shock of a great earthquake had, just at that period, rent the whole neighbourhood to its centre.' Though characterised as an 'earthquake', this devastation and ruination of 1840s Camden Town has little to do with nature. The catastrophe is the result of the monstrous, mechanical shadow being cast over Europe: the Railway
>
> (Dickens 1982: 120–1).

Throughout Charles Dickens' *Dombey and Son*, first serialised between 1846 and 1848, the transformation of natural and urban life by the advances of organised industrialism is demonically embodied by the railway, the arrival of which is marked by emotions that range from suspicion and fear to outright terror. Fear, terror and anxiety were quite common responses to the emergence of the railway system and the experience of rail travel in the period. Wolfgang Shivelbusch notes that until the novelty of rail transport was dulled by familiarity, travellers remained aware of an 'ever-present fear of potential disaster'. One passenger, in 1829, noted the difficulty of suppressing 'the notion of instant death to all upon the least accident happening' (Schivelbusch 1979: 131).

This general sense of terror is regularly underlined throughout *Dombey and Son* and culminates, towards the end of the novel, when the sense of foreboding and catastrophe is brutally manifested in death. The novel's schemer, Carker, is forced by 'the crash of his project' into a desperate flight (Dickens 1982: 872). On glimpsing his pursuer, Carker staggers and turns to run:

> He heard a shout – another – saw the face change from its vindictive passion to a faint sickness and terror – felt the earth tremble – knew in a moment that the rush was come – uttered a shriek – looked round – saw the red eyes, bleared and dim, in the daylight, close upon him – was beaten down, caught up, and whirled away upon a jagged mill, that spun him round and round, and struck him limb from limb, and licked his stream of life up with its fiery heat, and cast his mutilated fragments in the air.
>
> (875)

This is how it feels to be run over. Almost.

> Catastrophe is thus, through its association with industrialization and the advance of technology, ineluctably linked with the idea of Progress.
>
> (Doane 1990: 230–1)

In Dickens, that 'first shock of the great earthquake' reverberating through Camden Town heralds the arrival of a system that carves up the natural and built environment and replaces it with the mechanical imperatives of a commercial and industrial order, in the process transforming the realm of the aleatory and accidental from a meta-natural location to one that is 'asystematic' (Doane 1990: 237). *Dombey and Son*'s traumatic encounter with the railway system describes a 'sacrificial crisis' articulating – linking and separating – two orders of being: the chaos, confusion, and terror of the railway introduces a new system of mechanised existence through the catastrophe which serves 'to transcend the old violence and recreate a system of difference on another level of organization' (Attali 1985: 34).

A few years after Dickens wrote *Dombey and Son*, Dickens himself suffered a locomotive shock. On 9th June 1865, he was travelling from Folkestone to London when the train was derailed near Staplehurst. Though unaffected at the time, he finds it difficult to reflect on the crash: 'in writing these scanty words of recollection I feel the shake and am obliged to stop' (Dickens 1985: 151). Significantly, for the medical establishment, the trauma from which Dickens suffered was a new phenomenon in need of investigation: 'there are reports about railroad accidents that describe travelers as exhibiting signs of strong psychic disruption, phobias, obsessive actions, etc, without having suffered any actual injury' (Schivelbusch 1979: 137).

Noting the proximity between early accounts of technological shock and psychoanalytic theories of trauma, Schivelbusch turns to Freud for an explanation of both the habituation of travellers to new modes of transportation and the after-effects of accidents. Endorsing the hypothesis, in *Beyond the Pleasure Principle*, that organisms develop a 'protective shield' to cope with the excitations of external stimuli, Schivelbusch applies it to the experience of rail travel. As a new stimulus, the speed of travel and its effects on perception is a mildly distressing and irritating experience. With habituation, however, the velocity is 'psychically assimilated', the result of a thickening of the protective shield of consciousness. Shock thus becomes 'the shattering of a stimulus shield of convention' (Schivelbusch 1979: 158). Freud's abstract model, moreover, allows Schivelbusch to theorise the relationship between culture and technology so that 'social rules and technologically produced stimuli structure the individual in a similar manner, regularizing, regulating, shaping him according to their inherent laws' (Schivelbusch 1979: 158). While technological constructs manifest the external domination of nature, cultural conventions produce internal regulation according to the imperatives of civilisation and social order.

Urban Speed

The opening of Robert Musil's *The Man Without Qualities*, published a year before the outbreak of World War One, begins with a description of a car accident and its aftermath in order to demonstrate the systematic supercession of nature and experience through repeated proximity to a technological order, urban speeds, crowds and transport systems.[3] Accidents, like shock, becomes part of the system of modernity, the asystematic excess internal to its functioning repeatedly projected outside its field of operations. Walter Benjamin offers a materialist account: 'the shock experience which the passer-by has in the crowd corresponds to what the worker "experiences" at his machine' (Benjamin 1973: 178). The repetitive movements and jolts of the machine are reflected in the discordant and dislocating flows of everyday life. This is associated with the decline of auratic experience, in which the opportunities for reflection, imagination and uniqueness of individual experience, fuller in its sense of personal plenitude, permanence and presence than modern 'experience', is erased by mechanical reproduction's obliteration of distance. Experience is thus reshaped by the system of urban capitalist industrial organisation: 'technology has subjected the human sensorium to a new kind of training' (Benjamin 1973: 176). Here shocks operate not so much as technological breakdown, but as points of disjunction, puncta of articulation between speeds: they signal a speeding up, a reordering of the rhythms of the human organism according to the imperatives of the system of mechanical reproduction.

Benjamin's thesis, of course, is primarily concerned with the implications of photographic and cinematic representation. Film is more than an adjunct to the shocks of urban, industrial modernity, more than an aesthetic reflection of the experience of crowds and machines: as a technological invention, a mode of mechanical reproduction, it itself embodies and repeats those shocks. Film, visual traffic akin to urban and mechanical flows, constitutes part of the process of wiring the individual into the energy of modernity. Its shocks have two modalities. First, the 'shattering of tradition' quickly cedes to the shocks that form the basic operating principles of everyday cinematic experience. Second, film does not work to occlude or assuage the shocks of everyday life, but it repeats and intensifies them (Benjamin 1973: 177).

Reiterating the shocks, stimulation and sensation that define modern life, film does more than merely regulate or habituate workers and consumers to the speed and mechanical rhythms of urban, industrial systems; it does more than harden a shield already hard enough to signal, for Benjamin, the atrophy of experience. Instead, it breaks through that shield, allowing for an encounter, which, though destabilising the equilibrium of the viewer, produces sensations of heightened pleasure, repeating shocks on another level in order to overcome the sense of mechanical repetition dulling everyday experience. Cinematic repetition supersedes the repetitive jolts of experience in the crowd or at the machine by inscribing a degree of distance necessary to the process of overcoming feelings of impotence and subjection to the machines of everyday automation.[4]

Shock is thus incorporated. It functions as the asystematic interruption of aesthetic and urban industrial experience, in which the protective shield of consciousness is stimulated by the cinema screen. Accommodating experience to the rhythm of modern life, cinema also speeds up the process of sensation by penetrating the protective shield of consciousness. Given that repeated exposure to external stimuli also serves to harden the shield into an impenetrable shell of habituation, increased shocks are required to produce sensation and thrills. A negative dialectic of shock thus emerges at the abyssal core of modern experience: the more thrills that are presented, the more shocks and sensation there have to be to avoid the process of habituation and assimilation. Over a relatively short time, cinematic techniques are rendered familiar and mundane by their reiteration on the small screen. Entering everyday life in a more pervasive manner than cinema, the ubiquitous television amplifies the process of repetitive shock-pleasure in which thrills are introduced into the domestic space of the home.

Live Death

On 28th January 1986, with millions of Americans watching, the *Challenger* space shuttle exploded. After a stunned silence, television repeated the event again and again. Live death, repeated with the instantaneous force of the now, became the shock bodied forth by technology, about technology. The simultaneous screening of the explosion was intercut with its registration on the distraught faces of those, including the crew's families, gathered at the launch. Between a technological failure and a voyeuristic glimpse of personal drama, between the shuttle's spectacular disintegration and the capsule's impact off the Florida coast nearly three minutes later, there was time to ask how does it feel: 'we imagined from the audio tape the personal nightmare and terror inside the shuttle. Did they know? For how long?' (Mellencamp 1990: 255). But in the gap instituted by and in the televisual spectacle, shock is replaced by repetitive television therapy: 'Through repetition ... television implements on a technical level the organic modus of periodic "balancing out" of shock energies' (Schneider 1993: 141). Television brings the relation of shock and repetition closer than ever in the speed of access that it seems to provide to global events. For Patricia Mellencamp, TV is both 'thrill and preclusion'; it 'administers and cushions shocks, is both traumatic shock and Freud's "protective shield"' (Mellancamp 1990: 243, 254).

To watch death live on TV is not to experience it, but to enjoy 'participatory nonparticipation' (Mellancamp 1990: 262). Hence, on the spot reports must recuperate the event with endless statements from witnesses and victims, all asked the same question: 'how does it feel?' Live death, even as it bursts on the screen with the immediacy of the present, remains virtual, happening elsewhere, to others: despite the proximity, enough distance is inscribed to hollow out the moment of experience as an encounter that has just been missed.

Instant Experience

> Even NASA has been unable to avoid repeating the disaster for the sake of entertainment. One of the most popular exhibits at the new Space Center Houston, a $70 million attraction designed by the same firm that did Disney's Epcot Center, is a Nintendo-like exhibit that is a wall of computer simulators the visitor can use to attempt to land the space shuttle. The exhibit area resonates with loud crashing sounds when, as is the case more often than not, the visitor veers into the swamp or explodes on the runway.
>
> (Penley 1997: 48)

With virtual reality and computer simulations, the spectator is drawn into the image-event. Here, a new network of culture, shock and technology is manifested: a network of instantaneous communication, of virtual technologies and absolute digital speeds, replaces the orders of 'metabolic proximity' and 'mechanical proximity' with the imperatives of 'electromagnetic proximity' (Virilio 1998: 186). Systems that are defined by the relationship of mass and energy are succeeded by a network in which 'reality's third dimension' appears and is marked by 'the incredible possibility of a new kind of shock: *information shock*' (Virilio 1998: 189).

Accidents become essential features of informational living. And they are no longer limited to the specific instances of technological failure manifested in the traffic of the transport revolution. Instead, accidents become assimilated as the 'test' crashes integral to the drive for greater speed. For example, for Virilio, the introduction of 'unlimited highway speed' in Germany, in 1978, offers an index of the transformation of social and economic concerns through new technological imperatives: the whole nation is placed in the service of the automobile industry, 'highway casualties are casualties of Progress. Every driver has become a "test pilot" for technological expansion' (Virilio 1993: 213–4). Or a crash test dummy. The risks run by the driving public are undertaken 'in the name of product dependability': the maximum speed of cars – used or not – is a mark of durability and reliability and, hence, a sign of quality attractive to foreign markets with or without speed limits. Here, industrial performance is 'guaranteed by speeding' (Virilio 1993: 214). The effects of a system of technological speed on mode of production are also reflected in modes of consumption ruled by a 'law of stimulation in which humans become 'hyperactivated' beings' (Virilio 1995: 126). 'Superstimulants' that are 'the logical extension of a metropolitan sedentariness' serve to speed up the body for pleasurable as much as work-related performance (see Virilio 1995: 102–3). Shock takes the subject beyond judgement, reason or feeling, inducing an equilibrium of permanent disequilibrium that can no longer be simply correlated with an economy of pleasure.

Shock, once connoting the decline of modern experience, now becomes the only avenue of experience left. Without shocks there is no experience, no feeling, no excess that guarantees the fullness of the living being. Take a trip to Paris and pay a taxi driver to experience the pleasures of the 'Black Mercedes Tour'. And be driven at the correct speed – if the price is right. 'I have lived …' runs the refrain of a recent Playstation TV commercial. But living is not equated with the shots of workaday individuals going about their daily lives. Living is conquering armies and visiting new worlds. 'I have lived …', the young actors in the commercial speak in the past tense. To have lived, to have felt; the imperative of instantaneity precipitates and postpones fullness. The injunction to keep on shocking is thus a demand for feeling, for experience, understood as the speeding towards life's fullness, to the utmost, maximised potential of living glimpsed in the pregnant instantaneity of death: how does it feel to live life to the max? How does it feel to enjoy that once-in-a-lifetime experience, death? How does it feel … to feel?

Technical Ecstasy

According to *Billion Dollar Fun Fairs* (1998), a Carlton TV documentary, the construction of 'The Islands of Adventure' theme park was like 'building a city – with all the services, roads and restaurants you'd expect to support millions'. Apparently, the car parks are so huge that, like the Great Wall of China, they are 'visible from space'. Over 200 million people visit movie attraction theme parks in the US, perhaps in order to become oblivious, as Baudrillard famously said of Florida's Disneyworld, to the fact that all of the US is a movie attraction theme park. While the original cinema of attractions produced its aesthetic shock through conjuring a realist illusion that a train or car was about to plunge out of the screen, the movie attraction business immerses its audience *into* a screen-world that is more realistic, more vivid than actual everyday life. When interviewed by Carlton TV, Carey Cooper, a Professor of Psychology specialising in the therapeutic uses of movies and movie attractions, suggested that movie attractions have a beneficial effect in relieving the stress and boredom of quotidian existence. Cooper argued that, secure in the knowledge that their fears are being controlled and the risks are managed, the movie attraction customers can feel free to experience the thrills that are simulated for them, to the point that it 'makes them feel as if they were alive'. The implication is, curiously, that in their ordinary lives these customers are dead.

The level of terror needs to be continually raised as the paying customer seeks more thrills, in the process becoming the 'test pilot' of higher degrees of technological speed and complexity. The process of being made to 'feel alive', then, requires the production of more and more convincing crashes that don't quite happen, more near-death experiences that enable the rider to exceed the limitations of his or her earthbound, corporeal body. As Douglas Trumbull, creator of the *Back to the Future Ride*, 'the attraction by which all the others are judged', suggests: 'the *Back to the Future Ride* is like an out-of-body experience. It's like a dream. It's like some experience beyond reality'. Significantly, Trumbull realised the potential of themed experience when he worked, with Stanley Kubrick, on the final sequence of *2001*, a sequence that took the audience on a trip into space'. For him, this sequence 'wasn't about plot, narrative or character development': it provided an 'immersive cinematic experience'.

Though the *Back to the Future Ride* can simulate incredible speeds, twisting and turning, diving, veering away and accelerating at the imminent impact of some object or monster, during the ride the De Lorean never actually leaves the room – it goes nowhere. Yet the G-Force it appears to generate is as strong as a jet fighter. The makers of *Billion Dollar Fun Fairs* used a stunt fighter pilot, Sandy Rosel, to test the ride and see how it compared with the military jets he flies. Rosel was happy to confirm the 'realism' of the *Back to the Future Ride* and its duplication of his own workaday experience. Curiously, Rosel described his work in similar terms to Trumbull's description of his own ride's sublimity: 'When I'm in the aircraft I'm a completely different person. You're throwing caution and fear away. You're focusing so much on what you're doing. It's a tremendous feeling; it is almost an out-of-body experience. It is a sensation that is unlike anything else'. These rides, then, correspond to the work-experience of those at the heart of the military machine whose vehicles are also wired into the network of the 'electronic ecosystem' by the set of computers controlling the jet (see Adam 1991). When he 'tests' his plane, Rosel is also being taken for a ride. But his presence in the aircraft is crucial as the human stake in the testing of the technology. For the USAF, clearly, ecstasy equals efficiency. Rosel's 'inner experience' is a paradoxical one that involves the dissolution of his body in the apprehension of an impossible totality – the global network – in which he dissolves like sugar in water. It is the ecstasy of human disappearance within the machine.

Like fairground attractions, the movie attraction business provides therapy and training for the mass of suburban humanity who, for now, function within the interconnected machineries of the global mechanosphere. But as such, they function as an ecstatic excrescence, the foam that inseminates or lubricates the reproduction and development of technological systems. Like 'insects pollinating an independent species of machine-flower', humans merely service the evolution of a machinism beyond their ken (de Landa 1991: 3). Or their Barbie (SHaH, 1997). Human death provides the point of erotic friction, the shifting point of limitation, that, for now, speeds the desire and momentum of optimum performance. But further, the human imagination also demands, impossibly, that the machinery go faster. The audience wants still more, and the creative consultants wait impatiently for the technology to deliver. As Jan de Bont says in *Billion Dollar Fun Fairs*: 'I can't wait for the technology to go a little faster; it is still too slow for me. My imagination goes beyond what is possible yet'. In the theme park, then, the latest technology is tested to the limit; the eroticism of the crash is brought into play in order to facilitate an acceleration both beyond body, feeling, experience and towards the plenitude of a barely imaginable intensity.

'Oh! Mother will be pleased'.

Notes

1 This term, which refers to the counter-aesthetics of cinema developed by Sergei Eisenstein, succinctly incorporates both a concept of film as an accumulation of violent or intense moments, rather than a series of narrative climaxes, and a model of spectatorial interaction with the film, the sharply contrasting and heterogeneous images and events that pile into the viewer, frame after frame, shot after shot, leaving her or him dazed and reeling, attempting to reconstruct the images within some sort of narrative or interpretive framework (Eisenstein 1988, Vol. 1 (1922–1934): passim).

2 At this point Freud notes, 'When the child was five and three-quarters, his mother died. Now that she was really "gone" (o-o-o), the little boy showed no signs of grief' (Freud 1984: 286n).

3 Accidents are already treated disinterestedly here as mere figures: 'according to American statistics ... there are over a hundred and ninety thousand people killed on the roads annually over there, and four hundred and fifty thousand injured' (Musil 1995: 6).

4 Jeffrey Schnapp notes how the repetitive cycles characterizing the modern experience necessarily incorporate the crash as stimulant: 'the *kinematic subject* [...] finds himself caught in an addiction loop, threatened on the one hand by monotony and, on the other, by the need for ever new stimuli in order to maintain the same level of intensity: [...] the crash becomes a necessary feature of this loop structure, at once vouching for its legitimacy (by crystallizing the intensity for which it stands), serving as a regenerative device (by initiating a new cycle of hyperstimulation), and marking an absolute limit (death)' (Schnapp 1999: 4)

References

Adam, J. (1991) 'Warfare in the Information Age'. *IEEE Spectrum* September. 26–33.

Attali, Jacques (1985) *Noise: The Political Economy of Music*. Manchester: Manchester University Press.

Benjamin, Walter (1973) *Illuminations*. Tr. Harry Zohn. London: Fontana/Collins.

De Landa, Manuel (1991) *War in the Age of Intelligent Machines*. New York: Zone.

Dickens, Charles (1982) *Dombey and Son*. Ed. Peter Fairclough. Harmondsworth: Penguin.

—— (1985) *Selected Letters of Charles Dickens*. Ed. David Paroissien. London: Macmillan.

Doane, Mary Anne (1990) 'Information, Crisis, Catastrophe', in Patricia Mellencamp (ed) *Logics of Television: Essays in Cultural Criticism*. London and Bloomington: BFI and Indiana University Press. 222–239.

Eisenstein, Sergei (1988) *Writings*. Ed. Richard Taylor. London and Bloomington: BFI and Indiana University Press.

Freud, Sigmund (1984) *Beyond the Pleasure Principle*. Tr. James Strachey, *On Metapsychology*. Harmondsworth: Penguin.

Gunning, Tom (1989) 'An Aesthetic of Astonishment: Early Film and the (In)credulous Spectator'. *Art and Text*. *34*. 31–44.

—— (1996) '"Now You See It, Now You Don't": The Temporality of the Cinema of Attractions' in Richard Abel (ed.) *Silent Film*. London: Athlone. 69–84.

Mellencamp, Patricia (1990) 'TV Time and Catastrophe, or Beyond the Pleasure Principle of Television' in Patricia Mellencamp (ed.) *Logics of Television: Essays in Cultural Criticism*. London and Bloomington: BFI and Indiana University Press. 240–266.

Musil, Robert (1995) *The Man Without Qualities*. London: Minerva.

Penley, Constance (1997) *NASA/Trek: Popular Science and Sex in America*. London: Verso.

Schivelbusch, Wolfgang (1979) *The Railway Journey: Trains and Travel in the Nineteenth Century*. Tr. Anselm Hollo. New York: Urizen Books.

Schnapp, Jeffrey (1999) 'Crash (Speed as Engine of Individuation)', *Modernism/Modernity* 6(1) 1–49.

Schneider, Manfred (1993) 'Gott würfelt und schlägt den Takt: Über Unfälle und Zeitmaschinen' in Museum für Gestaltung Zürich (ed.), *Zeitreise: Bilder/ Maschine/ Strategien / Rätsel*, Frankfurt am Main: Stroemfeld/ Roter Stern. 132–145.

SHaH (1997) 'Incorporating the Impossible: A General Economy of the Future Present'. *Cultural Values* 1(2) 178–204.

Virilio, Paul (1993) 'The Primal Accident' in Brian Massumi (ed.) *The Politics of Everyday Fear*. Minneapolis: University of Minnesota Press. 211–220.

—— (1995) *The Art of the Motor*. Tr. Julie Rose. Minneapolis: University of Minnesota Press.

—— (1998) 'Continental Drift' in James Der Derian (ed.) *The Virilio Reader*. Oxford: Blackwell. 182–195.

Film and Television

Billion Dollar Fun Fairs (1998) w. Neil Richards. dir. Richard Blanshard. Carlton.

How It Feels To Be Run Over (1900) Hepworth Manufacturing Company. *Early Cinema: Primitives And Pioneers* Vol. 2. BFI.

Strange Days (1995) dir. Kathryn Bigelow. Universal.

4 Eye-Hunger: Physical Pleasure and Non-Narrative Cinema*

Karin Littau

> Flore was standing there, looking too. She loved accidents: any mention of an animal run over, a man cut in pieces by a train, was bound to make her rush to the spot.
>
> (Emile Zola 1890, *La Bête Humaine*)

Eye-hunger or *Schaulust*,[1] unlike voyeurism, is not about gratification at a distance, nor is it a private activity; the *Schaulustige*, unlike the voyeur, neither hides, nor is alone, but emerges in full view as part of the crowd, milling ever closer towards the intense pressure at its spectacular centre. Whether a crowd gathers spontaneously at the site/sight of an unforeseen accident, or comes together for the staged event of a head-on crash, the flirtation with disaster is about an 'urgent need for stimuli'. For Benjamin this 'was met by the film' where 'perception in the form of shocks was established as a formal principle' (1983: 132); for Kracauer, it was fulfilled by the miscellany of entertainments offered by the early moving picture shows where the 'total artwork of effects assaults every one of the senses using every possible means' (1987: 92).[2] When 30,000 people therefore paid to see the spectacle of the crashing train in 1896 at Crush City, Texas, it is not surprising that their fascination with motion, speed, and collision – in short, the aesthetics of shock – was also shared by the early cinema audiences who flocked to see train 'technology go out of control' (Kirby 1988: 120)[3] and film technology's 'illusion of motion' (Gunning 1994: 125) in features such as the Lumière brothers' *Arrivée d'un Train* (1895), Edison/Porter's *Uncle Josh at the Moving Picture Show* (1902), *The Photographer's Mishap* (1901) or Edison's *Railway Smash-Up* (1904). What interests me here is not so much the correlation between railway travel and cinema-going, but the crowd's assault by and reaction to the crash, be it real, staged, or simulated: this is to say, how the crash, as the very emblem of the thrill, shock and disaster, is not to be understood solely as an impact on our psyche, in that it might traumatize an eye-witness or fulfil a given spectator's fantasy of being run-over, but translates into a physical reflex, a bodily sensation for the *Schaulustige*.

---

* I would like to thank Richard Shackle of Colchester Public Library for his help in locating materials on the Colchester railway disaster of 1913.

What the now legendary story of the audience fleeing the scene of *Arrivée d'un Train* illustrates, is not so much that they mistook the screen image of the on-coming train for a real train that would run into them, that they were naive or psychotic, but that visual pleasure is physical sensation. The cinema is not just about absorption or identification, or to be explained from the perspective of an individual's psyche, and the pleasure of viewing is not just about getting lost in a fictional world; instead, cinemas from vaudeville to the multiplex have continued to be 'get-thrills-quick-theatres', to use Miriam Hansen's phrase (1991: 65), whose visual shocks send tremors through the body of the crowd. Since the thrills of the movies are 'nerve-racking' according to Hans Rost, which he sees as synonymous in 1916 with 'today's quest for images' (qu. Hake 1993: 13), we might seize on the *Schaulustige* as a model for spectatorship rather than the figure of the 'spectator-fish taking in everything with their eyes, nothing with their bodies' (Metz 1982: 97, qu. Williams 1994: 2), in order to de-emphasize both a psychoanalytic and a cognitive moment in looking, and re-emphasize that which excites the nerves and makes the flesh creep.

While it is true that the classic Realist cinema deploys narrative strategies of absorption, it by no means follows that the cinema *per se* lulls its subjects into a 'state of artificial regression' (Baudry 1999: 773). As Tom Gunning's historical work has shown, actuality filmmaking before the period of the nickelodeon is 'a cinema of instants rather than developing situations' (1994: 123), and as such displays rather than tells, astonishes rather than absorbs, placing 'emphasis on the thrill itself – the immediate reaction of the viewer' (1994: 122). Assessing the impact of *Arriveé d'un Train* on the audience, he writes,

> Rather than mistaking the image for reality, the spectator is astonished by its transformation through the new illusion of projected motion. Far from credulity, it is the incredible nature of the illusion that renders the viewer speechless. What is displayed before the audience is less the impending speed of the train than the force of the cinematic apparatus.
>
> (1994: 118)

It is not so much the quasi-Brechtian aspects of the early cinema which I want to pick up on here ('the spectator does not get lost in a fictional world and its drama, but remains *aware* [my emphasis] of the act of looking' [Gunning 1994: 121]), but precisely those aspects of what Gunning calls 'the cinema of attractions' which elicit an 'immediate reaction' in its spectator, rendering its 'viewer speechless', and which therefore imply a physiological dimension in the act of looking. What is significant about the reaction of audiences to *Arrivée d'un train*, I contend, is their prerational response to a possible danger, which is not the result of a naivete that mistakes the illusion for reality, but the result of a forgetting of the conscious self in favour of the physical self, and as such an index of the way in which film 'affects primarily the spectator's senses, engaging him physiologically before he is in a position to respond intellectually' (Kracauer 1960, 1997: 158), before he or she has the presence of mind to recognize, appreciate, or analyse the artistry of effect. Here also, the cinema of the crash makes itself felt; for, if anything, it wakes from hypnotic slumber and awakens stimuli, entices physical shock in its attempt to break through the protection shield of the skin, get under our skin so to speak. This is why spectating the crash becomes the paradigm case for *Schaulust* and its concomitant curiosity, the German *Neugier* – the lust, or appetite (*Lust*), to watch (*schauen*) and the craving (*Gier*) for novelty, for the new (*neu*) – terms in which inhere semantically the very physical pleasures of looking. '*Schaulust* celebrates its triumphs' here (Benjamin 1991: 572, my translation), because it remains irreducible to a merely psychological appropriation. Although flight appears to be the physical other of fright, or trauma, what the spectacle of the crash (real, staged or simulated) reveals is the physiological underpinnings of both.

At the junction of movement and vision is not just the new technology of the motion picture, but also the materiality of the city with its breathless traffic, railroads, cars and crowds, and the physical effects this environment has on its city strollers, train passengers and movie-goers alike. At this crossroads are also accidents, which is why Wolfgang Schivelbusch sees the 'ever-present fear of a potential disaster' linked with the invention of the railways (1986: 130) as a mode of transportation which was perceived as inhumanly fast. This fear is just as tangible in the crowded metropolis where, as Benjamin finds, 'moving through traffic involves the individual in a series of shocks and collisions' (1983: 132). The effect on the man in the crowd is that 'at dangerous crossings, nervous impulses flow through him in rapid succession' (Benjamin 1983: 132), just as nervous energies befall the traveller in the 'annihilation of space and time' (Schivelbusch 1986: 33) as the train hurries along the rails 'like a fierce storm sweeping all before it' (Zola 1977: 58). What is at stake here is not only speed and motion, that crashes are 'the work of a moment', as Thomas Mann's narrator tells us in 'Railway Accident', for which there is neither time to prepare, nor 'time to stop and think' (1997: 189–90),[4] but that pictures in motion are the work of a moment, too fleeting to be 'describe[d] verbally or rationalize[d] cognitively' (Charney 1995: 285). The fast pace of metropolitan life, which confronts its strollers, travellers and bystanders with the 'rapid crowding of changing images, the sharp discontinuity in the grasp of a single glance, and the unexpectedness of onrushing impressions' (Simmel 1997: 175), makes great demands on the organ of looking. Modernity makes itself felt as it 'pull[s] at the eyeballs on looking out of the window' of a moving train (Russel Reynolds 1884, qu. Schivelbusch 1986: 118), or gives an 'aching sensation to the eye' looking from a window onto the jostling crowds of the street (Poe 1986: 183). This is a hasty, impressionist kind of looking where faces on a passing train 'went by in a flash [so that] she was never quite sure she really had seen them; all the faces got blurred and merged one into another, indistinguishable' (Zola 1977: 56), and where the 'rapidity with which the world of light flitted before the window, prevented me from casting more than a glance upon each visage' (Poe 1986: 183). What these descriptions evoke, are not only how face upon face amasses into the urban crowd, but how image upon image, glimpsed from behind a window, mobilizes the eye.[5] Only a small step then from the street into the picture house, from the window to the screen, towards a 'filmic perception';[6] and yet a huge distance from 'the art of seeing' proposed by the cousin at the corner window in E.T.A. Hoffmann's tale (1992: 380) to the physiology of 'inflamed eyes, and headaches' (Franz X. Schönhuber 1918, qu. Hake 1993: 49) and 'an irritation of the retina caused by the confusion of images' (Dr Campbell 1907, qu. Kirby 1988: 115), attested to by cinema reformers and doctors alike.

The effects of the hectic environment on the nineteenth-century city dweller which Poe's *The Man of the Crowd* (1845) and Zola's *La Bête Humaine* (1890) describe, are not unlike the descriptions Kracauer gives of the cinema as a place where '[t]he stimulations of the senses succeed each other with such rapidity that there is no room left for even the slightest contemplation to squeeze in between them' (1987: 94). But if as Simmel suggests in 1903, this stimulation results in a kind of overload, whereby 'the nerves' are pushed 'to their strongest reactivity for such a long time that they finally cease to react at all' (1997: 178), it would follow that 'dulled senses demand powerful stimuli' as a survey surmises in 1909, for, 'exhaustion of the vital forces leads to a desire for crude, for violent excitation' (qu. Jowett 1983: 204). The cinema with its vaudeville multi-attention spectacles and its kinesthetic film sensations – alongside amusement parks, mechanical rides, or automobile stunts (see Singer 1995) – was just the kind of space to provide the necessary kicks by piling thrill upon thrill. The over-cranked projection of an attraction known as *The Runaway Train* may have merely induced vertigo in its audience (see Gunning 1983: 364), and the on-rushing locomotive of *Arriveé d'un Train* may have only given a hint of a potential collision, by the time an audience has seen *How It Feels to be Run Over* (Hepworth 1900), where a motor car 'dashes full into the spectator, who sees "stars" as the picture comes to an end' (from the catalogue description qu. Chanan 1996: 228), it is clear that the thrills and stimuli very much aim for physical effect. This is to say, if *Arrivée d'un Train* merely left its viewers sitting there 'with gaping mouths' (Méliès on the Lumière premiere, qu. Gunning 1994: 119), the kinesthetic sensation of the phantom ride, where a camera is strapped to the front of a moving vehicle and thus gives the illusion of moving through space, such as in the *Haverstraw Tunnel* film by Biograph (1897), made its spectators 'instinctively hold [their] breath as when on the edge of a crisis that might become a catastrophe' (review from 1897, qu. Hansen 1991: 32).

Crucially, the pleasure seems to emanate in the flirtation with a 'catastrophe'; a summary of a trade paper account from 1916 given by Raymond Fielding on the thrills of a Hale's Tour, which 'took the form of an artificial railway car whose operation combined auditory, tactile, visual and ambulatory sensations to provide a remarkably convincing illusion of railway travel' (1983: 117), demonstrates just this:

> the illusion was so good that when trolley rides through cities were shown, members of the audience frequently yelled at pedestrians to get out of the way or be run down. One demented fellow even kept coming back to the same show, day after day. Sooner or later, he figured, the engineer would make a mistake and *he would get to see a train wreck.* [my emphasis]
>
> (Fielding 1983: 124)

What is clear from such a description, to return to Simmel's point about the blunting of sensations, is that stronger sensations are called for, and that this means a cranking up

Figure 4.1 This titlecard used by SKY ONE shows a train enthusiast deliberately derailing a model train in order to photograph the crash. It also shows his evident pleasure in the crash he has caused; a pleasure in looking which is simultaneously framed by the real train rushing past in the background of the screen.

of the thrill: from a leisurely ride to the sensational crash. This is precisely the point argued by Ben Singer in his essay 'Modernity, Hyperstimulus and the Rise of Popular Sensationalism', when he traces the kinds of images which were taking hold in the popular press in the mid 1890s:

> It is telling that illustrations of accidents almost always employed a particular presentational schema: They were obliged, of course, to show the victim at the instant of most intense shock, just before death, but *along with this they almost always showed a startled bystander looking on in horror, his or her body jolted into a reflex action*. Such illustrations thus stressed not only the dangers of big city life but also its relentless nervous shocks.
>
> (1995: 83, my emphasis)

What is implicit in both Fielding's and Singer's accounts, is the figure of the *Schaulustige*, the passenger of the Hale Tour just as 'startled 'bystanders' are sensation-seekers who crave the sheer physical thrill. Nerves are therefore not just to be tickled through the sensation of movement, actual or stimulated, but when movement is violently arrested in the crash, another powerful stimulation makes itself felt. At its most extreme and pathological, it is 'the physical lust at the sight of this pathetic corpse', which makes the engine-driver, Jacques Lantier's 'heart [beat] furiously' (Zola 1977: 73) when he finds the 'crashed' body of Grandmorin by the side of the railway tracks; or the sexual lust which overcomes the male protagonist in *Un Chien Andalou* (1929) immediately after he has – in anticipation and 'evidently excited' (Dali & Buñuel 1994: 21) – seen the running-over of a girl in the street, when 'lustfully with rolling eyes' (5) he turns to the female protagonist, another witness of the crash, to touch her breasts.[7]

Such *reflex actions, physical lust or evident excitement* are not reducibly mental phenomena, they are profoundly bodily. Visual lust does not therefore tap into St Augustine's 'lust of the eyes' which wants to see in order to understand, a 'disease of curiosity [...] wherein men desire nothing but to know' (St Augustine 1969: 199).[8] Neither cognitive, nor, related to psychoanalysis' scopic arrangements whereby the distance between spectator and object looked at, must be maintained to prevent the spectator's 'pleasure of his own body' (Metz 1975: 61), *Schaulust* is of the body and as such opposes the kind of 'classical model of the spectator', of which Linda Williams says that 'whether psychoanalytic or ideological', it 'presumed a distanced, decorporealized, monocular eye completely unimplicated in the objects of its vision' (1994: 7). As Dr Edward Rees put it in *The Manchester Guardian* (26th February 1913), the cinema 'suddenly found the lust of the eye, and delights in the gratification of it':

> Every evening a magic carpet transports half of us, men, women, and children, to a region which we can explore with something of the joy of a traveller from chill northern lands in an unvisited country of tropical refulgence where it is always afternoon. [...] You sit in a pleasant torpor, only the eyes of you and what the physiologists call the visual centres awake [...].

As a result, movie-goers suffer from the condition of 'eye-hunger', as the German writer Friedrich Freska explains:

> Rarely has a time suffered so much from eye-hunger [*Augenhunger*] as ours. This is because the telegraph, newspapers, and lines of communication have brought the whole world closer together. Here, working people, bound to their chairs, are assaulted by a welter of images from all sides [...]. That is why we suffer from eye-hunger; and in order that we at least materially satisfy this hunger, there is nothing so fitting as the cinematograph. Eye-hunger is just as important for us in our time as once was the potato, which made it possible to feed the rapidly amounting mass of people.'
>
> (1912, 1984: 98, my translation)

In a similar vein, the Dadaist Walter Serner gives his treatise on the hunger of the eyes in his essay 'Kino und Schaulust' (1978: 53–58), published the same year as Rees' article and a year after Freska's, where he speaks not from the standpoint of the psychoanalyst, but that of the avant-gardist (see Schlüpmann 1990: 302), privileging precisely that which other discourses tend to ignore. Looking is not a disembodied gaze, but truly belongs to the eyes as an organ of the body. *Schaulust* for him is 'a terrible lust' with 'feverish' sensations that 'gush through the blood' and excite the 'flesh' (1978: 53, my translations). Such an analysis of the physiological underpinnings of spectatorship cannot be confined to fictional moments, since it is the very same 'horrible lust to look at atrocity, fight and death [...] which hurries to the morgue and to the site of the crime', and which also, according to Serner, 'pulls the people as if in a frenzy into the cinema' (1978: 54)[9] so that they might feast their 'starving eyes' on the 'exciting adventurousness of a tiger hunt', the 'wild mountain ride', or the 'death-daring car ride' and 'the breath-taking chase over the dizzyingly high roofs of New York [...]' (1978: 55). Nor is such an analysis restricted to kinesthetic motion (the speed of the car-ride, the chase); the physical thrill and intensity of feeling at the sight of the mangled corpse (at the street crash, in the morgue, by the railway tracks) induce 'feverish' sensations just the same.

The following example will serve to show the physical continuity of forms of spectating, irrespective of their fictional or factual status. The same year in which Rees' review and Serner's essay were published, appears this report of a train crash at Colchester North Station in *The Essex County Standard, West Suffolk Gazette*, and *Eastern Counties' Advertiser* (19th July 1913). It gives this 'vivid account' of an eye-witness' 'exciting experience':

> I went down to Colchester with my wife on Saturday for a quiet day in the country. I witnessed instead a spectacle that – seen as I saw it – was the most appalling thing *I could ever hope to imagine.*
>
> (my emphasis)

The train crash that this 'demented fellow' is lucky enough to get to see, is very much expressed in terms of his *Schaulust*, and the effect this 'amazing horror' had on him, is very much described in physiological terms, as he puts it:

> It left me rooted to the spot – dazed – trembling – sick; my wife put her hand to her face and fell on her knees. Remember, this amazing horror happened in an instant – in a space

> of time not greater than it takes to clap the hands together. [...] I think I drew my breath in tremendously – really I don't know what I did. I just watched [...].

What is evident in the detailed account of this 'thrilling story' is that all the immediate responses are processed physically, as manifest in his breathing, shaking, and feelings of nausea. As such, the moment of shock belongs first to sensation, as Leo Charney argues, 'and *then* to consciousness', for, '[i]nside the immediate presence of the moment, what we can do – the only thing we can do – is feel it. The present presence of the moment can occur only in and as sensation' (1995: 285, my emphasis). Charney's argument, in pointing towards two distinct moments, that of sensation and that of cognition, which 'can never inhabit the same moment' (281), is directly relevant to the on-looker's experience of the crash insofar as this unexpected 'work of the moment' – to echo Thomas Mann's words – only 'exists as felt, as experienced, not in the realm of the rational catalog but in the realm of bodily sensation' (Charney 1995: 281). When the eye-witness recounts his experience and states that 'I was too shaken, too incoherent, to tell him what happened' (*The Essex County Standard*) – it is not of course the case here that words fail the speaker altogether; rather they will not string into a coherent narrative. But then, '[w]hat is a word?', we might ask with Nietzsche, but 'a copy in sound of a nerve stimulus' (1988: 81); in the shock, stimuli overwhelm any potential

Figure 4.2 Commemorative Postcard of the Colchester Train Crash, showing the crowds (for which special transport was laid on to see the spectacle).

narrative, leaving its fascinated, arrested spectator stimulated and without verbal or cognitive issue: 'I don't know what I did'.

The Essex County Standard, on the other hand, is not stuck for words when it gives the details of the 'bruises', 'cuts', and limbs 'twisted in the iron work of the overturned engine', leaving little to the imagination. If the crash fulfils a fantasy to see with one's own eyes 'the most appalling thing *I could ever hope to imagine*', the movies could well have imagined this crash for him; so much so, that Ashok Chakravarti, a government official in the state of West Bengal, commenting on the head-on Gaisal Train Crash in India, can state that: 'It is the kind of scene you only see in the movies. You can't imagine how bad it is' (*The Guardian* 3. 8. 1999). The railway switchman in Edison's *Asleep at the Switch* (1910) tries to imagine just how bad it might be, if his wife hadn't alerted the on-coming train in the nick of time after he had fallen asleep whilst on duty. His horror fantasy, Lynne Kirby argues, is a projection of his guilt:

> The switchman wakes up too late, and, realizing his error, begins to hallucinate the probable outcome of his inaction. Inset in the upper left corner of the frame we see two model trains crash head-on, to the switchman's manifest horror. Later the window is filled with the rear-projected image of his would-be victims, who crowd the frame with arms outstretched. These psychic projections of guilt overpower the switchman, and he faints with remorse.
>
> (Kirby 1988: 127, see also 1997: 71)

Is this to suggest that his reactions are profoundly psychological then? However, by Kirby's own admission, the psycho-physical interaction has direct physical consequences; the whole organism of the switchman experiences a 'crash', not as a metaphor, nor simply therefore in an analogical response to a possible or fictive crash, but as reality. He faints, his mind literally shuts down with the overload of sensation. What is crucial here, is to determine whether the reaction of shock, and by extension whether trauma, is either to be explained from the perspective of the psyche (the switchman's guilt) or the body (the switchman's collapse).

A number of early films, which either feature the trauma of the railroad crash such as *Asleep at the Switch*, or the trauma of being run over such as *The Photographer's Mishap* (Edison/Porter 1901), or parody this fear as in *Uncle Josh at the Moving Picture Show* (Edison/Porter 1902), are all illustrative for Kirby of the various ways in which 'the railroad accident victim becomes in relation to early train films, and early cinema more generally, the film accident victim – a traumatized, and, in one sense, hysterical spectator' (1988: 116). This is evident in characters like Josh, who stands in front of a screen watching a train approaching (Edison's *The Black Diamond Express*, 1896), only then to flinch as it comes closer towards him in a 'naive' gesture of 'exaggerated fright, the bodily reaction to the train film' (1988: 125), which Kirby interprets as a hysterical gesture. She reads *The Photographer's Mishap* along similar lines. While setting up a tripod on a railway line, the photographer is run over by the on-coming train he is trying to shoot, but although he is hit by the train, and his camera is destroyed, he jumps back up and moves to another track, where he narrowly misses being run over again by another train. When at the end, however, he is taken away by two men, and 'breaks down, arms flailing, in a hysterical fit' (1988: 125), Kirby once more favours a psychopathological explanation: 'a man suffers an unbelievable accident, the result of which is not so much physical as emotional or mental trauma and shock – the joke being that he suffers no bodily harm being run down' (1988: 125). Does this really confirm that '[i]n theoretical terms, the assaulted spectator is the hysterical spectator' (Kirby 1988: 128)? What if we suggested that the trauma, be it that of the railroad victim, or that of the spectator featured as a victim of the 'train film', is not just a mental and emotional, but also a physical condition? In theoretical terms, this would imply that the assaulted spectator is not just the subject of psychoanalysis but also the subject of physiology.

The lack of visible physical injury, which indicates to Kirby that the photographer has suffered from mental trauma, constitutes the kind of psychological explanation which in the context of railroad accidents only became recognized in medical circles or for injury claims towards the latter part of the nineteenth century. As Schivelbusch illustrates the issue:

> From the early 1880s on, the purely pathological view was superseded by a new, psychopathological one, according to which the shock caused by the accident did not affect the tissue of the spinal marrow, but affected the victim psychically. Now it was the victim's experience of shock that was the main causative factor of the illness. By the end of the 1880s, the concept of 'railway spine' had been replaced by that of 'traumatic neurosis'.
>
> (1986: 135–6)

Despite the waning of the earlier 'material-mechanical explanations', and the shift therefore from "railway spine" to "railway brain", Schivelbusch notes, however, that 'there remained in the background, the continued notion that even the psychic cause ultimately had a "molecular" effect' (1986: 144); a point born out also by Hermann Oppenheim who having coined the term 'traumatic neurosis', physiologizes the condition by 'insisting that railway trauma gave rise to a nerve condition, with "electricity coursing through the nerves as the causative agent"' (qu. Kirby 1988: 123). The very same ambivalence between psychological and physiological explanations comes to the surface also in Freud, who 'saw more than the psychological aspect of trauma', Schivelbusch points out, when he 'developed a renewed interest in the kind of neurosis that is brought about in actual fashion, by means of violent events from outside' in *Beyond the Pleasure Principle*, and which as a consequence 'involved' him in 'a recapitulation of the original concept of traumatic neurosis' (1986: 148).

We might couch Schivelbusch's insights in slightly different terms here, that is, in terms of the shift that occurs in translations of Freud into English, whereby accident neurosis makes way for traumatic neurosis. While the German fairly consistently uses the term *Unfallsneurotiker* (see Freud 1990: 126 [in English, Freud 1991: 283]; 134 [293, 294]; 142 [304]) to refer to the person who suffers from traumatic neurosis, or uses the term *Unfallsträume* (1990: 134) for 'traumatic dreams' (1991: 294), thus embodying in the term the importance of the accident, the English just as consistently edits out any references to the *Unfall*, i.e. the accident, which lies at the root of the disturbance, in the above cited places of *Beyond the Pleasure Principle*. This would seem to suggest a psychologization of Freud, at least as the translator is concerned, by very subtly refusing to acknowledge the materiality of the accident itself which led to trauma (a strange emphasis in any case given this statement by Freud in *Beyond the Pleasure Principle*: 'A condition has long been known and described which occurs after severe mechanical concussions, railway disasters and other accidents involving a risk to life; it has been given the name of "traumatic neurosis".' [1991: 281]) If we refer to the French definition of trauma and traumatic, given by Dr A. Hesnard in the glossary to Freud's *Essais de psychanalyse*, we find in the definitions the kind of material Freud which the English seems to repress:

> *Trauma, traumatic*: said of a physical accident that damages health (a physical shock or impact). Meaning *extended* to emotional experiences (emotional shocks), particularly regarding children confronting sexuality: seduction by an adult, the spectacle of adult sexuality, and so on.
>
> (1986: 277; my trans. and emphasis)

It seems therefore that the English translation of *Beyond the Pleasure Principle* significantly contributes to a reading of Freud and by extension, psychoanalysis, whereby not just a certain materiality is removed, but physiology must make room for psychic phenomena; to put this into the language of the railways, the physiology of 'railway spine' gets absorbed under 'railway brain', or to put this into the language of film criticism, the spectator's body gets expelled by the inner eye of the 'spectator-fish'.[10] To remember Freud's own insistence, however, that '[p]sychoanalysis is unjustly reproached, Gentlemen, for leading to purely psychological theories of pathological problems' (1979: 113) or his acknowledgment of the 'deficiencies' which come from having to work with the descriptions 'peculiar to psychology' which, towards the end of *Beyond the Pleasure Principle* he speculates, 'would probably vanish if we were already in a position to replace the psychological terms by physiological or chemical ones' (1991: 334), would seem to indicate that physical sensations must share the fields of discourse with psychic phenomena. Comparing what he calls the 'old, naive theory of shock' to 'the later and psychologically more ambitious theory' offered by psychoanalysis, Freud states:

> These opposing views are not, however, irreconcilable; nor is the psycho-analytic view of traumatic neurosis identical with the shock theory in its crudest form. The latter regards the essence of the shock as being the direct damage to the molecular structure or even to the histological structure of the elements of the nervous system; whereas what we seek to understand are the effects produced on the *organ* of the mind by the breach in the shield against stimuli and by the problems that follow in its train.
>
> (1991: 303, my emphasis)

Freud speaks here of the brain as 'the organ of the mind', he also, following the insights of cerebral anatomy, 'locates the "seat" of consciousness in the cerebral cortex [*Gehirnrinde*]' (Freud 1991: 295), just as Kant before him, had described the brain – 'the seat of representation' (Kant 1979: 193) – as an 'organ of thought' (207), an emphasis which together with references to vesicle and skin layers, as the impact zones of stimuli and excitatory processes, would seem to beg the question of just how physical the mental is in this case. To put this back into the context of railway travel, cinema-going, railway crashes in the world *and* the world of the movies, we might ask whether the assault on the senses makes the passenger a 'victim of railway brain', just as the spectator is said to be a 'victim of cinema brain' – the very correlation Kirby establishes (see 1988: 126) – or rather, whether the brain is in any case just a cortical extension of the spine.

The decision to read Freud materially, constitutes a mode of reading which is culturally in tune with the discourses of that time, which, as references to many thinkers of the German-speaking world cited here have shown, are saturated with concerns about neurology and physiology (see Ben Singer's excellent thesis on the '*neurological* conception of modernity', 1995: 72–99). Film theory's debt to psychoanalysis is unquestionable; however, with its emphasis on the individual's psyche, on the subject's dreams, fantasies and processes of identification, and the spectator's submission, and loss of body, to the camera's ubiquitous eye, psychoanalytic film theory tends to divorce the mental from the physiological, thereby ignoring Freud, the *Nervenarzt* (literally 'nerve-doctor'), and opting to translate him into the 'mental specialist', the modern-day 'psychiatrist', rather than the turn-of-the-century 'neurologist'. Furthermore, by individualizing the experience of spectating, when conversely it is an experience in and as part of a crowd, the spectator remains just a disembodied gaze, as opposed to a member of a gathering, the *man in the crowd* who 'refuses to be alone' (Poe 1986: 188), and who 'has given up elbow room' (see Gunning's reading of Poe 1997: 29) to nuzzle closer to the scene of the spectacle. Being in a crowd is in itself a bodily and electrifying experience, as is clear from the old man's reactions in Poe's tale, when he 'threw himself amid the crowd' (1986: 186). Thus immersed in the spectacle, he abandons himself to sensations: his 'spirits [...] flickered up, as a lamp which is near its death-hour' (187), and, he 'spoke no word, and looked at all objects with a wild and vacant stare' (185).

Whether the crowd gathers at the crash site or gathers for a crash film in the cinema, it is their readiness to be thrilled which has brought them together. Thus, whether the crash film has quickened the audience's heartbeat through kinesthetic motion (*The Haverstraw Tunnel*) or confused their retinas through the collision of images in montage sequences (*Un Chien Andalou*), or conversely, has commented on spectatorial sensation (*Uncle Josh at the Moving Picture Show*) or on the thematized *Schaulust* within the fiction of the filmic text (Cronenberg's *Crash*, 1996), with all these diverse films we find, to a greater or lesser extent, instances of the physical pleasure in looking (be it for the spectator in the auditorium, or the spectators-within-the-fiction). This is why crashes from Edison's deliberately staged head-on train collision in *The Railroad Smash-up* to the obligatory Hollywood car chases, which generally end in a cop-car pile-up, provide for a viewing experience, which relates more to the rollercoaster ride at the fairground, or immersion in VR s(t)imulations, than to the traditions of the theatre and its reinvention in narrative film.

When Tom Gunning characterized the early 'cinema of attractions' (until 1908) as a 'cinema of instants' which 'favoured direct visual stimulus over narrative development' (Gunning 1998: 218), it was to emphasize that this cinema 'rather than telling stories, bases itself on film's ability to show something' (Gunning 1991: 41). The crash within a film, then as now, is such an instant, which, rather than truly developing situations, primarily wants to thrill, and as such is paradigmatic of Gunning's assessment of the non-narrative cinema. Equally, the 'ability to show something' is what the action film of today exploits: subordinating the story to the thrill, the narrative to the spectacle. What is said of the early cinema of attractions is also true of the cinema of crashes: it is about presentation rather than representation (Hansen 1991: 34), about exhibitionism rather than voyeurism (Gunning 1990: 57). From the cinema of the turn-of-the-century to the current Hollywood blockbuster, from footage shown on the Cinematograph to the home VCR: from R.W. Paul's fantasy film *The ? Motorist* (dir. Walter R. Booth, 1906) to the sporting highlights of 'the most *breathtaking*' and 'the very best and the worst thrills & spills, spins & bashes, smashes & crashes' which announces the 'adrenalin inducing' *Crash Impact* video tape (Telstar 1997), the aim has been to satisfy the eyes' hunger for sensation and stimulation. And all this is addressed to a flesh-and-blood audience. I don't mean the 'real' person from which Cultural Studies' ethnographic research elicits meanings and counter-readings, but the physiological being who sits at the edge of their seat and whose pulse is racing and whose spine is tingling.[11]

This essay was just a reminder then that watching a film is also physiological, just as reading a book was once thought of as a physical act. To read a book was not just to 'devour', 'digest', or quite literally to eat it 'day by day and leaf by leaf, between two sides of bread and butter' (see Darnton 1990: 172), but, one hundred years prior to the birth of the cinema, 'reading-rage' (*Lesewut*) or 'reading-addiction' (*Lesesucht*) was thought to cause a whole host of physiological side-effects:

> susceptibility to colds, headaches, weakening of eyes, heat rashes, gout, arthritis, hemorrhoids, asthma, apoplexy, pulmonary disease, indigestion, blocking of the bowels, nervous disorder, migraines, epilepsy, hypochondria, and melancholy.
>
> (J.G. Heinzmann 1795, see Darnton 1990: 171–2)

On a more positive note, if 'doctors in ancient times used to recommend reading to their patients as a physical exercise on an equal level with walking, running, or ball-playing' (Dom Jean Leclercq 1961, qu. by McLuhan 1962: 89), such a prescription does not betoken passivity. The spectator who reads images is not 'immobile', 'silent' or 'motionless' as Baudry or Metz would have us think (see Williams 1995: 2), but 'the "mental vertigo" which befalls the spectator and the "physiological tempests" raging in him' and her (Gilbert Cohen-Séat 1946: 154–5, sum. Kracauer 1960, 1997: 159), and which express themselves with each jolt, gulp, scream, or hollow feeling in the stomach, are signs of just how much, to use the words of a medieval Englishman, 'the whole body labors'.[12]

Notes

1. Unlike the English scopophilia (see Strachey's [1991: 127] rendition of Freud's *'Schaulust'* 1990: 53), or its translation into the 'joy of watching' (see Zohn's rendition [1983: 69] of Benjamin's *'Schaulust'* 1991: 572), consider the connotational field of these definitions given of the term in the *Wahrig Deutsches Wörterbuch* (my translation and emphasis given): *'Schaulust* (noun): *Lust* [lust, desire, appetite], *Freude am Zuschauen* [pleasure in looking], *bes. an Vorgängen auf der Straße* [particularly with regard to occurrences in the street]; *seine ~ bei einem Unfall befriedigen* [to satisfy one's 'hunger to see' at an accident site]. (Adjective) *schaulustig: gern anschauend* [likes looking], neugierig [curious]; *eine ~e Menge hatte sich angesammelt* [a 'sensation-seeking' crowd had gathered]'.
2. Tom Gunning's work on the early cinema draws extensively on Benjamin's and Kracauer's ideas; this essay in turn draws extensively on his insights, and would not have been possible without his ground-breaking research.
3. While the crash at Crush City was the first of its kind, Lynne Kirby also points out that until the 1920s many such 'train wrecks [were] staged at county fairs in the US' (1988: 120, 129 n13). Information such as this, together with her detailed analyses of the numerous train (crash) films of that period have made Kirby's work on the relations between railway travel and the cinema, a rich and invaluable source for my own argument (see also Kirby 1997).
4. Mann's story is about a writer involved in a railway crash who fears he may have lost the manuscript of his book and searches for it in the debris, an incident which echoes Charles Dickens' train accident where he has to crawl back into the carriage to recover his manuscript (see Schivelbusch 1986: 138).
5. This phrase echoes Aumont's 'mobile eye in an immobile body' (1997: 236), who, albeit very differently from the argument suggested in this essay, is also working towards a corporealized looking (see also the commentary by Charles O'Brien in the same collection 1997: 259–262). The only other argument I have come across which emphasizes the importance of the body in human vision is Jonathan Crary's. In tracing the suppression of the bodily in the history of classical theories of vision, he turns to early nineteenth century discourses on physiology and anatomy in order re-discover 'the "visionary" capacities of the body' (1995: 27). While Aumont largely draws on the history of painting, and Crary on the insights of the physical sciences, both carry within their arguments, more or less explicitly, critiques of theories of the gaze; neither, however, offset their physiological insights against the 'mentalist' biases of psychoanalytic film approaches.
6. This is Schivelbusch's term (1986: 42), which he uses with specific reference to the annihilation of space and time in railway travel, and forms the crux of Kirby's (1988: 114) work on the related experiences of railway-travel and cinema-going.
7. Both these incidences beg not just a feminist analysis, but might also have become the starting point for a consideration of the importance of sexual difference in the act of looking, not along Laura Mulvey's lines, but according to the terms of physiology suggested here; the project of a gendered *Schaulust* falls unfortunately outside the scope of this essay.
8. Tom Gunning uses this section from St Augustine on curiositas to support a 'metapsychology of attractions' (see 1996: 75): he suggests that '[t]he taste for thrills and spectacle' is 'the particularly modern form of curiositas' and as such it 'defines the aesthetics of attraction [...]' (1994: 128, see also 124); a claim which I am gesturing against because of the epistemological, rather than the physiological, claims St Augustine makes.
9. See Vanessa Schwartz's fascinating essay on visiting the Paris morgue as a pre-cinematic family spectator-sport (1994: 87–113).

10 While it is true, of course, that neither the spectator nor the actor suffers dangerous physical injury, when compared to the crash victim's bleeding, open wounds, this does not, however, mean that there is no physiological reaction, that heartbeats don't race or pupils don't dilate. We might say, it is all 'in the degree of violence' (see Schivelbusch on the perceived severity of railroad crashes compared to other accidents, 1986: 139).

11 Mention should be made of the film *The Tingler* (William Castle 1959), because it quite literally gives a body to fear in a creature called the tingler. What is significant in the context of our argument is that this parasite, which roams the movie theatre feeding of the audience's fear, and would kill if the audience failed to relieve their tension by screaming, lives in the spinal column, and not in the darkest corners of our consciousness. As such, this would seem to underline the physiological aspects of fear, rather than its psychological dimension. The screenings of this film provide another interesting angle insofar as certain effects, such as electrical charges under given seats, were installed in order to physically enhance the viewing experience of the 'real' audience of the film, in effect 'assaulting' them in a parallel gesture to the assaults within the screen fiction.

12 This quotation by Orderic Vitalis is on the physicality of writing in the Middle Ages (in Clanchy 1979: 90, qu. Ong 1982: 95). For a sustained examination of the relation between the physiology of reading and looking, see my forthcoming book *Theories of Reading* (Polity Press).

References

Aumont, Jacques (1977) 'The Variable Eye, or the Mobilization of the Gaze', Charles O'Brien & Sally Shafto, trans. in Dudley Andrew, ed. *The Image in Dispute: Art and Cinema in the Age of Photography.* Austin: University of Texas Press.

Baudry, Jean-Louis (1999) 'The Apparatus: Metapsychological Approaches to the Impression of Reality in Cinema [1975]', Jean Andrews and Bernard Augst trans. in Leo Braudy and Marshall Cohen, eds, *Film Theory and Criticism: Introductory Readings.* Oxford: Oxford University Press.

Benjamin, Walter (1983) 'Some Motifs in Baudelaire [1939]', *Charles Baudelaire. A Lyric Poet in the Era of High Capitalism.* Harry Zohn, trans. London: Verso.

Benjamin, Walter (1983) 'The Paris of the Second Empire in Baudelaire [1938]', *Charles Baudelaire: A Lyric Poet in the Era of High Capitalism.* Harry Zohn, trans. London: Verso.

Benjamin, Walter (1991) *Gesammelte Schriften.* Band I: 2. Frankfurt: Suhrkamp.

Breuer, Joseph & Sigmund Freud (1974) *Studies on Hysteria.* Vol. 3. James & Alix Strachey, trans. Harmondsworth: Pelican.

Buñuel, Luis and Salvador Dali (1994) *Un Chien Andalou.* Phillip Drummond transcribed and introduced. London: Faber and Faber.

Chanan, Michael (1996, 1980) *The Dream that Kicks: The Prehistory and Early Years of Cinema in Britain.* London: Routledge.

Charney, Leo and Vanessa Schwartz, eds (1995) *Cinema and the Invention of Modern Life.* Berkeley: University of California Press.

Christie, Ian (1994) *The Last Machine: Early Cinema and the Birth of the Modern World.* London: BFI.

Cohen-Séat, Gilbert (1946) *Essai sur les principes d'une philosophie du cinéma. I. Introduction générale: Notions fundamentales et vocabulaire de filmologie,* Paris.

Crary, Jonathan (1994) 'Modernizing Vision', in Linda Williams ed. (1994) *Viewing Positions. Ways of Seeing Film.* 46–71.

Darnton, Robert (1990) *The Kiss of Lamourette.* London: Faber and Faber.

Fell, John ed. (1983) *Film Before Griffith*. Berkeley: University of California Press.

Fielding, Raymond (1983) 'Hale's Tours: Ultrarealism in the Pre-1910 Motion Picture', in John Fell ed. (1983) *Film Before Griffith*. 116–130.

Freska, Friedrich (1984) 'Vom Werte und Umwerte des Kinos [1912]', in Fritz Güttinger (ed.) *Kein Tag ohne Kino*, Frankfurt: Deutsches Film Museum, pp. 98–103.

Freud, Sigmund (1990, 1978) 'Jenseits des Lustprinzips [1920]', *Das Ich und das Es und andere metapsychologische Schriften*. Frankfurt: Fischer.

Freud, Sigmund (1991, 1984) 'Beyond the Pleasure Principle [1920]', *On Metapsychology: The Theory of Psychoanalysis*. Vol 11, James Strachey, trans. Harmondsworth: Penguin.

Freud, Sigmund (1979) 'The Psychoanalytic View of Psychogenic Disturbance of Vision [1910]', *On Psychopathology*. Vol 10, James Strachey, trans. Harmondsworth: Penguin.

Gunning, Tom (1983) 'An Unseen Energy Swallows Space: The Space in Early Film and Its Relation to American Avant-Garde Film', in John Fell ed. (1983) *Film Before Griffith*. 355–366.

Gunning, Tom (1990) 'The Cinema of Attractions: Early Cinema, Its Spectator and the Avant Garde', in Thomas Elsaesser, ed. *Early Cinema: Space Frame Narrative*. London: BFI.

Gunning, Tom (1991) *D. W. Griffith and the Origins of American Narrative Film*. The Early Years at the Biograph. Urbana: University of Illinois Press.

Gunning, Tom (1994) 'An Aesthetic of Astonishment: Early Film and the (In)Credulous Spectator [1989]', in Linda Williams, ed. (1994) *Viewing Positions: Ways of Seeing Film*. 114–133.

Gunning, Tom (1996) '"Now You See It, Now You Don't": The Temporality of the Cinema of Attractions [1993]', in Richard Abel, ed. *Silent Film*. New Brunswick, NJ: Rutgers University Press.

Gunning, Tom (1997) 'From the Kaleidoscope to the X-Ray: Urban Spectatorship, Poe, Benjamin, and Traffic in Souls (1913)', *Wide Angle* 19 (4) 25–61.

Gunning, Tom (1998) 'Heard over the Phone: The Lonely Villa and de the Lorde Tradition of the Terrors of Technology [1991]', in Annette Kuhn and Jackie Stacey, eds *Screen Histories: A Screen Reader*. Oxford University Press.

Hake, Sabine (1993) *The Cinema's Third Machine: Writing on Film in Germany, 1907–1933*. Lincoln: University of Nebraska Press.

Hansen, Miriam (1991) *Babel and Babylon: Spectatorship in Early American Film*. Cambridge Mass: Harvard University Press.

Hesnard Dr, A. (1986, 1975) 'Glossaire', in Sigmund Freud, *Essais de psychoanalyse*, Dr S. Jankélévitch, trans. Paris: Petite Bibliothèque Payot.

Hoffmann, E.T.A. (1992) 'My Cousin's Corner Window [1822]', in *The Golden Pot and Other Tales*, Ritchie Robertson, trans. Oxford: Oxford University Press.

Jowitt, Garth S. (1983) 'The First Motion Picture Audiences' in John Fell, ed. (1983) *Film Before Griffith*. 196–206.

Kant, Immanuel (1979) *The Conflict of the Faculties*, Mary J. Gregor, trans. New York: Abaris Books.

Kirby, Lynne (1988) 'Male Hysteria and Early Cinema', *Camera Obscura* (17) 113–131.

Kirby, Lynne (1997) *Parallel Tracks: The Railroad and The Silent Cinema*. Exeter: University of Exeter Press.

Kracauer, Siegfried (1987) 'The Cult of Distraction: On Berlin's Picture Palaces [1926]', Thomas Y. Levin, trans. *New German Critique* 40 (Winter) 91–96.

Kracauer, Siegfried (1997) *Theory of Film. The Redemption of Physical Reality* [1960], intro. Miriam Bratu Hansen, Princeton, Princeton University Press.

Mann, Thomas (1997) 'Railway Accident [1907]', *Little Herr Friedemann & Other Stories*. London: Minerva.

McLuhan, Marshall (1962) *The Gutenberg Galaxy: The Making of Topographic Man*. London: Routledge & Kegan Paul.

Metz, Christian (1982) *Imaginary Signifier: Psychoanalysis and the Cinema* [1975], Celia Britton, Annwyl Williams, Ben Brewster, and Alfred Guzzetti, trans. Bloomington: Indiana University Press.

Metz, Christian (1975) 'The Imaginary Signifier', Ben Brewster trans. *Screen* 16 (2) 14–76.

Nietzsche, Friedrich (1988) *Philosophy and Truth,* Daniel Breazale, trans. New Jersey: Humanities Press.

Ong, Walter (1982) *Orality and Literacy: The Technologizing of the Word*. London: Methuen.

Poe, Edgar Allen (1986) 'The Man of the Crowd [1845]', *The House of Usher and Other Tales*. Harmondsworth: Penguin.

Schivelbusch, Wolfgang (1986) *The Railway Journey: The Industrialization of Time and Space in the 19th Century* [1977]. Leamington Spa: Berg.

Schlüpmann, Heide (1990) *Unheimlichkeit des Blicks: Das drama des frühen deutschen Kinos*. Frankfurt: Stroemfeld / Roter Stern.

Schwartz, Vanessa R. (1994) 'Cinematic Spectatorship before the Apparatus: The Public Taste for Reality in Fin-de-Siècle Paris', in Linda Williams ed. (1994) *Viewing Positions: Ways of Seeing Film*. 87–113.

Serner, Walter (1978) 'Kino und Schaulust [1913]', in Anton Kaes, ed. Kino-Debatte: *Texte zum Verhältnis von Literatur und Film 1909–1929*. Tübingen: Niemayer.

Simmel, Georg (1997) 'The Metropolis and Mental Life [1903]', Hans Gert, trans., in David Frisby and Mike Featherstone, eds, *Simmel on Culture*. London: Sage.

Singer, Ben (1995) 'Modernity, Hyperstimulus and the Rise of Popular Sensationalism', in Charney, Leo and Vanessa R. Schwartz, eds (1995) *Cinema and the Invention of Modern Life*. 72–99.

St. Augustine (1969) *The Confessions of St. Augustine* [397]. New York: Airmont.

Williams, Linda, ed. (1994) *Viewing Positions: Ways of Seeing Film*. New Brunswick, NJ: Rutgers University Press.

Zola, Emile (1977) *La Bête Humaine* [1890], Leonard Tancock, trans. Harmondsworth: Penguin.

5 Crashed-Out: Laundry Vans, Photographs and a Question of Consciousness

Ben Highmore

The Death of the Author

The death of the author Roland Barthes occurred in March 1980. A month earlier Barthes was hit by a laundry van while crossing the road. A month prior to this, his book on photography, *Camera Lucida,* was published. This juxtaposition of traffic-accident and photography might seem an arbitrary collision (itself an 'accident') if it wasn't for its uncanny repetition in the writing of modernity. In this writing (and I'm thinking specifically of the work of Simmel, Benjamin and Jünger) the difficulty of negotiating traffic in a culture saturated by photographic images provides a constellation that figures the modern everyday as dangerous, technological, and *endlessly* mediated. But if such writers find vivid moments of modernity in 'the advertising pages of a newspaper or the traffic of a big city' (Benjamin 1983: 132), what connections could be made between the two that would provide something more than circumstantial evidence for Barthes' death? Surely to find an immediate correspondence between the imaginary realm of the image and the brutal actuality of traffic is to conflate two separate registers? Wouldn't this effectively break a fundamental rule of a theory of representation: to mistake the re-presentation of actuality for actuality? Wouldn't this constitute a kind of wrong headedness in relation to language (both visual and scriptural) that Paul de Man points to when he writes; 'no one in his right mind will try to grow grapes by the luminosity of the word "day"' (de Man 1986: 11)?

Writing about the affective detail (the *punctum*) that he finds in certain photographs, Barthes could just as easily be writing about car crashes: 'this element that rises from the scene, shoots out of it like an arrow, and pierces me' (Barthes 1984b: 26). For Barthes, the photograph's *punctum* is an 'accident' that can 'wound'. Such moments do not succumb to the business of decoding; they do not offer themselves up for interpretation. Similarly, if traffic accidents can be considered 'meaningful' then Barthes' (much earlier) description of the photograph might be appropriate: to be hit by a van is to be hit by 'a message without a code' (Barthes 1984a: 17). *Camera Lucida* ends by offering a choice for attending to the photographic image: 'To subject its spectacle to the civilized code of perfect illusions, or to confront in it the wakening of intractable reality' (Barthes 1984b: 119). Barthes' early work is mainly spent preoccupied with the first choice, in *Camera Lucida* he has opted for 'intractable reality.' The first choice Barthes describes as being 'tame' his other option is 'mad'. That such a mad choice could result in his being run-over would, apparently, seem absurd: a mad claim that clearly wouldn't stand up in court.

'Tame' and 'Mad' Choices

It is a commonplace to note a general cultural ability in reading images. We decode complex advertisements, movies and soap operas with sophistication and speed. For the most part (thankfully) we are adept at crossing the road as well. The link between these two abilities might be as simple as a willingness to read and act according to cultural conventions, to buy into a general sign system, a social semiotics. The child learning the green cross code (or any other set of road safety instructions) is being given an introduction to semiotics that will be continually developed and extended in classrooms and playgrounds. In later life the same child might be introduced to 'semiotics' (by name) as a theoretical approach to the representational world. In such introductions the coded nature of everyday life is inevitably exemplified by reference to 'traffic lights' (Hall 1997: 26–28). The pay-off for all this semiotic training might include being able to watch TV, pass a driving test or make a Hollywood blockbuster.

In the light of the two choices that Barthes gives us, the deployment of any semiotic system, must be a 'tame' choice. The word is not arbitrary. Traffic and signs are circulating pell-mell. The helter-skelter careering of such material as it bombards our bodies and brains (our sensorial consciousness) gets 'tamed' and managed in a number of ways. Here it is enough to point to two inter-related form of management: traffic control and semiotics. Both are used to delimit the excess of a production, to calm the dizzying affects of a spectacular emission. The cinemascope billboards that turn cities into picture palaces that screen thousands of movies simultaneously are greeted with 'a handbook on the decoding of advertisements'. Diverting, riveting and clamorous, seductive and repulsive, the phenomenal shock of the image is answered by a lesson in textual analysis. Likewise, the souped-up silver dream-machines, filled with high explosives and the latest in power handling are met by sleeping policemen and other forms of 'traffic calming'. Modernity would mean little if the ceaseless proliferation of images and traffic and their affects were not recognized. Traffic wardens and image decoders join hands as amnesiacs of modernity.

Perhaps it is enough to suggest that the failure to abide by such a tame and taming response to modernity is enough to get you run-over. Would it be surprising that, in refusing to read images according to conventions, you might also refuse the conventions of road crossing? Could the denial of rudimentary lessons in visual semiotics result in playing fast and loose with the law of the road? Would Barthes' 'mad' choice of seeing images as 'the wakening of intractable reality' lead to a general un-learning of the rituals of road safety?

Perhaps. But Barthes' 'mad' choice is something more than a disrespect for this 'law of the land'. Barthes is 'ill'; his perceptions refuse to accord sense material their 'proper' place. 'I have a disease: I *see* language. What I should simply hear, a strange pulsion – perverse in that in it desire mistakes its object, reveals it to me as a "vision"' (Barthes 1977: 161). And just as hearing triggers visual perception, visual material, such as photography, result in haptic (tactile, bodily) sense perceptions: 'A photograph's *punctum* is that accident which pricks me (but also bruises me, is poignant to me)' (Barthes 1984b: 27). If we had to diagnose Barthes' 'mad' choice (his disease) we could liken it to the sensory perception of the synaesthete who might smell a colour or taste a sound. Synaesthesia (as a named condition) emerges in the 1890s (Kern 1983) at a moment of intense modernization. The synaesthete's response to modernity is a sensory system that 'leaks' (Buck-Morss 1992). Such leakage might be a purposeful reaction to the scientific separation of the senses in modernity, or it might be that the upshot of modernity's continual sensory bombardment is a 'leaky vessel'. Barthes' synaesthetic choice (his 'mad' choice) evidences a number of refusals: the refusal to adopt the 'proper' protocols for attending to sense data (you do *this* with images, you do *that* with sounds) and the refusal to categorically distinguish between representations and phenomenal reality (images 'bruise' and 'prick'). But if such wrong headedness turns him into a 'poor' semiotician, it generates an approach to phenomenal reality (bulldozers *and* billboards) that is, potentially, both materialist and historical. Barthes' mad materialism connects him to a tradition of writing modernity.

Materialism and Urban Modernity

Distant echoes come crashing over the textual airwaves. Marx writes about consciousness and its cultural forms as being *determined*. He also writes about modernity. For Marx the material base determines the cultural superstructure just as the form of social being determines consciousness: 'it is not the consciousness of men that determines their being, but, on the contrary, their social being that determines their consciousness' (Marx 1968: 181). Much ink has been spilt on semantically negotiating these terms. What does Marx mean by the 'base'? What could consciousness mean in relation to being? Is determination causal or something less direct, more mediated? In a desire to short-circuit this discussion and avoid too much ink spilling (while acknowledging that I am also riding roughshod over the history of Marxism), let us state categorically that the 'base' must include the material and phenomenal condition of modernity. Such a condition (which would include the reckless movement of cars and laundry vans *and* the phenomenal shock of images) would *be* social being. The determined superstructure and its sensorial consciousness would include the 'tame' forms for managing and negotiating such a base. It would seem clear that such a short-circuit has worked to make any clear distinction between the base and superstructure *as distinct materials* problematic. Much of what gets called culture would be both base *and* superstructure, both 'social being' *and* consciousness. For example, a gigantic billboard of a speeding car could be seen as providing a phenomenal shock while at the same time offering some of the semiotic material for managing that shock. An 'actual' car screeching along a road – deafening, dirty and dangerous – is a material fact registered by a range of senses. But it too is not easily separable from systems of traffic control, from the social imaginary of car consumption, and from the cultural conventions that make cars understandable as ordinary objects rather than as unexploded bombs. A materialism that is suspicious of over-hasty designations of 'base' and 'superstructure' is unlikely to hold much truck with categorical separations between 'illusion' and 'reality', 'representation' and 'actuality'.

Looked at through the prism of other, later writers of modernity, Marx offers an introduction to the cultural anthropology of industrial modernity. Resolutely historical, Marx's determining relations figure the scene of urban modernity as the material base, the material form of social being. The industrial factory can be seen as the historical instance for such relations to emerge: the crashing machinery and the estranging conditions (including, of course, a division of labour between machines, managers and workers) are part of the material circumstances that determine an alienated consciousness. Writers such as Simmel will posit the material conditions of the modern metropolis as determining. For Simmel, writing in 1903, 'the sensory foundations of mental life' are created 'with every crossing of the street, with the tempo and multiplicity of economic, occupational and social life' (Simmel 1971: 325). There is something in this phrase 'the sensory foundations of mental life' that corresponds to a notion of 'sensorial consciousness' – a form of consciousness that is both sensual and mental, that would emerge as a result of an insertion into the material conditions of the modern world. In Simmel's writing the material base of modernity is found (as it should be) everywhere: in fashion, in trade exhibitions, and emphatically in urban culture. There is no attempt to 'tame' the brutal actuality of representations (money, images or exhibits). It is in the sensual cacophony of the city that the sensorial consciousness is determined but not in any *pre*determined form. For Simmel, the sensory foundations of the metropolis are likely to fashion a divided set of responses: neurasthenic and agoraphobic on the one hand; cold, calculating, rationalist and blasé on the other. Modernity in its base and sensual forms offers a challenge: 'shape up or ship out'; 'whatever doesn't kill you will make you strong'. Modern individuals bombarded on all fronts by intensified stimuli will either become numbed to such stimuli and successfully parry the blows to consciousness (the blasé attitude), or they will become over-sensitized, jumping at every car horn, jolted by every 'shock of the new' (neurasthenic). The synaesthete (who as well as seeing smells and hearing colours treats representation as actuality) offers a third option. It is a disposition that in opening-up to the sensory attack of modernity radically questions our ability to dodge the moment of impact. If a heterogeneous base modernity (photographs, factories, trains, traffic, toxins, telephones, etc.) ambivalently conditions consciousness, then the forms of consciousness that result (the blasé semiotician, the hypersensitive neurasthenic, the mad materialist synaesthete, etc.) will offer different negotiations of modernity. Who will 'safely' navigate this urban everyday? Who will feed on its dangers? Who will fall foul of its contradictions?

For the mad materialists of the 1920s and 1930s the assault on sensorial consciousness that is offered by metropolitan culture will find its apogee, not in the streets of Berlin or New York, but in the scene of modern industrial warfare.

The Fragile Body and the Urban War-Zone

Writing after the First World War, Walter Benjamin conjured a vividly modern scene: 'in a field of destructive torrents and explosions, was the tiny, fragile human body' (Benjamin 1973: 84). The juxtaposition of an industrial, technological and destructive force, with the 'unprotected' human body sets the scene not just for modern warfare but for modern life in general. In his essay, *The Storyteller*, Benjamin is puzzling how it is that the surviving soldiers of the first world war 'returned from the battlefield grown silent – not richer, but poorer in communicable experience' (Benjamin 1973: 84). The reason for this is that, for Benjamin, modernity is the contradiction of communicable experience – here 'social being' (industrialized warfare) determines a mute consciousness. In this same passage Benjamin relates the contradiction of communicable experience to traffic: 'A generation that had gone to school on a horse-drawn streetcar now stood under the open sky in a countryside in which nothing remained unchanged but the clouds' (Benjamin 1973: 84). Of course Benjamin is talking about the battlefields of Europe, but he could just as easily be talking about the modern city where an industrial technology had also left nothing unchanged.

It is easy to imagine that when writing about the experience of the modern city, writers such as Benjamin and Simmel were figuring the metropolis as the war-zone of modernity. The city as war-zone offers a compelling image of the urban pedestrian negotiating endless bombardments by cars, laundry vans and a fully technologized image-track. In a passage from his writing on Baudelaire, Benjamin recognizes that photography and the traffic of a big city (image technologies, transport technologies) both combine in the general shock of modern life: 'the camera gave the moment a posthumous shock, [...]. Moving through this traffic involves the individual in a series of shocks and collisions. At dangerous crossings, nervous impulses flow through him in rapid succession, like the energy from a battery' (Benjamin 1983: 132). This generalized urban technology has a determining effect on sensorial consciousness. Writing about how modern traffic has meant that pedestrians are obliged to 'cast glances in all directions' he suggests that 'technology has subjected the human sensorium to a complex kind of training' (Benjamin 1983: 132). The technology of traffic (cars, lorries, but also traffic lights and zebra crossings) has generated an adjustment of the human sensorium, so that pedestrians practice a form of hyper-perceptivity that can handle an array of multi-directional and intense stimuli. But it is the possibility of technology (especially film and photography, but why not traffic?) to determine a potentially *critical* sensorial consciousness, that won't simply be armoured against the war-zone of modernity but might intervene in it, that holds-out a redemptive promise for Benjamin. Cinema, especially, suggests the possibility of an anthropology of everyday life, which through the techniques of slow motion or time-lapse photography might provide the material for an analytic approach to the choreography of the everyday. The gestures and flows of modern living could be attended to with the enhanced perceptional possibilities offered by film that will at once de-familiarize them whilst also opening them up to potentially critical scrutiny. Thus the technologized environment of modernity is both poison and cure: it's what sets nerves jangling, but in its role as a transformer of perception it offers the possibility of a consciousness critically adequate to this environment. While Benjamin's position is hugely suggestive it is, in the end, difficult to see how such a consciousness would emerge as *necessarily* critical and what kinds of practices it would result in; we are left with hints, suggestive possibilities and the occasional practical remark. Writing at the same time as Benjamin, but articulating a completely different political instrumentality, Ernst Jünger's work offers a more practical demonstration of the determining effects that technology might have.

Protectionism and Total Mobilization

If some soldiers returned from the Front Line mute, when Jünger came back he couldn't shut up. In 1920 he published his war diaries as *In Storms of Steel*, and what followed was an avalanche of writing with combat as its central motif.

In 1931 he introduced and helped publish a collection of photographs and texts entitled *The Dangerous Moment*. The photographs in this volume 'depict shipwrecks, natural catastrophes, wars, strikes, and revolutions as well as violent sporting accidents' (Werneburg 1992: 50). In his introductory essay to this volume, 'On Danger', Jünger poses 'the question of whether a space of absolute comfort or a space of absolute danger is the final aim concealed in technology' (Kaes et al 1994: 371). Explicitly arguing the case for the latter (the former being irredeemably bourgeois for Jünger) he claims a link between *all* technology and war while reminding us that 'inventions like the automobile engine have already resulted in greater losses than any war, however bloody'. The 'passionate struggle' is given a particular technological dimension in the modern era: 'Thus does the daily accident itself, with which our newspapers are filled, appear nearly exclusively as a catastrophe of a technological type' (Kaes et al 1994: 372). But for Jünger, as for Benjamin, technology isn't simply part of the material catastrophe, it has determining effects for consciousness.

The idea of a photographic and technological consciousness is an insistent feature of European culture between the wars. Whether it is the filmmaker Vertov's assertion in 1923 that 'I am kino-eye, I am a mechanical eye' (Michelson 1984: 17), or Christopher Isherwood's written account of 1930s Berlin that starts with the claim 'I am a camera with its shutter open' (Isherwood 1977: 11), photographic consciousness seems to be more than a convenient metaphor for a realist style. Writing three years after the publication of *The Dangerous Moment*, Jünger reflects on the relationships between photography, consciousness and pain. For Jünger 'the photograph stands outside the realm of sensibility', it 'registers just as well a bullet in mid-air or the moment in which a man is torn apart by an explosion' (Phillips 1989: 208). For Jünger photography *alone* doesn't result in a particular form of consciousness it must also be seen as 'an expression of our characteristically cruel way of seeing'. Photographic consciousness is modern consciousness determined by a technological and violent form of 'social being'. For Jünger the result is a 'human type that is evolving in our time' and who possesses a 'second, colder consciousness [that] shows itself in the ever more sharply developed ability to see oneself as an *object*' (Phillips 1989: 207). Such a 'type' is not that distinct from Simmel's 'blasé type', except that Simmel is *describing* the psychological affects of the metropolis while Jünger is *prescribing* the attitude to be adopted by 'worker-soldiers' as they prepare for 'Total Mobilization'.

The Dangerous Moment can thus be seen as a training-manual for seeing as 'an act of aggression'. Immersion in this barrage of 'industrial accidents' seen by 'an insensitive and invulnerable eye', would set the scene for a defensive-aggressive consciousness: protected and defended against the pain of catastrophe (through self-objectification) while aggressively armed with an analytic weapon. This at any rate might be the implicit rationale for the publication of this collection. The fascistic nature of this seems clear. But when picturing the male body in combat with modernity, we are not offered visions of an armoured (machinic) body competing with a 'slave revolt of technology' (Benjamin in, Kaes et al 1994: 159). Instead photographs from the collection show bodies responding to sudden impact with the graceful and fluid movements associated with dancers.

The man thrown from the racing car (figure 1) performs the movements of classical ballet, while the man jettisoned from the boat (figure 2) responds to collision with a jazzy leap. Whilst the viewer who is submerged in this onslaught of visual crashes might or might not be arming themselves for 'mobilization', the choice of images also suggests other desires: for a masculine body not constrained by the repertoires of industrial and military movement. What is being pictured is not the disciplined bodies of worker-soldiers, but the lithesome and mutable body of the dancer. The crash releases the body from the constraint of a certain attitude, it allows for another manner of being. Jünger projects a desire for a future 'machinic' sensorial consciousness (defensive-aggressive) whilst imagining the limber body of the dancer.

Barthes, on the other hand, is looking elsewhere. More Proustian than predatory, Barthes' photographic consciousness is not defensive-aggressive. It is a consciousness prone to reminiscence, to an awkward self-awareness, to the historicity of the present.

Figure 5.1 The last second.

Figure 5.2 Los Angeles. A motorboat runs down a rowboat, whose occupant is flung into the water by the impact of the collision.

Image Repertoire

Flicking through the pages of *Camera Lucida* I am startled by a shocking realization: I am not looking at these images, they are looking at me. Out of the twenty or so photographs that are included in the book, the vast majority of them are pictures of people staring directly at me (or you, or Barthes). *Camera Lucida* orchestrates a gallery of piercing, scrutinizing, judgmental, joyous, troubled, calculating, castigating, perplexing stares. The book prepares us well: on looking at a photograph of Napoleon's youngest brother, Barthes writes: 'I realized then, with an amazement I have not been able to lessen since: "I am looking at eyes that looked at the Emperor"' (Barthes 1984b: 3). *Camera Lucida* is a phenomenology about the weight of the past as it presses on the consciousness of the present.

No writing insists more emphatically on the lived actuality of 'the image' than the last few books of Barthes. No writing is more stymieing of attempts to separate the imaginary from the real. No writing conjures up the material reality of an imaginary culture more forcefully, more vividly and more *inescapably*. The phrase Barthes (or his translator, Richard Howard) uses to insist on a weaving of the real through the threads of textuality is 'image repertoire'. It is to this that we are condemned. Examples of what this means are peppered throughout *A Lover's Discourse: Fragments* and his autobiography *Roland Barthes by Roland Barthes*. In *A Lover's Discourse*, Barthes sets out a 'scenography of waiting' for a lover. This is a scene with 'no sense of proportion' (Barthes 1979: 37). In response to the non-arrival or late arrival of the lover, Barthes 'decide[s] to "take it badly"'. The quotation marks surrounding the emotional expenditure of 'taking it badly' should alert us to a scene of the image repertoire. To 'take it badly' has been enacted before; to perform it now is to be caught up in the cultural scene of the lover's discourse and all the possible images that circulate in it. The fact that for Barthes this is a 'decision' shouldn't preclude the recognition of the inevitability of this scene: if not this image repertoire, then another. This is not a scene of pure volition – the pick and mix identity games much loved in the 1980s by promoters of a certain sense of postmodernism (shall I wear my business suit or my technoid-punk ensemble?). For Barthes, 'The power of the Image-repertoire is immediate: I do not look for the image, it comes to me, all of a sudden' (Barthes 1979: 214) – like a truck.

The image repertoire is the lived-ness of culture as it articulates and enlivens your body. It is culture played out in the minute twitches and gestures of your arms and legs. It is the inescapable staging of history in the muscle spasms which produce this smile and not another. The image repertoire allows for the recognition (but not the simple naming) of culture in the body's reflexes. It demands a history: the history of the sneeze or the yawn.

Camera Lucida finds the image repertoire not in the staging of certain kinds of cultural acts, it finds it reflected back on the reader, the viewer. Faced with this jury of enervating and unanswerable stares, *Camera Lucida* refuses the innocence and naturalness of posture, pose and gait. The faces staring out from the pages of *Camera Lucida* scrutinize our bodily attitudes and mannerisms and find them saturated with history.

Coda: Stepping off the Curb

If the phenomenal realm of Barthes' images (and the 'mad' form of attention that is offered) determines a certain kind of consciousness, what kind of consciousness would it be? On the one hand it would be a consciousness beset by reminiscences. These wouldn't have to be the kind of personal reminiscences detailed by Barthes; they could be more general, more social, less the result of private experience. The social being that Barthes suggests would determine a consciousness filled with hallucinations from the archive of lived imaginary culture. Like David Bowie's alien visitor in *The Man Who Fell To Earth*, sepia-tinted scenes of frontier history (only 'known' as part of imaginary culture) would be seen while driving stretch-limousines. On the other hand what is being determined is a *self*-consciousness hyper-aware of its own cultural conditions. Every gesture is measured, weighed and releases an overflow of cultural associations. Such hyper self-consciousness does not suggest an easy negotiation of modernity – 'what does it mean to step off the curb like this?'

If Jünger propels an armoured consciousness crashing into the future, Barthes' consciousness is closer to Benjamin's angel whose 'face is turned toward the past' and sees 'one single catastrophe which keeps piling wreckage upon wreckage and hurls it in front of his feet' (Benjamin 1973: 259). The question of consciousness is determined by a sensorial-mental position in relation to the brute matter of modernity. A sensorial consciousness under-prepared by either the taming practices of semiotics or the total mobilization of the worker warrior, steps out into the road. A sensorial consciousness where 'the tradition of all the dead generations weighs like a nightmare on the brain of the living' (Marx 1968: 96). A body, whose fleshy fragility is shot through with history, plunges into traffic. The 'mad' consciousness of the synaesthete has the capacity to chronicle the gamut of modernity's different registers. But the cost is high; such a consciousness might be left vulnerable to the deadly impact of modernity. More is at stake here than the interpretation of images. It would seem that in looking resolutely backwards (or forwards) it is no wonder that we might forget to 'look left, look right, look left again.'

References

Barthes, Roland (1977) *Roland Barthes by Roland Barthes*. Trans. Richard Howard. New York: Hill and Wang.

—— (1979) *A Lover's Discourse: Fragments*. Trans. Richard Howard. London: Jonathan Cape.

—— (1984a) *Image, Music, Text*. Trans. Stephen Heath. London: Flamingo.

—— (1984b) *Camera Lucida*. Trans. Richard Howard. London: Flamingo.

Benjamin, Walter (1983) *Charles Baudelaire: A Lyric Poet in the Era of High Capitalism*. Trans. Harry Zohn. London: Verso.

—— (1973) *Illuminations*. Trans. Harry Zohn. London: Fontana.

Buck-Morss, Susan (1992) 'Aesthetics and Anaesthetics: Walter Benjamin's Artwork Essay Reconsidered'. *October* (62) 3–41.

De Man, Paul (1986) *The Resistance to Theory*, Manchester: Manchester University Press.

Hall, Stuart (ed.) (1997) *Representation: Cultural Representation and Signifying Practices*. London: Sage.

Isherwood, Christopher (1977) *Goodbye to Berlin*. St. Albans: Triad/Panther Books.

Jünger, Ernst (1996) *The Storm of Steel: From the Diary of a German Storm*. New York: Fertig.

Kaes, Anton, Martin Jay and Edward Dimendberg (eds) (1994) *The Weimar Republic Source Book*. Berkeley: University of California Press.

Kern, Stephen (1983) *The Culture of Time and Space 1880–1918*. Cambridge, Mass.: Harvard University Press.

Marx, Karl and Frederick Engels (1968) *Selected Works in One Volume*. London: Lawrence and Wishart.

Michelson, Annette (ed.)(1984) *Kino-Eye: The Writings of Dziga Vertov*. Trans. Kevin O'Brien. London: Pluto Press.

Phillips, Christopher (ed.) (1989) *Photography in the Modern Era: European Documents and Critical Writings, 1913–1940*. New York: The Metropolitan Museum of Art / Aperture.

Simmel, Georg (1971) *On Individuality and Social Forms*. Chicago and London: The University of Chicago Press.

Werneburg, Brigitte (1992) 'Ernst Junger and the Transformed World'. *October* (62) 43–64.

6 Crash: Beyond the Boundaries of Sense

Jane Arthurs

If I want to argue that the shocked reaction to the film of *Crash* (Cronenberg 1996) can only properly be understood as *both* a psychologically and socially produced event, it immediately creates difficulties. Lacanian theory has been the privileged discourse in film studies through which the transcendent psychological positioning of the film spectator has been understood, whereas audience research has used various forms of language-based discourse analysis as a means to understand the historical and social specificity of people's varied responses. Both are highly contentious fields of research in themselves, but they are also widely regarded as antithetical, and few academics cross the divide between them. Yet, on reading Freud's *Beyond the Pleasure Principle* (Freud 1920) while engaged on an Economic and Social Research Council (ESRC) empirical research study of the audiences of *Crash*,[1] I found in the speculative concept of the 'death drive' a compelling way to explain, not only the film text itself, but also the public reaction to it – that is, as a form of trauma management following a catastrophic event.

This approach is made possible by a change of emphasis in the uses made of Lacan for film analysis: moving away from the relation between the imaginary and the symbolic, and towards a concern with the relations between the imaginary and the real – a move which Hal Foster argues is centrally important to 1990s culture:

> This shift in conception – from reality as an effect of representation to the real as a thing of trauma – may be definitive in contemporary art. Let alone in contemporary theory, fiction, and film.
>
> (Foster 96: 146)

In this model we protect our imaginary selves, the subject of representation from 'the real as a thing of trauma', through the symbolic 'screen' of cultural conventions. The subject is threatened by the 'gaze' of the material world which precedes and exceeds the subject. It has to be tamed through the codes of visual culture.

> To see without this screen would be to be blinded by the gaze or touched by the real.
>
> (Foster 1999: 140)

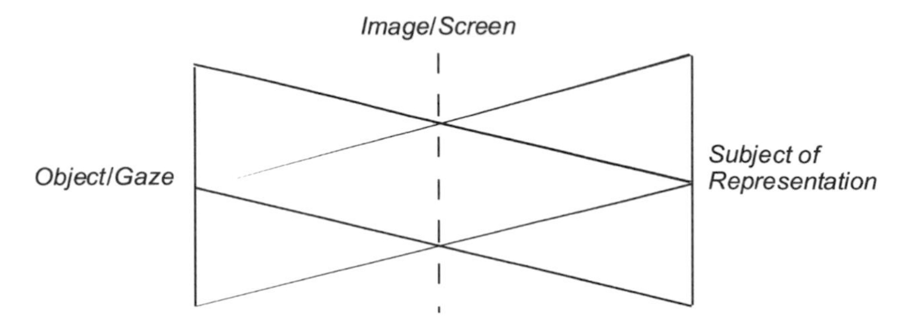

(Foster 1999: 139)

This is the model which informs Parveen Adams' Lacanian reading of *Crash* (Adams 1999), in which the film is analysed as a deliberate assault on the 'screen' which serves to confirm our subjectivity, producing a more profound experience in which the boundaries of the self are dissolved.

> What is at stake here is not pleasure, but *jouissance*. Indeed pleasure is the barrier to jouissance. Anyone who has seen *Crash* will recognise that it sets out to smash that barrier.
>
> (Adams 99: 62)

Cut to an (imaginary but plausible) exchange in an audience research interview:

Researcher: Tell me, what did you like or dislike about *Crash?*
Interviewee: Well, I found it pretty boring actually, but I can't stop thinking about it. I found it pretty disturbing in some ways -- I wish I knew what it was trying to say.

In what ways can we use this socially produced discourse as an index pointing to the viewer's unconscious psychological relation to the text? Discourse analysis of any kind depends on an implicit or explicit theoretical model of the relation between language and subjectivity, not simply on empirical evidence provided by the spoken words (Billig 1997). I have no exclusive commitment to a Lacanian model, but in this case it helped me to 'make sense' from what was otherwise a (threateningly) unmanageable mass of contradictory discourses which posed a challenge to any 'mastery' of them within a single theoretical frame. I acknowledge, however, that using this interpretative strategy will inevitably leave 'a remainder' – the outside of my explanatory discourse – on whose repression its truth effect depends.

If we then widen the 'text' to which audiences are responding to include the discursive network within which the film came to be embedded following its first exhibition in 1996, I want to argue that the boredom, the confusion, the fascination and the disturbance is produced not simply by the film itself but by the management of the trauma occasioned by the film in the public sphere (the press, the politicians and the

British Board of Film Classification (BBFC). The political and moral scandal produced a mountain of discourse behind which the film itself disappeared from view, both literally in that its distribution was delayed for over six months, and in the sense that the 'real' of the film was replaced by a 'screen' of conventional representations used to tame its initial impact. Once the film had been released for distribution, the controversy attracted a wider audience than might otherwise have chosen to see it. Amongst these people were those who, unused to Cronenberg or 'art film' more generally, and in the absence of generic markers, were at a loss to find any meaning in the film at all. This led many to the conclusion that not only was it boring, but also abhorrent, deviant, depraved. The whole process of trauma management had begun again.

The Trauma of the Real

> What is at stake then in the sexuality of *Crash* is an experience beyond representation, an experience of pure libido. The film explores this gap.
>
> (Adams 1999: 61)

Lacan's concept of the death drive differs from Freud's in that it is the fictive ego which is subject to death not the biological organism (Boothby 1991: 84). Lacan proposes the idea that in the trauma (the crash) we encounter the invisible face of the real, the realm of unbounded energy (libido) which lies outside representation (an imaginary gestalt of the body with which we identify). The real, although impossible to represent, is intimated in images of the body in bits and pieces (the wounds and scars). The threat to the ego comes from the fact that these forces lie outside the existing imaginary structure of the ego and so threaten its integrity. For Lacan, the death drive is the pressure of expressing these unsymbolised forces. The effect is to threaten the psyche with a wave of unmastered energies, which it then works to master retrospectively – to bind the traumatic impressions – that is, to find a mode of representation for libidinal forces which are compatible with the ego, so that the energy can be discharged and a pleasurable equilibrium restored. It can be productive of the most profound pleasure, the satisfaction of an untamed libido, but in its unbound state the force of the death drive is not experienced as pleasure. In this model, sexuality can be traumatising, can constitute a force of death to the extent that it threatens the bound ego (Boothby 1991: 87).

Accordingly in Parveen Adams' reading of the film (Adams 1999), Vaughan, the central character in the film, is driven by the desire to experience pure libido, the terrible *jouissance* of the real, without sacrificing his imaginary ego. This he can only achieve by becoming a legend after death in a famous car crash. The other main protagonist, James, following his encounter with the shock of the real in a fatal car crash, moves through a sequence of only partially satisfying sexual encounters, interspersed with car crashes, in the hope of reaching fulfilment. James finds instead that he is simply destined to repeat: 'Maybe next time, darling', which he whispers in Catherine's ear as she lies injured in the final scene, after he has shunted her car off the road. *Crash*, in this reading, is about the 'subject who has seen through the illusions and substitutions of desire' and 'wishes to be precipitated beyond desire and beyond the object into the ending of desire' (Adams 1999: 72).

As in much contemporary art, the evocation of the real in *Crash* is achieved through a focus on the abject – that which operates spatially and temporally as a threat to the differentiation on which subjectivity depends (Kristeva 1982). In *Crash*, the spatial boundaries of the body are represented as broken, wounded, scarred, turned inside out (semen, blood) or invaded by the object to the point where distinctions between the self and the other, figure and ground are lost. Temporally the abject is represented by the corpse, the body transformed into an object, soon to be returned to the undifferentiated matter from which it temporarily emerged. But it is most insistently represented in the loss of differentiation between humans and machines, the animate and the inanimate. The cars become more and more like people, their 'bodies' breathing steam, getting old and imperfect, body fluids getting absorbed into their material, their surfaces scarred by crashes. Meanwhile, people's bodies become more and more like machines, from the sleek metallic surfaces of the women's underwear to the prosthetic hybrid of Gabriella, who is part machine, part organic body. Her skin has been ruptured with a deep gash from the penetration of the car body into her flesh.

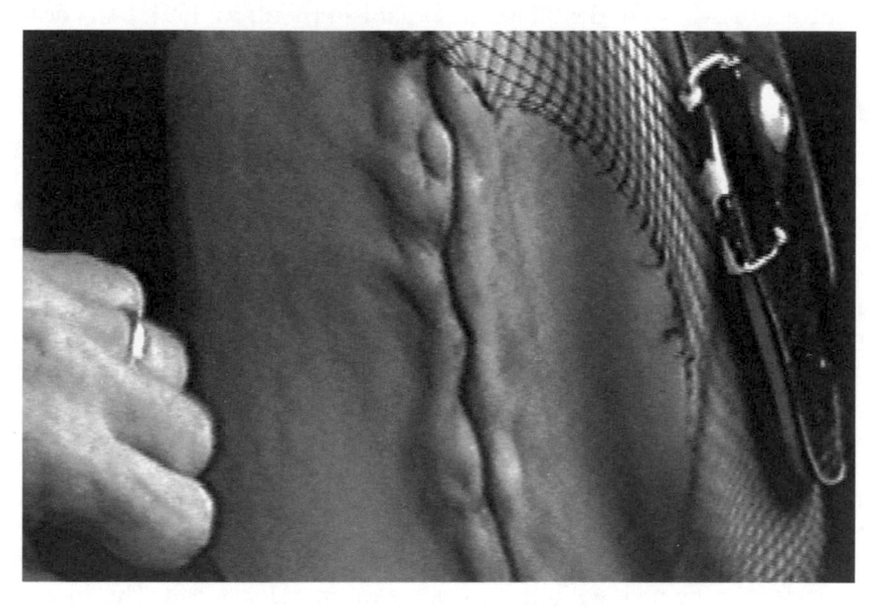

Figure 6.1 Gabriella's leg wound'. *Crash*, (Cronenberg 1996).

These wounds, even when healed into a scar, are an object of fascination and excitement to the characters in the film. Adams argues that this is because the wound signifies the moment in the crash when the libido passes beyond representation – the libido unbound, moving from the imaginary to the real. As the film progresses:

> Repetition follows repetition in order that the wound is kept open. The wound is the boundary between life and death but it refuses to be the boundary and allows life and death to communicate in an alarming space. The wound marks the spot where death nearly realised itself in an accident.
>
> (Adams 99: 66)

The constant return to these images of the broken body is both an invocation of the shock of the real, and the need to defend the ego against it, as with the repetitious traumatic dreams of shell-shocked soldiers which first led Freud to speculate on the existence of the death drive and the processes of binding, through repetition, it necessitates:

> The real cannot be represented; it can only be repeated, indeed it must be repeated.
>
> (Foster 1996: 132)

Repetition and the disruption of representation are also at work in the film, forbidding spectator identification with the characters, an effect rendered by denying the three-dimensional space of the 'other' in the camera work and editing:

> and thus the spectator is thrown back again and again on the moment of seeing.

rather than:

> being engaged at the level of the psycho-dynamics of the individual in sexual relation with the Other.
>
> (Adams 1999: 71)

This repetition of raw seeing both obstructs interpretation of the characters' behaviour and prevents the spectator channelling the body's energies into an imaginary gestalt, thus denying the pleasurable fantasy of wholeness and mastery that Hollywood narrative normally provides. Instead the spectators are returned again and again to the surfaces of bodies and cars and to the wounds which scar them. They too, like the characters in the film, are confronted with the dissolution of the self in the face of the trauma of the real. What happens as a result is of little interest to Adams:

> Spectators will deal with their experience of the film in their own ways but the logic of the film remains unequivocal.
>
> (Adams 99: 66)

I want to take up the analysis where Adams leaves off and discuss how this way of understanding the film can make sense of its reception, seeing in people's reactions to the film their attempts to manage the shock of the real through a process of discursive 'binding'. This process has both an individual and cultural dimension as people search for a conventional discourse through which to 'screen' the film in ways which are compatible with an imaginary self.

The Scandal

> A movie beyond the bounds of depravity.
>
> (Evening Standard 1996)

> Ban this car crash sex film!
>
> (Daily Mail 1996)

In the political arena, the film became symbolic of a struggle to establish the hegemonic political subject, polarised here as a struggle between the authoritarian subject of a conservative tradition founded on strongly defined and policed boundaries and the permissive subject of a libertarian tradition founded on the transgression of boundaries. This was also represented as a class struggle between the bourgeois middle class and an intellectual elite. James Ferman, the director of the BBFC, responded by trying to diffuse the political conflict by making the film safe. He allowed time for the shock to be assimilated, delayed the release of the film by six months, and tested the film on 'expert' audiences who could give re-assurance of its safety for public consumption. In effect the BBFCwere seeking to avoid any responsibility for causing harm through a quasi-scientific calculation of the risks. A group of the physically disabled attested that the BBFC had no need to be concerned on their behalf. A forensic psychologist reassured that it would not break the laws of obscenity, having failed to find in *Crash* any incitement to depravity or corruption (BBFC 1997).

Those cultural critics intent on giving the film a positive cultural value for the elite, intellectual audience, could most easily tame the film through a discourse of 'auteurism'. In this approach the film is understood through its imaginary unified point of origin in the person of the creator, who thereby provides a substitute for the absent points of identification in the film. As an adaptation of a famous book, *Crash* has two potential points of origin: Cronenberg and Ballard. Cronenberg did what he could to provide a point of identification by giving many, many interviews in the course of the film's distribution. In Britain these were timed to coincide with the film's first exhibition at the London Film Festival (LFF). The first of these interviews appeared in *The Guardian Weekend* just prior to the opening (Shelley 1996). This was followed by a press conference, and then by an interview with J.G. Ballard for the LFF, published later by the *Index for Censorship* (1997). Cronenberg characterises the film as a serious, philosophical work of art which was intended to disturb people's existing conceptual frameworks. He was quite deliberately developing a unique style, building on some of the same themes as his earlier films but leaving behind the horror conventions used in them. However this attempt to place the film firmly within the category of 'auteur' cinema was overturned by the 'middle England' press reaction to the film, which actively undermined this discourse. As a result the film opened to a much wider audience for whom Cronenberg, if he meant anything, came to stand as a pornographer with entirely venial and debased motives.

Although couched in the conventional discourses of British censorship, the scandal can be understood as a process of abjection, a means to reassert the boundaries of the subject in the face of a threat by classifying it as disgusting rubbish which must be thrown out. This process was instigated by Alexander Walker's review in the *Evening Standard* (Walker 1996), filed from Cannes in June but taken up and developed by Nigel Reynolds in the *Daily Telegraph* (Reynolds 1996) and Chris Tookey in the *Daily Mail* (Tookey 1996) at the time of the film's exhibition at the London Film Festival in November. Walker accused the film of being pornography 'in effect if not in intention' whose characters, like Cronenberg, have lost any sense of moral boundaries; they are 'urban sophisticates' who have become detached from normality and their own feelings. Headlined 'A movie beyond the bounds of depravity', Walker's article came to define how the film was discussed in Britain. The *Daily Mail* defined it as a test case for the system of film censorship in Britain, calling for the BBFC to ban it on the grounds that it was pornographic and violent. Drawing on established discourses of censorship, the film's sexual imagery was classified as 'obscene', as likely to deprave and corrupt; while the car crashes and injured bodies were regarded as a potentially dangerous incitement to road rage or sado-masochism (Tookey, 1996, 1997). The *Mail* claimed to be acting on behalf of the 'ordinary people' that make up its readership, who believe in the importance of making moral judgements about films, in order to counteract the liberal belief in the 'freedom of the artist' held by a decadent urban elite (Mooney 1996). The only way to make it safe was to ban it, to remove it from circulation so it could not harm the vulnerable.

This reaction can be explained psychoanalytically if we think of the film as 'obscene', in the way that Foster uses the term, rather than as conventionally pornographic. He defines the obscene in abject art through the relations of the object to the visual codes of its representation. He distinguishes it from the pornographic by the different set of spatial relations employed. Where pornography stages the object in such as way as to distance the viewer, to create a voyeur, the obscene object is presented 'as if there were no scene to stage it, no frame of representation to contain it, no screen' (Foster 1996: 149). The object comes too close to the viewer and threatens dissolution, not only of the boundaries between self and other but also, in the absence of mediating codes, of meaning. This conceptualisation helps to explain viewers' scandalised responses to the bodily images in *Crash*, and in particular their reactions to images of sexual activity, including the sexualised fascination with wounds and scars. If it had merely been pornographic, there would not have been the same scandal – it is a genre with highly predictable conventions. It is the unreadability of these images, the absence of a 'screen', which provokes the processes of abjection.

Multiple Crashes: the audience researched

Intimations of the psychological disturbance produced by *Crash* can also be read in the socially produced discourses captured in the interviews of the ESRC *Crash* audience research project (Barker, Arthurs, Harindranath and Haynes 1999). Amongst these discourses, there was a polarisation between at one extreme an intense, disturbed and positive fascination with the film and at the other extreme either a bored and negative dismissal or an engaged and passionate disgust, of the sort which had been demonstrated by the journalists and politicians. In trying to explain these reactions, I offer here a few examples, interpreted at a more detailed level, using the Lacanian framework already established. I choose them as particularly suggestive examples of talk which evidences the processes of 'binding' in operation.

My first example is a group of two men and one woman (who was the partner of one of the men). They were all in their thirties and defined themselves as having liked the film. Any disturbance felt by this group was to do with a shared uncertainty about what the film meant, but they were all, to varying degrees, gripped and fascinated by it. They had expected it to be more visually explicit in its depiction of violence and sex, given the level of fuss about it in the press, and were slightly disappointed that it wasn't. The couple in particular actively seek films which transgress social taboos. The woman in the group put it like this:

> I was expecting to see blood, gore, umm, maybe children, sort of, you know, with an arm hanging off or something, you know, it was going to be really (intake of breath). Especially after the first scene, well, not the first scene, but, sort of, **when the body comes through the window,** you expect it to grow on from there'

Its refusal to conform to being a conventional 'shocker' makes it more, not less, disturbing; the body came through the window, tearing the screen, but without its expected generic frame, this viewer is left uncomfortably disturbed.

However, this is worked through by the group during the course of the discussion as they search for a workable code with which to make sense of the film. Eventually they decide that it must be an art film and therefore must have a meaningful conceptual purpose, even if they weren't quite sure what it was. It remains as fragments in their minds. Their inability to fully articulate the film's meaning isn't

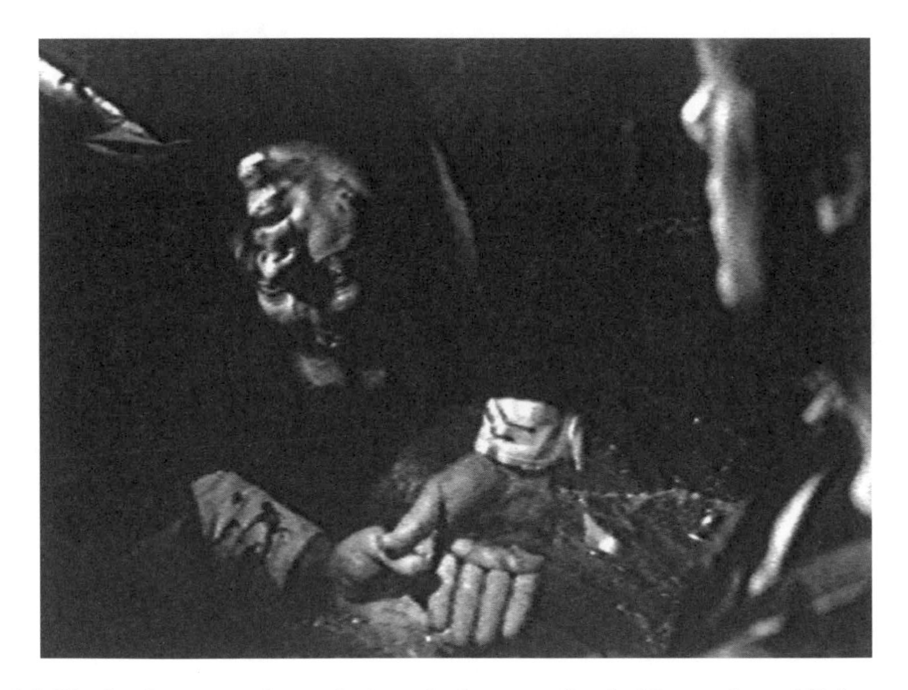

Figure 6.2 The body comes through the windscreen. *Crash*, (Cronenberg 1996).

taken as the film's failure, but theirs – they just haven't been able to fathom it yet. In fact, it is their very inability to make sense of it which fascinates. Again the woman in the group expresses her uncertainty and ambivalence:

> I mean, from a fascination point of view, as I said, I was bored by it. But then I sort of kept thinking, well, I was fascinated from the point of view that ... did I not see something in it, an undercurrent sort of meaning to it, or **that, sort of, I was missing**. So, sort of, it drew you on to, sort of, keep looking and to keep, sort of, finding another channel to it.

The dissolution of subjectivity she experiences, the inability to identify with the film, instigates a process of searching for a discourse through which to bind the experience. If it is art then maybe they should look to the artist as the source of meaning? Then the fragments could be synthesised into a whole through the subjectivity of the author, but none of them have the familiarity with Ballard or Cronenberg, or published accounts of the film, to locate the meaning in this way. One of the men in the group, a photographer, eventually suggested a way out of their confusion by comparing it to contemporary art:

> I don't know you can analyse these things. It's like art, isn't it. Someone looks at half a fish or half a cow in a tank and thinks, God, how horrid – a cow in a tank. How horrendous.

And

> Should we not actually view it as conceptual art, when going through it? **It is what it is** and come away and that was it.

This recognises the 'real' of the film, an experience which can never be represented in words. Instead they need to view it again ... and again:

> You'd **need to see** the film three or four times.

What is it that enables these viewers to tolerate the uncertainty and discomfort the film engendered without it provoking immediate abjection? I would argue from the way that they talked that it is because the willingness to go beyond the imagined boundaries of the self was constitutive of their sense of self. This means they were open to the idea of being transformed by the experience of watching *Crash*. These are people for whom life is conceived as a journey of exploration which opens into unknown futures, rather than being tied to tradition and social conventions, as in the moral discourse through which the film was understood in the popular press. Sexuality is one aspect of this experimentation, and in their view, shouldn't be restricted by fixed regulation about what should be experienced and shown. This is especially true of the photographer:

> I'm not a great one for 9–5, 45 years of your life, die and end up with a miserable pension.

His position in relation to the social and symbolic order is consciously transgressive, an identification which is manifest in his liking for 'subversive' films. His lack of investment in conventional modes of film representation eventually allows him to bind the film to a notion of conceptual art which works outside verbal and narrative articulation, which acknowledges the excess of the visual. In reaching this conclusion, he has found a way of not only placing the film within a workable discourse of interpretation but also of affirming his social identity as a photographer with access to this kind of specialist interpretative knowledge.

For some of the people who were antagonistic towards the film, the process of abjection had already taken place before they actually viewed it. Such was the man in his seventies who came to see *Crash* already armoured by his reading of the *Daily Mail* and its moral condemnation of the film. He moved quickly to bind the film to these prior conceptualisations, which were consistent with his Christian fundamentalism; he was able to develop an impassioned and elaborated condemnation of the film based on his firmly held moral, philosophical and religious views. He professed to being 'appalled' by the film; he had to go and wash his mouth out with beer afterwards because it made him feel unclean. He says very little about the film itself, mentioning only two scenes in any detail:

> The emphasis upon the **prosthesis of the injured woman was particularly offensive**.

Because to focus on any injury is 'obscene'; a dignified response is to ignore it. But even worse were:

> **the homosexual and lesbian scenes (which) are offensive** to those of us who believe that these are abominable acts

He justifies his attitude by quoting chapter and verse from the Bible.

These abject images questioned the distinctions on which he has constructed his sense of self, developed in the course of a life in the army in which he travelled to Mozambique, Madagascar, and the Solomon Islands and witnessed for himself what he regarded as the necessary boundary between the civilised and the primitive. He is afraid that viewers will be dehumanised by seeing these images, that having achieved the pinnacle of the hierarchy of civilisation we will descend via primitivism to the slime of undifferentiated matter. Culture should uplift mankind not debase them, because it is very hard to preserve these distinctions and, once lost, to regain them. He felt angry that we were wasting public money researching such a film; we are a Faculty of Humanities not a Faculty of Animal Behaviour:

> Toads can on occasion be seen attempting to mate with dead or dying members of the same species. But **human beings are not toads** and you're part of a Faculty of Humanities.

And as such we should, instead, be contributing to the higher development of man's capacity as human beings.

His discourse is a neo-Victorian mix of Christianity, political economy and Social Darwinism. He even shares Freud's theory of an economy of psychic energy and the regression to entropy on which his theory of the death drive depends:

> I believe that when you make a jump, as it were, from one level to a lower level, it's not a question of gradually crawling up again. You can't do that, you've got to obtain **the energy to promote yourself out of that depraved or decayed state**.

He was well prepared against the film's imagery, but the music and sound track had insinuated its way into his mind and stayed there, perhaps reminding him of the drums of the primitives he had once lived amongst and what lay beyond the tightly drawn boundaries of his Christian subjectivity.

> The music, I thought, could have been associated with a much better film. **The music itself er ... the drum beats and the sort of cacophony of sounds to suggest sexual activity and so on and lust, the ... these things, actually was quite well done**. And as I say, at one point there was just a hint of us being lifted to something which is ... higher ... er ...

He comes to this aspect of the film without a prior discourse of revulsion to bind it to, nor does he feel the need to defend himself in this way. Perhaps the soundtrack side-steps this need because of the primacy of the visual and the linguistic in the formation of the bounded ego.

My last example, drawn from an interview with two policemen in middle age, is chosen to examine what happens to viewers for whom *Crash* remains unintelligible, who as a consequence find the sexual imagery in *Crash* 'gratuitous' and in the absence of detectable narrative motivation or generic code 'pointless' and therefore 'obscene'. Although again it is the homosexual sex and James's penetration of Gabriella's leg wound which they found particularly 'sickening', it is the failure of the film to make any sense which really offends them:

> I found it so dreadfully boring, but I wanted to see if there was a point. **I was desperately looking for a point** and I was thinking 'Am I the only person in this cinema who can't see the point of this film?'

Combining sex and crashes in one film violates their sense that these are subjects made intelligible within their own proper genres. They expect films about car crashes to have a public service function to warn against the dangers of bad driving. The advance publicity had led them to expect pornography, but they soon realised that it failed to conform to the conventions with which they were familiar (having worked in the Vice Squad). It wasn't that the images were too explicit that made them obscene, in fact it was their lack of explicitness which was the problem because it broke the pornographic code within which they would be intelligible as 'images designed to arouse'.

Furthermore, *Crash* violated their expectations of an entertainment film. They compare it unfavourably with *Basic Instinct*, which

> had a lot of sex in it, but **it didn't disgust me like this film did** ... **at least there was a story-line to it.'**

The characters in *Crash* were experienced as two-dimensional, their motives obscure. In comparison to Hollywood films the sex was obscene because it didn't allow for the kind of psychic investment in the characters which would make the sexual imagery legitimate. Again it is only through the music that they can respond positively to being 'disturbed' because it signifies without recourse to a visual relation or a language-based systems of meaning on which their egos are founded:

> I could **see a point to the music really** – could leave you feeling quite disturbed, I think, the music.

They would prefer other people not to have the chance to see the film because, in their social roles as policemen, they see it as their duty to protect the general public from harm, and this film might provoke copy-cat behaviour both in encouraging perverted forms of sexual behaviour and reckless driving. It also challenges their sense of their own sexual identity. One explains that he considers himself 'a straight husband. I wouldn't do anything like that'. These are both people for whom maintaining and policing boundaries between the normal and the deviant are central to their sense of self, in both their private and professional lives.

Afterword

Long after the public scandal about the film had dissipated, *Crash* has settled into a longer term pattern of occasional exhibition in independent cinemas and we can see how the initial shock caused by the escape of the film into the mainstream has given way to reverential canonisation. University lecturers have adopted the film into degree courses, encouraged by the quick availability of academic articles on the film (Adams 1999, Botting and Wilson 1998, Creed 1998, Grant 1998). Iain Sinclair's book on the film has been published in the BFI *Modern Classics* series (Sinclair 1999); a recent showing of the film at the *Arnolfini* art centre in Bristol was preceded with a talk and slide show based on the book. Sinclair calls it 'a film without context', which he rectifies by evaluating the film in relation to the historical particularity of the novel on which it is based. He takes Cronenberg to task for smoothing over the raw energy of Ballard's novel, for making the pornography safe and elegant, its Dionysian frenzy of sex and death mediated by the cool Apollonian perfection of the formal codes through which he interprets the film:

> His carefully positioned characters show how a scene should be read by studying the angles of the head.
>
> (Sinclair 1999: 70)

This mediation allows for the cool, distanced appreciation which maintains the integrity of the viewer's subjectivity. He therefore considers it ironic that the film attracted censure which the book escaped. Now the figure of Cronenberg the pornographer has given way to Cronenberg the artist, the film 'tamed' within a set of specialist discourses known only to the few. Only in the video shops do bemused customers still return it in disgust.[2]

Notes

1 This essay draws on materials gathered during an 18 month project on the viewing strategies of the audiences for *Crash* funded by the Economic and Social Science Research Council. It was a team project consisting of Dr Martin Barker as project director, myself and Dr Ramswami Harindranath, with Jo Haynes as our research assistant. We gathered and analysed an extensive collection of reviews and newspaper reports on *Crash,* interviewed many of the journalists and other key people involved in the controversy, and interviewed 63 people selected from an audience of 167 attending a specially arranged screening of the film. The results are published in Barker, M., Arthurs, J., and Harindranath R. (2001) *The Crash Controversy: Censorship Campaigns and Film Reception.* London and New York;Wallflower Press. The use I have made of the materials here is quite separate from the team project and represents my personal selection and interpretation of the data collected.

2 Informal information gleaned from my local video retailers in Bristol.

References

Adams, P. (1999) Cars and Scars. *New Formations 35,* 60–72 .

Ballard, J.G. interview with Cronenberg (1997), *Index of Censorship 3,* 91–97.

Barker, M., Arthurs, J., and Harindranath R. (2001) *The Crash Controversy: Censorship Campaigns and Film Reception.* London and New York;Wallflower Press.

Barker, M. (project director), Arthurs J., Harindranath, R., Haynes, J. (1999) *What viewing strategies were adopted by different audiences of the film* Crash. ESRC Project: R000222194.

Billig, M. (1997) From Codes to Utterances: Cultural Studies, Discourse and Psychology. In Ferguson, M and Golding, P. *Cultural Studies in Question,* 205–226.

Boothby, R. (1991) *Death and Desire: psychoanalytic theory in Lacan's return to Freud.* London and New York: Routledge.

Botting, F. and Wilson S. (1998)Automatic Lover, *Screen* 39:2, 186–192.

British Board of Film Classification (1997) *Crash* Press Release, 18th March.

Creed, B. Anal Wounds, *Screen* 39:2, 175–179.

Daily Mail (1996) *Ban this car crash sex film.* November 9th, 1.

Evening Standard (1996) *A movie beyond the bounds of depravity.* 3rd June, 16.

Foster, H. (1996) *The Return of the Real: the avant-garde at the end of the century.* Cambridge Massachusetts and London: MIT Press.

Freud, S. (1920) Beyond the Pleasure Principle. *Standard Edition of the Complete Psychological Works of Sigmund Freud, 18.* 1–64.

Grant, M. Crimes of the Future; *Screen* 39: 2, 180–185.

Mooney, B. (1996) I am proud to call myself a liberal, but I cannot see why freedom of expression must mean freedom to peddle violence and pornography. *Daily Mail,* 30th November.

Reynolds, N. (1996) 'Depraved' film to be released in Britain, *Daily Telegraph,* 8th November, 1.

Shelley, J. (1996) Always crashing the same car, *The Guardian Weekend,* 2nd November.

Sinclair, I. (1999) *Crash.* London: British Film Institute.

Tookey, C. (1996) Morality dies in the twisted wreckage. *Daily Mail.* 9th November, 6.
Tookey, C (1997) Does anything appal this man? *Daily Mail.* 20th March 1997,14–15.
Walker, A. (1996) A film beyond the bounds of depravity. *Evening Standard.* 3rd June, 16.

7 Sexcrash

Fred Botting and Scott Wilson

For as long as people have defined themselves as'human', Technology, or the figure of the machine, has provided the inhuman element which lies at the extreme core of identity – the engine of desire. Once upon a time, woman (as Courtly Lady, doll, automaton or corpse) provided man with an inhuman partner worthy of his machinic desire, an object of powerful sublimation for which he would create beauty, amass fortunes, conquer the world, make a name for himself. Now the machine is its own metaphor, which suggests that this metaphor has been reduced to a literalism that renders desire purely and machinically metonymic. Without an end, desire 'careers' along a chain of objects, across a grid of network connections, until it crashes. At that point, identity is formed retroactively, according to the outcome of the crash: celebrity, notoriety, anonymity, a sudden rocketing success, or a disastrous collapse. Since the 1960s, a number of notable texts have appeared which are particularly symptomatic in their literalization of machinic desire, representing or actualizing a desire to impact with, become scarred and mutilated by, or annihilated by machines. In different ways, these texts presuppose the existence of some kind of unspeakable machinic *jouissance* to which there is no access except through crashing.

Baudrillard has hailed J.G. Ballard's novel *Crash* as 'the first great novel of the universe of simulation, the one with which we will all now be concerned – a symbolic universe, but one which, through a sort of reversal of the mass-mediated substance (neon, concrete, car, erotic machinery), appears as if traversed by an intense force of initiation' (Baudrillard 1994: 119). It is strange to hear Baudrillard speak of a 'great novel' in the universe of simulation that was supposed to have totally integrated the art-work into the commodity-sign, but Ballard's book is a peculiarly lush work, with a degree of figuration and lurid imaginings that is at odds with those sleek chrome surfaces fetishized by the characters. The book is almost Lawrentian in the redemptive force that it grants to the phallic power of the automobile, in which sexuality is celebrated in a 'bloody eucharist' with the machine. Ballard's book is locatable at a point of transition: it is a fantasized 'initiation' (complete with symbolic mutilations and scarification) of an entry into a new order of machinic sex which is imagined in an all–too-human way, in terms of the hard, virile penetration of vulnerable human flesh. The crash celebrates a 'fierce marriage' of 'eroticism and fantasy' (Ballard 1995: 79). Victims' scars become 'a potent metaphor for the excitements of a new violence' (Ballard 1995: 135). It is bound up with a technological imperative, as Ballard, in the novel, notes: 'I thought of being killed within this huge accumulation of fictions, finding my body marked with the imprint of a hundred television serials ...' (Ballard 1995: 50). Cronenberg's sympathetic rewriting, too, invokes the energy of an apocalyptic, violent and sexualised coupling with machines, having Vaughan speak of the crash as the advent of the future, 'a liberation of sexual energy that mediates the sexuality of those who have died with an intensity impossible in any other form' (Cronenberg 1996: 42). The intensity of the impact which takes sexual energy beyond sex is a quasi-mystical illusion, a precipitation of fantasy that marks bodies with a machinic otherness, in the same way that the scars tattooed on the thigh and abdomen of Ballard and Vaughan are said to hold a 'prophetic' significance (Cronenberg 1996: 54). From sex to death, the crash promises a new order of intensity, beyond pleasure and the possibility of return.

Michel Foucault, too, finds pleasure somehow unsatisfying and incomplete without an intensity that is 'related to death'. Indeed, beyond the circuits of a pleasure principle, the intensity draws the subject towards a fullness which sacrifices life and, significantly, depends on a moment of catastrophic interruption of everyday experience:

> Because I think that the kind of pleasure I would consider as *the* real pleasure would be so deep, so intense, so overwhelming that I couldn't survive it. I would die. I'll give you a clearer and simpler example. Once I was struck by a car in the street. I was walking. And for maybe two seconds I had the impression that I was dying and it was really a very, very intense pleasure. The weather was wonderful. It was 7 o'clock during the summer. The sun was descending. The sky was very wonderful and blue and so on. It was, it still is now, one of my best memories [*Laughter*].
>
> (Foucault 1988a: 12)

The near death experience caused by a car accident offers an intensity unavailable to the world of normal pleasures and touches on a profundity heterogeneous to daily life. Foucault's description, moreover, colours the scene in distinctly conventional romantic tones and then punctures the bubble with a burst of ironic laughter; a romanticism of death charged with intensity does not quite lift the experience onto an extraordinary plane, nor does it escape the circuits of pleasure and attain the velocity necessary for obliterating the conditional tense preceding the description. If sex ceases to retain the mysterious power of heterogeneity, then death, too, fails at the point of fantasized fullness. Indeed, Baudrillard's account of *Crash* evinces a similar ambivalence: his praise for the novel is counterbalanced by a recognition that, in the new world of a pervasive hyperrationality the accident becomes the rule and exposes 'the banality of the anomaly of death' (Baudrillard 1994: 113).

Rather than endorsing an accelerating quest for a truly intense instant in which the crash materialises, on the point of machinic annihilation, the pregnant pinnacle of human plenitude, there is another direction – of banality, repetition, and boredom – which structures experience according to different technological relations. In art that slightly predates and anticipates *Crash* in its apparent infatuation with machinic processes of communication, imaging and production coupling with the glamour of dead personalities, a different technological imperative manifests itself. Andy Warhol's work in the early sixties – his images of Jackie, Liz, Marilyn, electric chairs and car accidents, the 'Death in America' series – clearly embodies the machinic process that strips tragic images of any human depth. These images also incorporate the means by which that process still manages to enlist identification, and, to a degree, desire. In his analysis of these works, Hal Foster demonstrates how the process of enlistment operates, and in so doing repeats a mode of identification characteristic of David Cronenberg's film of Ballard's novel.

In *The Return of the Real*, Hal Foster develops the category of 'traumatic realism' through a discussion of Warhol's early work. Beginning with Warhol's famous motto 'I want to be a machine', Foster psychoanalyses it as a response to the shock *of* the machine, a repetition unconsciously employed to protect consciousness from the shock of automation (Foster 1996: 130–1). Similarly, other famous mottos of Warhol's 'quasi-autistic persona' – 'I like boring things', 'I like things to be exactly the same over and over again' – are read as a deliberate draining of significance and affect to protect against the violence of the traumatic event. The argument is essentially the same as Bart Simpson's response to his sister's complaints about the repetitive violence on American TV: 'How are you ever going to become desensitized to the violence on TV if you don't watch TV?' Hence, Warhol's subject matter: the scenes, victims and instruments of violent death that are subjected to the same mechanical processes of production and reproduction as Brillo Boxes, Campbell's Soup tins or bottles of Coca-Cola. *Car Crash* (1963), *White Car Crash* (1963), *White Car Crash Nineteen Times* (1963), *Orange Car Crash Fourteen Times* (1963), *Ambulance Disaster* (1963), *White Disaster* (1963), *Green Disaster # 2* (1963), *Green Disaster Ten Times* (1963), *Saturday Disaster* (1964), *White Burning Car I* (1963), *White Burning Car Twice* (1963), *White Burning Car III* (1963), *Five Deaths Twice II* (1963), *Five Deaths Three Times* (1963), *Five Deaths Seventeen Times in Black and White* (1963), *Five Deaths on Red* (1962), *Five Deaths on Orange* (1963). And so on. How many crashes, disasters, deaths was that? The repetitive process of reproduction becomes little more than a statistical tally devoid of affect. Mechanical reproduction with its automation of the same operates a kind of mechanical destruction: there is nothing outside its procession, no affect, no depth, nothing, indeed, beyond the sequence of images.

Though there may be nothing outside the process of mechanical reproduction, there may be a disturbance, and some affect, within it. Foster argues that trauma is indeed disclosed by Warhol's images precisely through the process of their production and the flaws and glitches, minor 'crashes' occurring to and within the mechanised images themselves. These mistakes or errors, indicative of the mechanical process of their production, function as a kind of '*punctum*' in the Barthesian sense, providing an uncanny point of identification that arrests and fascinates the gaze. Barthes locates, in still photographs, the *punctum* in details of content, whereas Foster finds it both in content and in technique. For example, in Warhol's *White Burning Car III* (1963) Foster locates the *punctum* both in the indifference of the passer by to the crash victim impaled on the telephone pole and in the 'galling' repetition of that indifference that the multiple reproduction of the image itself repeats. The *punctum*, Foster states,

> works less through content than through technique, especially through the 'floating flashes' of the silkscreen process, the slipping and streaking, blanching and blanking, repeating and coloring of the images. To take another instance, a *punctum* arises for me not from the slumped woman in the top image in *Ambulance Disaster* (1963) but from the obscene tear that effaces her head in the bottom image.
>
> (Foster 1996: 134)

Here it is the purely technological accidents, machinic errors, and repeated wounds that serve as points of identification for Foster. In an increasingly automated world where crashes are frequently assumed to be the result of *human* error, these glitches render the mechanical process curiously human, thereby providing an uncanny point of recognition. Using Lacanian terms, Foster calls them 'visual equivalents of our missed encounters with the real' (Foster 1996: 134). But these are precisely not human parapraxes, slips or scars that disclose the real through repetition, even when they shield the trauma of that missed encounter. On the contrary, these are purely machinic 'pops' or 'pokes' through which, Foster suggests, 'we seem almost to touch the real' (Foster 1996: 135). The real is virtually experienced as an effect of a mechanical process of reproduction, precisely when that process malfunctions. The substance of the experience of almost touching the real remains an effect of an equivalence in which Warhol's pictures disclose the mechanical way in which the real impacts with the human subject. This suggests that human beings are real only insofar as they are failed machines, insofar as they are the living effects of machinic failure. The irony is that this affect is produced as an effect of a desire for absolute homogenization: 'I don't want it to be essentially the same – I want it to be *exactly* the same' (Warhol, cited in Foster 1996: 131). Only through total assimilation with the machine will a human being really be able to experience the crash that enables them to 'touch' the real.

> It is because the sexual act has become so easy and available to homosexuals that it runs the risk of quickly becoming boring, so that every effort has to be made to innovate and create variations that will enhance the pleasure of the act.
>
> (Foucault 1998b: 298)

If boredom threatens homosexual sex, which is still residually charged with the energy that comes of normative prohibition and taboo, then heterosexual sex, repeatedly represented and readily available to any consumer, must already have suffered the fate that comes from instant accessibility and immediate gratification: the extinction of mystery, prohibition and desire. Sylvère Lotringer, in a study of sex clinics in the USA, notes how the sexual saturation of culture leads to a voiding of significance and value, a steady immersion in banality: 'sex has ceased to be extraordinary, even for ordinary people. Psychologists report that it is fast becoming America's dominant social activity. Everywhere sex is taken casually as legitimate entertainment' (Lotringer 1988: 8). As with TV, movie-going, videos and computer games, sex is consumed on a plane of equivalence that is divested of value, which is to say, desire. Its consumption within the orders of mundane commodified existence, for Lotringer, manifests a new imperative at work:

> In the last years of his life Foucault used to say, 'Sex is boring'. Boredom therapy highlights the curious dilemma of our postmodernity: pleasure, not pain, consumption not prohibition, have become our punishment. Repetition is the norm, and the cure. Who can truly say that he is not copying lines as children used to do at school, and as adolescent offenders now do at the clinic. The end of the century is getting closer, and the end of world remains an open-ended question. But at least we've managed to be through with something: the 'secret' of sexuality. Sexuality is no longer repressed, but no longer desirable. It is what's left to be desired when desire amounts to nothing.
>
> (Lotringer 1988: 176–7)

Haunted by a remainder, an excess that sex can no longer satisfy, the absorption of subjectivity into the repetitive circuits of pleasure and consumption allows no room for the transgressions which once crossed and established the limits of cultural prohibitions; nothing is desired – the nothing that comes precisely from the machine.

For Baudrillard, *Crash* exhibits a process of incorporation: 'everything is hyperfunctional, since traffic and accident, technology and death, sex and simulation are like a single, large synchronous machine. It is the same universe as that of the hypermarket, where the commodity becomes "hypercommodity", that is to say, itself always already captured, and the whole atmosphere with it, in the incessant figures of traffic' (Baudrillard 1994: 118). In Cronenberg's *Crash*, the characters are driven by their investment in this universe; from a tedious plateau of sexual saturation, the automobile becomes not the vehicle of an initiation, but the point of entry, or assimilation, into a hyperhomogenizing machinic network. The film starts from the premise that sex is boring. Boredom, indeed, is the film's milieu. Generically, *Crash* combines the stylized ennui of a seventies German urban alienation film with the grainy, low-tech, humourless repetition of a seventies German porn film. Set in a Canada that seems to consist totally of motorways and tower blocks, the film's opening sexual encounters present sex as a matter-of-fact, workaday activity: an automatic emptying of the liberation of sex into the free-floating realms of consumer capitalism, a 'pornographic culture' of materialized appearances, mechanical labour and copulation (Baudrillard 1990: 34). On a balcony overlooking jammed motorways, James and Catherine Ballard compare notes on the day's sexual encounters: 'How was work today darling?' is replaced by the equally perfunctory 'Who did you fuck at work today, darling?' and shortly followed by the question, 'Did you come?' Sex becomes the same dull daily grind as work: a banal, repetitive, mundane event absorbed in the pleasure-boredom principle of the productive and consumptive economy. Sex, work and pleasure, but no *jouissance*, at least not that day, according to the Ballards' negative response to their own inquiries. An everyday routine, sex has been divested of desire, freed from any morality other than the imperative to enjoy, a joyless, superegoic command to keep on fucking.

Cronenberg's film addresses the injunction to and extinction of sexual desire, in line with J.G. Ballard's project in his novel *Crash* and other works. In *The Atrocity Exhibition*, for example, Ballard has one character speak of the need 'to invent a series of imaginary sexual perversions just to keep the activity alive' (cited in Lotringer 1988: 5). For Vaughan, in *Crash*, the automobile serves as a sex aid. As the film's sex-guru, Vaughan recruits his disciples, the Ballards and Helen Remington, by setting their car accidents in a photo-narrative, thereby giving their physical trauma a new, erotic meaning. In a short time, the characters begin to share Vaughan's interest in car crashes, an interest manifested in precipitating, photographing, recording, and re-enacting automobile collisions. In his workshop, he speaks of a 'benevolent psychopathology' of the car crash as a 'fertilizing event'. Credited as the film's dominant character by the others around him, the master of ceremonies who connects crash victims, Vaughan explains events and stages their ritual observances. As a paternal or phallic figure, however, he remains suspect. Elias Koteas's performance of Vaughan as the dangerously charismatic, virile American is so excessive (often recalling Nicholson and De Niro at their most deranged) as to successfully hint at the deficiency that determines his obsession. Far from being the intoxicating, sinister figure he appears to be for Helen Remington and the Ballards, he merely evokes incredulity, and fails to provide the point of identification that could enliven his project for a cinema audience. Looked at another way, he's simply 'a dickless piece of shit who fucks with cars' (Vincent Vega in Tarantino 1994: 42).

Absent or not, Vaughan's dick is an object of curiosity in the film. Ironically, in the one scene of normal 'bedroom' sex between the Ballards, pleasure comes as an effect of persistent, probing inquiries into another fantasized sexual scene: Catherine Ballard interrogates her husband about Vaughan's penis: What does it look like? Is it circumcised? Is it badly scarred? Would her husband like to suck it ? Moving from his scars to his penis, from his sexual habits to the semen smell of his car, from his anus to the idea of sodomizing him, the escalating series of questions and speculations spices sex with a quite literal instance of perversion – in the Lacanian sense of a turning towards the father (*père version*) that foregrounds the symptom or object, *a* supporting the paternal function (Lacan 1982: 167). However, as Catherine Ballard later discovers, Vaughan's penis, if not already severed after 'the motorcycle accident' that was supposed to have damaged it, is not an organ he employs in the film (Cronenberg 1997: 37). When he's not ramming someone with his car, he fucks with his fists, leaving behind a trail of cuts and bruises; as Catherine Ballard discovers, sex with Vaughan is just another kind of car crash.

Vaughan occupies a central place in the libidinal economies of the film's characters, then, as their point of *père version*, in the form of a quasi-phallic, yet penis-less, figure who sits in his car as the scarred metaphor of a 'real' castration that precisely discloses the excessive *failure* of traditional symbolic castration. Liberated from any taboo that might once have given it meaning, all 'normal' sexual activity disappears, and the phallus (the taboo) is desired precisely as a body that has been beaten black and blue, scarred with twisted metal. Imagined and fetishized as the signifier of the desire of an Other now seen as machine, the battered and broken body is the last remnant of a human erotic imaginary in the face of a fully automated form of desire. As the bedroom is replaced by the car, sexual organs and erogenous zones are replaced by scars in a technological supplementation of quasi-erotic energy and intensity. Ultimately, cars, scars and signifiers conjoin to sever sex from bodies and organs.

Signifiers of the collision – the wounds and scars – are photographed, collected, simulated and fetishized first by Vaughan, then by his disciples: Catherine's interest in Vaughan's scarred body; Ballard's impatience to touch the healed gash along the back of Gabrielle's thigh; Ballard's ardent sensitivity towards his wife's battered and bruised body; Ballard's and Vaughan's passionate kissing of each other's bruised tattoos. Eventually the entire film is dominated by a generalized medico-pornographic gaze that is turned in on itself as a symptom of its own psychopathology. Scars endow bodies with a value they would not otherwise possess. As scar-screens, the empty units of visual identification ('characters' is too strong a word) are marked by the traces of an unspeakable automotive *jouissance* unavailable to a human culture determined by the restricted economy of the pleasure principle. At the point linking and separating horror and eroticism, crash scars announce a splitting of subjectivity that comes of the transformation of bodies and their reinscription in a new order of desiring. *Crash*, however, seems to do no more than fetishize a generalized lack. Without any privileged place of identification, the film is plotted along a chain of scars signifying the displacement of the fetish from its 'original' location as the substitute for maternal lack, to a fetishistic repetition and universalization of lack: all figures are all-too-obviously castrated, scarred, clumsy, limping bodies, mobile only with the aid of vehicles, sticks and callipers. The effect is similar to that noted by Laura Mulvey who suggests that the fetishistic and close representation of the female image breaks the cinematic spell, freezing the male look, rather than allowing it to assume a masterful and superior distance (Mulvey 1975: 18). Similarly, in Slavoj Žižek's version of the pornographic gaze, the discomforting of the position of viewer as voyeur evacuates the attenuation of any secure authority (Žižek 1991: 108). The wounds, bruises and scars repeatedly thrust by the camera into watching faces serves to abject, rather than incorporate or elevate, the look. Visual pleasure is not restored by the jubilant identification of meaning; the spectator is not returned to the comforts of a recognisable resolution which fills cinematic lack. Instead, all that is seen is a pornography of scars that either leaves one cold or becomes a horrible limit beyond which one cannot bear to look. It is from the overt presentation of a generalized castration, perhaps, that the censorious morality which surrounded the release of the film in Britain takes its bearings, since any moral concern expressed in regard to the likelihood of cinematic seduction or childish emulation (this is not a film advocating sex in cars) is quite untenable.

If sex in *Crash* disappears in the back of a car, it does so as an effect of its generalized *automation*. Significantly, the car crashes do not take place as part of a compelling narrative. Stylistically and technically, *Crash* refuses to evoke or simulate the sensational and spectacular effects that one would expect of a film that draws an equivalence between sex and car crashes. There are no big bangs, no sensuous slow motion smashes, no romantic chases or erotic duels on the open highway. The crashes take place as a series of bumps that occur as an effect of sudden accelerations or minor deviations amidst packed lanes of commuter traffic. Since sex has become work, it has become just one functioning part of the regulative synchronous machine that articulates the circulations, exchanges and communication of so many bio-mechanical vehicles that are visualized in the film's recurrent shots of traffic flowing. It is a movement, relentless and aimless, that seems to be simply there, underscored by the omnipresent background noise of internal combustion engines. 'I somehow find myself driving again', Ballard remarks to Helen Remington (Cronenberg 1997: 21). No purpose or reason informs his decision, only a kind of automatism that is reinforced by their mutual, stupefied sense of the monotonous increase in heavy traffic. Cars replace human subjects, equivalent units of mechanical and automatic motion. In *Crash*, driving, work, sex, and pleasure have become hyperhomogenised into the same productive-consumptive economy determining the flows of communicational vehicles. Sex, work and pleasure are bound up with driving and are absorbed by the repetitive, automatic insistence of a signifying chain. Everything accedes to a new order of automaton, a social symbolic machine working with and absorbing the intensities and erotic energy previously associated with enjoyment and *jouissance*.[1]

In the hypersexualized and desexualized setting of *Crash*, sex is associated with the circulation of communicational vehicles and invested with the erotic charge of the crash. That sex is still synonymous with some sort of 'crash', therefore, does denote its survival or reinvention as a mode of nonproductive expenditure opposed to the world of work and traffic flows, even as it is dependent upon them. Indeed, as Joan Copjec argues, sex appears where words and categories fail, in the gaps of signification where desire articulates and separates beings (Copjec 1994: 204). But of course it is not the human characters who are the vehicles of sexual identity, nor are they the conduits of desire; they don't have the sex. Rather, they suffer the *effects* of autosex, they become its 'victims' and they eroticize themselves precisely as such in the form of their wounds and scars. Strangely, this is where *Crash* connects with a problem of so-called 'political correctness'. This is not so much to do with the suggestion that, in its sexy depiction of a paraplegic, *Crash* shows a commendable willingness to affirm that the differently abled can also enjoy healthy relations on screen. Rather, the increasing juridical, governmental and corporate concern, in North America, with unauthorized incursions into the 'personal space' of employees (particularly the various degrees of sexual harassment) has, in common with *Crash*, the close identification of work and *jouissance* and an interest in intensifying sex, and the social activities around it, as something that may seriously damage your health – or psyche. It is no longer taboo, or transgression, then, that returns some interest to sex, but the location of sex as the scene of potential disaster: sex as a kind of car crash, computer crash, financial crash or lifestyle crash, physical, psychic or system violation, malfunction, illness, break down or burn out – the catastrophic point where one's life, identity or career crashes.

Hollywood, of course, has a history of disaster films and of film careers arrested, destroyed or immortalized in one kind of crash or another. These provide the conventional means by which the crash and its victim may be romanticized by an image; , *Crash* makes explicit reference to this tradition with its photographs and photographed reenactments of the celebrated deaths of James Dean and Jayne Mansfield. The photographic image becomes the only means by which the hypermodern subject can verify its existence imaginarily and symbolically in an umbilical connection to a reality 'that has been' (Barthes 1984: 96). Absolutely bound up with a hyperhomogenizing system whose only point of fissure is the 'crash' itself, crashes become, for the hypermodern subject, simulations of the traumatic (missed) encounter with the real.[2] This is why they must be photographed. The photograph functions as a scar in time, freezing the moment when the mortal being becomes Other, fully transformed into pure image. Vaughan's photographs not only capture the instant when bodily parts are indelibly imprinted by mechanical components, they inscribe the image on another technological surface: the subject is moved along a chain of mechanical production and reproduction; created by the machine's signifier – the scar – being becomes machinic when registered through light, lens, enlarger and chemicals, on photographic paper. 'Photographic film', observes Baudrillard, 'is part of the universal, hyperreal, metallized, and corporeal layer of traffic and flows' (Baudrillard 1994: 117). As Hollywood has known for years, one's life and destiny is *realized* on film. Vaughan is another prophet of this destiny, aspiring to die in a celebrated and much photographed crash. (In the novel, he plans to die in a crash which also kills Elizabeth Taylor).

In Cronenberg's film, however, Vaughan fails, in his own fatal crash, to guarantee his own photographic immortality by impacting with a film star. Nevertheless, after his death, the Ballards carry the torch with their own brand of car sex, presided over by the spectre of Vaughan, in a repetition and displacement of earlier patterns. Having bought and rendered roadworthy Vaughan's 1963 black Lincoln, the final sequence of the film documents their own romantically-paired car chase. With their scars and cars, sex between the two has become fully automated. Ballard is seen furiously driving Vaughan's car-phallus-scar machine, the object of pursuit being his wife's grey sportscar. He catches up to ram the smaller car repeatedly from behind, until it careers off the road. The Lincoln halts hurriedly. Ballard, apparently shaken, gets out and stumbles down the grassy roadside to the overturned car to peer down into the camera. As he kneels, his prostrate wife comes into shot. She is not dead. He inspects her injuries and strokes her head, breathes her name and asks if she is OK. In reply, she murmurs his name and says that she is OK. With a consolatory air, he tenderly kisses her and whispers 'Maybe next time, darling … maybe next time'. They have sex where they are lying. The camera rises, with a warm crescendo of orchestral strings, above the lovers' ardent embrace on the grassy bank. A romantic climax and the end of the film.

The ending rewrites the story as the rediscovery of the illusion of a sexual relation. Vaughan's death governs the reborn sex life of the Ballards, renewing desire with the promise of an unimaginable *jouissance*. 'Maybe next time'. Maybe next time Catherine will attain fatal bliss in the orgasmic instant of the crash. Maybe next time. *Jouissance* remains postponed, but the recovery of its possibility, its fantasy, constitutes the occasion for the reappearance of desire. From being a mechanical failure of diminishing returns, sex is transformed by the crash and becomes, again, a liberating experience. Maybe. What sustains the illusion is the intensity given by death, a fantasised *jouissance* in which the thrill of a fatal crash reinvigorates desire through loss of control and of oneself. But the practice enjoyed by the Ballards has already been commodified. For Virilio the pleasures of dangerous and extreme sports and pastimes such as bungee-jumping simulate the near-death experience of the crash (Virilio 1995: 93). Death, even one's own, saves one from boredom by being incorporated into the imminent banality of another interactive entertainment package.

Where fantasy restores the illusion, deferral and the coming promise of a sexual relation in the film, there is no fantasy or place for it made available on the screen: the audience watch a relentless series of similar acts with steadily diminishing interest, divested of curiosity, desire or identification. The screen discloses itself to be an empty space of repetition: sex, sex, sex, car, crash, car, sex, sex in car, sex, crash, cars, sex in car, crash ... and so on. Just as there is no sexual relation, so, in *Crash*, there is no cinematic relation, no fantastic unification between audience and moving images – scars having become too visible as vicious visual slashes severing voyeur and screen. Indeed, instead of the pleasurable cinematic spectacle of a narcissistic urban alienation, *Crash* offers only the relation of non-relation, an experience of redundancy in the face of endless work-sex-pleasure that unfolds on film in the absence of a *jouissance* that is always missed, that occurs elsewhere, in another scene, at another time, beyond human comprehension in the missed instantaneity of the crash.

Notes

1 *Jouissance* includes Lacan's sense of the 'getting' of meaning ('enjoy-meant') and 'erotic bliss' (Lacan 1990: 16; 89), and his account of the discharges of sexual and bodily energies exceeding symbolic law, that is, 'beyond the phallus', 'God and the *Jouissance* of The [under erasure] Woman', (Lacan 1982: 137–48); Bataille's general economic notion of excessive expenditure, sacrificial consumption and inner experience (Botting and Wilson 1997); and Lyotard's 'acinema' of the libidinal intensities of the drives and the wasteful and pyrotechnical dissipation of energy and images (Benjamin 1989: 169–80)

2 For a discussion of the distinction between 'hypermodern' and 'postmodern', see the issue on 'Hypervalue', *Cultural Values* 1: 2 (1997).

References

Baudrillard, Jean (1990) *Seduction*. Brian Singer, trans. London: Macmillan.

—— (1994) 'Crash', in *Simulacra and Simulations*. Sheila Faria Glaser, trans. Ann Arbor: Michigan University Press: 111–9.

Ballard, J.G. (1995) *Crash*. London: Vintage.

Barthes, Roland (1984) *Camera Lucida*. Richard Howard, trans. London: Fontana.

Benjamin, Andrew (1989) *The Lyotard Reader*. Oxford: Blackwell.

Botting, Fred and Scott Wilson (1997) *The Bataille Reader*. Oxford: Blackwell.

Copjec, Joan (1994) *Read My Desire*. Cambridge MA: MIT Press.

Cronenberg, David (1996) *Crash*. London: Faber & Faber.

Foster, Hal (1996) *The Return of the Real*. Cambridge MA: MIT Press.

Foucault, Michel (1988a) 'The minimalist self', in *Politics, Philosophy, Culture: Interviews and Other Writings 1977–1984*. Lawrence D. Kritzman, ed. London: Routledge.

—— (1988b) 'Sexual choice, sexual act: Foucault and Homosexuality', in *Politics, Philosophy, Culture: Interviews and Other Writings, 1977–1984*. Lawrence D. Kritzman, ed. London: Routledge.

Lacan, Jacques (1982) 'Seminar of 21 January 1975', in *Feminine Sexuality*. Juliet Mitchell and Jacqueline Rose, eds. Basingstoke and London: Macmillan.

Lacan, Jacques (1990) *Television.* Denis Hollier, Rosalind Krauss and Annette Michelson, trans. New York: Norton.
Mulvey, Laura (1975) 'Visual Pleasure and narrative cinema'. *Screen* 16(3).
Tarantino, Quentin (1994) *Pulp Fiction.* London: Faber & Faber.
Virilio, Paul (1995) *The Art of the Motor.* Julie Rose, trans. Minneapolis: University of Minnesota Press.
Žižek, Slavoj (1991) *Looking Awry.* Cambridge MA: MIT Press.

8 Cyborgian Subjects and the Auto-Destruction of Metaphor

David Roden

The Other Side of Hyperspace

Since the publication of Donna Haraway's essay *A Manifesto for Cyborgs: Science, Technology and Socialist Feminism in the 1980s*, the figure of the cyborg, 'creatures simultaneously animal and machine who populate worlds ambiguously natural and crafted' (Haraway 1989: 174), has emerged in philosophy and cultural theory as a foil for 'logics of identity' which normalise relations of domination and their correlative oppositional constituencies. Whereas identitarian logics articulate essences and subjects (human, machine, animal, male, female, capitalist, worker, etc), the cyborg begins life technically as an assemblage.[1] For cyborg ontology, 'cultures' and 'identities' no longer strive for completion or mourn lost origins; cyborg politics likewise disclaims universal history, eschewing dreams of reconciliation in favour of local alliances and opportune struggles:

> The cyborg would not recognise the Garden of Eden, it is not made of mud and cannot dream of returning to dust. Perhaps that is why I want to see if cyborgs can subvert the apocalypse of returning to nuclear dust in the manic compulsion to name the enemy.
>
> (Haraway 1989: 175)

Cyborg theory itself lives in transition between science, science fiction, philosophy and 'social reality'. It is, thus, to be expected that critics of Haraway's manifesto feel entitled to seize on sci-fi prototypes, such as the 'console cowboys' of *Neuromancer*, to fuel accusations that the cyborg myth legitimates the 'masculine' colonisation of a recalcitrant, female-coded flesh. As Jill Marsden shows in her essay 'Virtual Sexes and Feminist futures', such objections presuppose the very dualistic distinctions between organism and artifice that Haraway's trope seeks to conflate; locating the cyborg 'within a pre-critical understanding of the machinic' (Marsden 1996: 8). For Haraway, there is no eudaimonic state not *already* constituted by cultural, technological or biotic systems; rendering it both possible and, as a functioning assemblage, massively contingent:

> No objects, spaces, or bodies are sacred in themselves; any component can be interfaced with any other if the proper standard, the proper code, can be constructed for processing signals in a common language.
>
> (Haraway 1989: 187)[2]

The 'onto-logic' of the cyborg is of couplings which transect the notional boundaries of systems, rendering identity hybrid, problematic. Within the systems of a cyborgian nature/culture, 'hybrid "identity"' is 'entirely coextensive with … functioning' (Marsden 1996: 7). The meaning of a term or thing is coextensive with its role in mediating between inputs (perceptions) and outputs (actions).

Poststructuralists have argued that this 'incarnation' of the operational code implies the utter indigence of its analytical distinctions, even, as Baudrillard suggests, the possibility of its 'symbolic' resolution and destruction. Like Baudrillard, Haraway accepts that the hypertrophy of operational variants – recombinant strings of DNA, the commutation of fashion-bodies – erodes lines between derivative and original, sign and referent. When technically produced 'models' attain this threshold of finesse (the *hyperreal*) objects become iterable without limit as *simulacra*: 'copies without originals' (Haraway 1989: 185–189). A simulacrum – for example, that postmodern lab rat, the serially-implemented neural network – has no self-circumscribed reference or distinction from the field it replicates. From the purview of Haraway and Baudrillard the question 'Does a net "trained" to categorise faces according to family resemblance and gender only model human recognitional capacities or does it, *in fact*, recognise?' (see Churchland 1995, 1998) is facile. It asks for a determinate truth value where there is only a 'hyperspace' of variation in which the real ('recognition') is absorbed by its models and by whatever 'boundary projects' they subtend (Haraway 1991: 201). As Marsden points out, this denial of transcendent systems (essences) complicates the normative basis of Haraway's disarmingly irenic socialist-feminism:

> The conditions for cyborg politics are merely "formal" and in no sense prescriptive … To ask what makes a cyborg alliance liberating rather than oppressive or parasitic may be to reinscribe an extrinsic moral vantage point, thereby misunderstanding Haraway's philosophy of immanence.
>
> (Marsden 1996: 13)

'Cyborg politics', she goes on to suggest, may have to be theorised in terms of self-organising systems re-designing boundaries according to local specifications – 'degrees of control, resistance, rates of stability and changes in flow' – not some vain pursuit of ethico-political Ideas. However, Marsden's proposal suggests, in turn, the fantasy of a politics without judgement, and of the reduction of language to *code*.

This philosophical impasse highlights the problems associated with a 'cyber-monism' wedded to a 'pre-critical understanding of the subject'. As ontology, it is insufficiently reflexive. Its alludes to an internally complex *real* (Marsden 1996: 7) which cannot be represented (representation having faded from a universe defined by the transpositions of simulacra). Dialectically, then, cyborg philosophy gravitates towards an *asemia* unthinkable in terms of its much touted operationalism of coded difference, 'degrees of control, resistance, rates of stability …', feedback, etc, since, as a metaphysics denuded of prescription, its engagement with the real can only be speculative, not generative.

The second-level discourse of 'cyborg politics' thus cedes to a different 'order of being' to the operational/machinic cyborg: no longer of the real, but of the *symbolic*. In its migration across the texts of Lévi-Strauss, Lacan, Baudrillard and, latterly, Žižek, the symbol is always an excess over the semantic or performative dimensions of language. For Baudrillard, it is also exorbitant to the 'cybernetic' regime of simulation. Instead of the coded equivalences of simulacra, 'symbolic exchange' involves the 'festive' cancellation and sacrifice of differential-value; as in the uncoded dispersion of graffiti across urban space (Baudrillard 1993: 82). In *Symbolic Exchange and Death* its formal strategy is exemplified in Saussure's early studies of ancient poetry, which he claimed to be governed by exact rules for the coupling/distribution of phonemes. Each vowel is cancelled by a 'counter vowel in some other place in the verse'. Any 'remainder' (unpaired element) must be resolved in the following verse of the series. Finally, verses are constrained to 'diffract' the name of a god or hero in anagrammatic form: e.g. *AA*SEN ARG*A*LEON *ANEMON AMEGA*RTOS AUT*ME* (*AGAMEMNON*) (Cited in Baudrillard 1993: 196; see also Gane 1991: 118–9). Baudrillard takes Saussure's speculations to illustrate the principle that any combinatory of elements into well-formed sequences can be 'exterminated' by over-writing singular (*anagrammatic*, hence *uncodified*) distributions of its elementary units. Modern signifying practices are thus 'haunted', for Baudrillard, by an aleatory reversion of the code in ambivalence, the notional 'death' of determinate subject positions, the 'ritualistic ... deconstruction' of value in the cyclical play of appearance (Baudrillard 1988: 150).

For Lacan, on the other hand, the term 'symbolic' applies to *any* structure which conjugates the desire of the subject via 'metaphorical' substitutions between signifiers (Lacan 1977: 207; MacCannel 1986, Chapter 6). It is the genetic basis of the 'modern' structural subjectivity (subject = labour of idealization/repetition) first delineated by Kant. Although the systemic character of the Lacanian symbolic might appear to align it more closely to cyborg ontology, it does not reduce to the complexity of cybernetic systems because its 'tokens' are pure units of repetition whose 'identity' is always surplus to their structural role (Žižek 1995: 148–161). The symbolic, in this sense also, addresses the *radically different*, which can, in some sense, be desired, presupposed, encountered, struggled over, etc, but is not operationalisable in terms of 'local destinies' or historically situated networks.[3] With regard to Haraway, this point is made very well by Mary Anne Doane in *Cyborgs, Origins and Subjectivity*, where she criticises Haraway's 'myth' for dissallowing a subjectivity inflected by loss, absence or displacement: that is, for confusing the subject with its humanist ejecta (Doane 1989: 210–11).

Cyborg ontology deconstructs conservative terror-reflexes (phantasms of ecological, bodily or national integrity, etc) in the face of the 'overkill technologies' unleashed by global capital. However, without a place for the symbolic the 'cyborgian' insistence upon constitutive hybridity tells us nothing of how these technologies might vehiculate the strategies and desires of cyborg subjects. It is only where there is an under-coded circulation of redundant tokens (symbols in the Baudrillardian or Lacanian sense, Lévi-Strauss' 'floating signifiers') that the 'blurrings' of cyber-life can be addressed socially, aesthetically or politically, since their effects are fundamentally ambivalent. Missing this layer of reflexivity, Marsden mistakes Haraway's symbol for a schematic.

How then does 'cyborg' become 'symborg': a technically imbricated subject? This 'semio-engineering' problematic can be diffracted instructively through a rhetorical reading of J.G. Ballard's implacable cyborgian romance: *Crash*. Ballard's novel, as I will show, contains the speculative germ of a desire that is mediated by technical prostheses, but never saturated by their operations and protocols. I will begin by detailing a 'cyborg' reading of *Crash* that is formally (if not politically) in tandem with Haraway's account of cyborg identity: namely, Baudrillard's celebrated chapter on the novel from *Simulacra and Simulations*. In the following section I will show how attending to figural structures of Ballard's text – which Baudrillard either ignores or excludes – allows us to limn a cyborgian subject which dreams of catastrophes both equivalent to and alien to those which Haraway hopes to forestall.

Ballard, Baudrillard and the Anagrammatized Body

In *Crash* the technology of the car has become the adjunct to a violent sexuality. Its erotic focus and ideologue, Vaughan, is an ambulance chasing ex-TV presenter whose career as a glamorous 'hoodlum scientist' has been cut short by his disfigurement in a motorcycling accident. Marking the details of vehicle collisions and casual sexual encounters with Polaroid and cine camera, Vaughan is a social being of sorts, assembling around him a crew of co-experimenters whose sexuality has been activated by 'the perverse eroticisms of the car-crash'. The novel's narrator, James Ballard, recounts his induction into the crashpack: first through a motorway accident, then via a succession of techno-erotic duels and excursions, culminating in Vaughan's attempted 'seduction' of the actress Elizabeth Taylor in the environs of London Airport.

In his introduction, Ballard describes *Crash* as 'the first pornographic novel based on technology'. However, its concatenations of sectioned bodies and industrial artifacts are construed in his self-reading as emblems of a cautionary fable. Ballard poses the automobile as a 'total metaphor' for the collapsing universe of late modernity; the vistas of cosmic exploration adumbrated by Asimov and Clarke having been 'annexed' by technologically mediated lifestyles and identities. Freud's distinction between manifest and latent content of dreams, Ballard writes, 'now needs to be applied to the external world' (Ballard 1995: 5). Analysed accordingly, the reality of the present is, for Ballard, a pathological abstraction which fragments the narrative time of nineteenth-century 'realism'. It is to be acceded to, if at all, only through the most formal and estranged aesthetic devices.

As Mike Gane has observed, the media-soaked world of *Crash* is perhaps closer to the Baudrillardian hyperreal than that of any other literary text (Gane 1991: 19). In his reading of the novel, however, Baudrillard detects an epistemological inconsistency between the novel's omnivorous violence and the dystopianism of Ballard's introduction. For Baudrillard, Ballard's novel stages the 'deconstruction' of a traditional philosophical view of the body; a 'perspective' in which the body is only an instrument for the rational transformation of nature, and technology its prosthetic extension. In *Crash*, the precarious system of erogenous zones, localised during the passage into adulthood, is displaced by a *semiurgy* in which genitalia are generalised into wounds, sections, nodes, coincidences of planes, raw membranes and torn surfaces; 'death and sex are read identically on the body, without phantasms, without metaphor, without sentences …' (Baudrillard 1994: 113). Ballard's introduction portrays the endless recapitulation of wounds in terms of the perversion of an 'intimate time and space' of the body and the irruption of narcissistic violence. According to Baudrillard, this self-reading succumbs to the very model of socialised desire whose order is exceeded in *Crash*. And it can be exceeded because it is a differentiated structure with prescribed rules:

> Sex as we conceive it is only a narrow and specialised definition of all the symbolic and sacrificial practices by which the body can open itself, no longer by nature, but by artifice, by the simulacrum, by the accident.
>
> (Baudrillard 1994: 113)

In effect, this passage applies the anagrammatic principle abstracted from Saussure: wherever a system is articulated by a combinatory it can be symbolically co-opted, generating concatenations devoid of precedent, metaphor or rule. Sexual dispositions are articulable against technological sites, surfaces and interstices, not because of some dangerous and untapped libidinal reserve, but because of the enormous combinatory power of a machinic society. The accident constitutes, as Vaughan says, 'a fertilizing event': a specific redeployment of sexuality from an external field rather than a violent transgression of limits – 'a strategic organisation of life that starts from death' (Baudrillard 1994: 113). The relations between bodies and technological artifacts in *Crash* – pre-eminently those associated with the automobile – *physically antecede the desire for their conjunction*; desire being conveyed in a language for which the traditional 'erotic loci' – penises, breasts, vaginas – are topologically resituated. This erotic formalism is, in fact, serially thematised in the text; for example, where James Ballard arouses his wife Catherine with accounts of imaginary sexual acts between himself and Vaughan:

> His attraction lay not so much in a complex of familiar anatomical triggers – a curve of exposed breast, the soft cushion of a buttock, the hair-line arch of a damp perineum – but in the stylisation of posture achieved between Vaughan and the car. Detached from his automobile, particularly his own emblem-filled highway cruiser, Vaughan ceased to hold any interest.
>
> (Ballard 1995: 117)

When James has sex with the crippled social worker, Gabrielle, following a visit to the Earls Court motor show, it is not the authorised conjunctions of the gendered body which determines their erotic itinerary but the abrasions and indentations of flesh and leg-brace, the coincidence of the body and an intimate design technology. The wounds incised on their bodies by their collisions become the 'abstract vents' of a new sexuality (Ballard 1995: 179).

This erotic combinatory has parallels in the structural eroticism that Roland Barthes elicits in his essay on Georges Bataille's *Story of the Eye*. Barthes shows that the erotic effects of Bataille's narrative arise from a 'metonymic' crossing of terms from two metaphoric series: that of the 'eye' which establishes the series *eggs, head, testicles, sun* ...; that of 'liquid' (*blood, milk, egg yolk, sperm, urine, intestines, light* ...). The metonymy consists in jarring contiguities which interchange the two series. Thus the eye of the matador Granero, spurting from his head 'with the same force as innards from a belly' (Bataille 1987: 54), and the eye of the priest Don Aminado placed in the body of Simone, interchange with the cat's saucer of milk of the opening chapter, as with the liquifying head of the female cyclist severed in collision with the lovers' car (Bataille 1987: 10).

However, while the metonymy of Bataille's text is tightly constrained by the two metaphoric 'rows', Baudrillard sees the juxtapositions of Ballard's novel as devoid of metaphor: their principle of concatenation being the accident and the anagrammatic potential reposing in the micro-differences of technological systems. An apparent confirming instance would be James Ballard's beatific recollection of a flight from London Airport to Orly while recovering in hospital from the crash which first catalyses his obsession. His reverie is mediated by 'the languages of invisible eroticisms, of undiscovered sexual acts' reposing in the equipment of an X-ray ward (Ballard 1995: 40–1). A hoary simile likening aircraft to 'silver penises' conjoined with 'an air hostess's fawn gabardine skirt' inaugurates juxtapositions which *owe nothing* to analogies between genital objects and technological artifacts: the 'dulled aluminium and areas of imitation wood laminates' of the airport buildings, the coincidence of a 'contoured lighting system' and the bald head of a mezzanine bartender. When confronted in hospital with Dr Helen Remington, the wife of the chemical engineer killed in the impact, Ballard is incited by 'the conjunction of her left armpit' and the 'chromium stand' of the X-ray camera (Ballard 1995: 44). For Baudrillard, the crash becomes the disruptive figure of a syntax in which 'blood' crossing 'the over-white concrete of [an] evening embankment', ruptured genitalia, luminous drifts of shattered safety glass, copulating bodies sheathed in 'glass, metal and vinyl', skin incised by underwear and chromium manufacturers' medallions, prophylactic 'dead' machines, casual 'leg stances' and crushed fenders become interchangeable without remainder or significance (Baudrillard 1994: 113).

Baudrillard's reading of *Crash* thus pre-empts Haraway's universe of generalised exchange, where 'any component can be interfaced with any other'. Its *sexualité sans antécédent* no longer a function of the somatic body or the yearning for authenticity. In Ballard/Baudrillard's socio-technical anagram bodies have become estranged not only from the biological goal of reproduction, but *jouissance* (enjoyment) – a trite affair compared to the glittering conjunction of bodies and technique (Baudrillard 1994: 116).

As Bradley Butterfield has argued, Baudrillard's essay on *Crash* can be seen to exemplify a negaesthetic strategy of 'reversal': co-opting the logic of systems to the point at which they 'reciprocate' with their extinction. The microelectronic universe of simulation, which grows from the cultivation of technique, of 'cybernetics', destroys the modern order of functionality; senselessly proliferating beyond the point at which any finality or purpose can be assigned to it (Baudrillard 1994: 118–9). For Butterfield, this 'hyperfunctionality' precipitates a resolution of the estrangement and banality of simulation via an orgiastic symbolic exchange between life and death, the body and technology (Butterfield 1999: 73).

If the crash were a form of symbolic exchange in Baudrillard's sense of this term, it would assuredly supply a principle of radical difference irreducible within the functionalist cyborg ontology we have been considering. As the principle of the 'extermination' of value by fabulously *uncodifiable* events and acts, it enjoins the destruction not only of the subjects and identities of traditional philosophy and political theory, but also a kind of systemic collapse of the 'situated' subjectivities explored by Haraway, Marsden and others. Within Baudrillard's Manichaean universe, 'symbolic death' would be the one 'political' response to the banality of signs. For this reason, Baudrillard's reading of *Crash* implies an 'immanent critique' of Haraway's affirmative response to the universe of simulation. *Crash*'s symbolic violence would claim 'social relevance' by iterating the logic of the social beyond the point at which its technically mediated imaginary could be sustained (Butterfield 1999: 73–4).

Terminal Metaphor

Baudrillard's 'symbolic' arguably involves a reification of structure which under-emphasises the degree to which the slippage of difference conditions the function of signs in all contexts.[4] Without this inflation of the 'code' the very idea of its asemic 'other' becomes dialectically self-stultifying. However, if there is a defect in Baudrillard's reading of Ballard's novel, it is not its philosophical ellipsis – the hyperfunctional is surely not the 'other' of the functional – but its peremptory elision of metaphor. While Baudrillard's incendiary logic ascribes to the crash the function of extirpating the social façade of functionality, a sufficiently close reading of Ballard's text shows that it also operates as the *terminal metaphor* of an entirely different polity: a virulent 'algorithm' fermenting desire from excremental fragments.

This synthetic function is best exhibited in terms of what I will call, after Derrida, *Crash*'s 'radical metaphoricity'[5]. My emphasis upon metaphor might seem to run counter to what has been claimed concerning the anagrammatic basis of its charnel conjunctions. Baudrillard's denial that they possess any metaphorical significance is certainly justified in so far as the 'human' teleologies of biology, freedom or Oedipal compulsion lend no depth to its sexual calculus. However, metaphor has a self-positing character which is not accounted for in terms of pre-symbolic sense or referential domain. Ballard's novella *Myths of the Near Future* provides a wonderfully perverse illustration of this principle; formulating a deranged 'metametaphorics' for which pornography and a kind of autistic *bricolage* function as the privileged figures of knowledge. *Myths* relates the epidemiology of a mysterious schizoid condition that appears to emanate from the abandoned Kennedy Space Centre in Florida. When its protagonist, the Orphic architect Roger Sheppard, constructs a notional 'time machine' from pornographic videos of his dead ex-wife and reproductions of Ernst and Delvaux, he cites one of the empty swimming pools of Cocoa beach as its 'power source': 'It is', he remarks to an indulgent clinical psychologist, 'a metaphor to bring my wife back to life' (Ballard 1985: 32).

In calling this assemblage a 'metaphor', the metaphor 'a machine', illness 'an extreme metaphor with which to construct a space vehicle' (Ballard 1985: 14) Ballard pragmatically circumvents semantic criteria of metaphorical aptness. Sheppard's pornography is an 'effective' vehicle of resurrection because, like space itself, it is 'a model for an advanced condition of time ...' (Ballard 1985: 14). This is not because the genre's formal qualities are (or are held to be) analogous to a spatialised time, but because the text equates pornography with modern dislocations of the continuum: 'Space exploration is a branch of applied geometry, with many affinities to pornography' (Ballard 1985: 30). Sheppard's time machine is a 'good' metaphor because it is a work of pornography, and pornography (in *Myths*) is a paradigm of hermetic technology by dint of its metaphoricity.

Crash, like *Myths*, inaugurates its own metaphorics. Its conjunctions are 'metaphors of metaphor' in the Derridean sense; that is, 'modules' of an order or 'code' for which there is no extra-systemic formulation. Thus the juxtapositions in James Ballard's 'X-ray' reverie are terms of *languages*. His encounter with Gabrielle is a preliminary to savage fantasies in which the erotic valences of bodies are enlarged by the disproportionate violence of late-twentieth-century technologies: 'thermonuclear reaction chambers, white-tiled control rooms, the mysterious scenarios of computer circuitry' (Ballard 1995: 179). These overkill bodies with their 'dozens of auxiliary orifices' harbour 'codes' *which only a car crash could release*. Incest would become, for Ballard, an inconsequential derivation of their permissive syntax (Ballard 1995: 180).

There is no basis for attributing to Ballard's characters a *masochistic* desire to escape the (Lacanian) symbolic order of gender identification and genital sexuality; re-experiencing the lost/wild body of the helpless infant in the collision (See Foster 1993). The crash configures the body with an enlarged repertoire of orifices; but it is the desire vehiculated in the conjunctions afforded by these new control surfaces which 'drives' the characters of *Crash*, and not pre-genital nostalgia. For this reason, however, it *is* appropriate to employ Lacan's conception of the symbolic in a reading of Ballard's text as long as it is understood, with Žižek and McCannel, as the abstract engine of subjectivity. It is not necessary for the objects and investments which articulate the drives to be markers of sexual difference or retroactive constructions of a pre-Oedipal body to act as tokens in a symbolic nexus. *Crash*, rather, enacts the displacement of one parochial order by a Cyborg-Symbolic for which the imaginary of sexual difference is vestigial.

The significance of Vaughan within the Cyborg-Symbolic is, as I have already suggested, that he is its ideologue; the one who gives expression to its exigencies. Vaughan is entirely a creature of spectacle and masquerade (Ballard 1995: 168—9, Lacan 1977: 193). It is for this reason that James Ballard must experience his incised body – 'a collection of loosely coupled planes' – as an object of desire. The formation rules which authorise the exchange of signifying modules are 'memorialised in the scarred contours of his face and chest' (Ballard 1995: 147). In the classic Lacanian formula, James desires the desire of the Other: 'to be involved in a second collision, this time under Vaughan's eyes' (Ballard 1995: 146).[6] It is only insofar as Vaughan '[mimes] the equations between the styling of a motor-car and the organic elements of his body' (Ballard 1995: 170), modulating the symbolic requirements of Ballard's narrative with his histrionics, that he can remain its primary sexual focus. This is the 'metaphoric' import of the erotic formalism noted above in our discussion of Baudrillard's essay. These impersonal 'equations' mediate every affective relationship between the characters and *Crash*'s residual city of multi-storey car parks, airport termini, hermetic suburbs and motorway slip roads. They are expressed in a language of excremental objects – 'aluminium ribbons', Gabrielle's thigh wound, Vaughan's sectioned nipples, torn fenders, scars, etc. – whose very lack of quotidian function commends them as arbitrary tokens in the symbolic algebra.

The crash underpins this wholly imaginary economy by providing its indisputable (because tautologically closed) exchange standard; the singular point at which the information flows between traffic systems and organic bodies succumb to what Haraway terms the 'privileged pathology' of the cyborg universe: *communications breakdown* (Haraway 1989: 187). The crash stands in for the cyborg *real*: the thing that cannot be coded, interfaced, or controlled, monitored through feedback or subjected to recombinant logics. It can be represented only as that recalcitrant X which resists the affinities of cyborgs and thus 'belongs' to the cyborg universe as a consequence of its repeated failure to knit together as a whole. In a reading of Kant and Lacan, Slavoj Žižek argues that the *real* – 'the mythical object whose encounter would bring about the full satisfaction of the drive' – must not be reified, but is symbolised retroactively by its imaginary substitutes (Žižek 1995: 35–7). If we define the crash purely as a logical argument place – the catastrophic state of auto-affection[7] which, *per impossible*, would fulfill cyborg desire – then there are no crashes in *Crash*, only its metaphorically displaced tokens.

Ballard's observance of this logic is exemplary. The crash is always figured as something other; as a pornographic assemblage, a media simulation, or (though this is much the same thing) as an ontological disaster. More decisively, we are informed in the novel's opening paragraph that the one collision which *ought* to have solved the equations inscribed on the bodies of its characters will have signally failed to occur:

> Vaughan died yesterday in his last car-crash. During our friendship he had rehearsed his death in many crashes, but this was his one true accident. Driven on a collision course towards the limousine of the film actress, his car jumped the rails of the London Airport Flyover and plunged through the roof of a bus filled with airline passengers. The crushed bodies of package tourists, like a haemorrhage of the sun, still lay across the vinyl seats when I pushed my way through the police engineers an hour later. Holding the arm of her chauffeur, the film actress Elizabeth Taylor, with whom Vaughan had dreamed of dying for so many months, stood alone under the revolving ambulance lights. As I knelt over Vaughan's body she placed a gloved hand to her throat.
>
> (Ballard 1995: 7)

There is nothing less accidental than this *one true accident*. As Baudrillard emphasises, the actual crashes in *Crash* are variations upon a impurely repeatable model, like the simulated impacts at the Road Research Laboratory in which the 'anticipated injuries' of mannequins are marked 'in carmine and violet …' (Ballard 1995: 122), or the imaginary collisions in Vaughan's psychometric montages of the crash-death injuries of the rich and famous (Baudrillard 1994: 117). This fatality of repetition and simulation is evident in the motorway pile-up in which the stunt driver Seagrave is killed. The impact is presaged by 'garbled references' on police broadcasts to 'the multiple injuries of the screen actress Elizabeth Taylor' (Seagrave has in fact collided with a minor television celebrity). The stunt driver is able to pre-empt Vaughan's final assault upon the imaginary because, *were it to occur*, it would only be an additional FX sequence, a supplementary module in the text's metaphorical immolation. Conversely, the status that Taylor's sex-death assumes in the novel is dependent upon the impossibility of it *having occurred* within the time line of late-sixties/early-seventies England which forms its historical locus. The name 'Elizabeth Taylor' designates an individual who – unlike Albert Camus, Jayne Mansfield or James Dean – had not been a crash fatality prior to the book's publication. The radically different event that could saturate Vaughan's desire – that of every character in *Crash* – is foreclosed; thus *only symbolisable* in an iterative sexual notation. In a 'labour of the negative' lucidly expounded by Žižek, the overkill bodies of *Crash* become transmuted by the impossible satisfaction represented by Vaughan's demand. Each module is, as Žižek puts it:

> a kind of "positivisation", filling out, of the void we encounter every time we are struck with the experience of "This is not *that*!" In it, the very inadequacy, deficiency, of every positive object assumes positive existence, i.e., becomes the object.
>
> (Žižek 1995: 122)

Vaughan thus demonstrates a certain insight into the dialectical predicament of the crashpack when he says of Taylor:

> Everything lies in the future for her. With a little forethought she could die in a unique vehicle collision, one that would transform all our dreams and fantasies.
>
> (Ballard 1995: 130)

For Vaughan, and for those he involves in his experiments, each conjunction of body and technique, no matter how trivial, is a formal 'element' of this singular auto-disaster; an assassination weapon (Ballard 1995: 182). Structurally, the impossible event would overcharge the mechanism which furnishes Ballard's cyborg community with its symbolic nexus, erasing this 'positivisation' of its absence. Seagrave's parodic collision merely reconfirms the necessity of its irresolvable, endless duplication. When it becomes apparent that the modules can never ameliorate the lack designated by the projected collision, James Ballard can at last conceptualise his love for Vaughan as an 'offering' of equivalents: 'the automobile injuries carried by my own body in place of those imaginary wounds he wished upon the actress' (Ballard 1995: 184). While James' wounds are no less imaginary for being actual, this does not vitiate his offer. It is the condition of its possibility and, by extension, of the whole cyborg *socius*.

Drive Theory

Crash displays a philosophical insight well in advance of much 'cyborg theory' because it fabricates an autonomous field of desire, signified by techno-erotic conjunctions rather than routines of a 'natural', reproductive body. These junctions *drive*, but not because the cyborg desires of *Crash* are co-extensive with the technological networks which generate them. Each cyborgian subject is constituted by the failure of metaphorical substitutions to finalise in a state of catastrophic auto-affection: an 'enjoyment', such as the 'optimum sex death', ceaselessly deferred by the endless relations of equivalence among modules: 'units in a new currency of pain and desire' (Ballard 1995: 134). *The crash has not taken place.* Ballard's novel rigorously programs its exclusion. In its place there are recombinant bodies, which, as Baudrillard emphasises, over-write the utilitarian calculus of 'function/dysfunction' (Baudrillard 1994: 118). Baudrillard is correct in claiming that Ballard's text 'deconstructs' the anthropocentric conception of technology as an intrinsically indifferent 'means' to humanly specifiable 'ends' – if premature in hailing the 'seductive … innocent' transgression of finality (Baudrillard 1994: 113, 119). The dazzling, auto-destructive circuitry of *Crash* exhibits the logic by which a technology becomes normative through its hyperfunctional indices. The monstrosity of Ballard's cyborg is not the ethical ambiguity celebrated by Haraway's partisans, but its phantasmic embodiment of an *order* which, like Vaughan, might already have us enlisted in its projects.

Notes

1. Gray 1995 provides a useful sourcebook for the industrial and political genealogy of the cyborg.
2. As attested by the homeostatic politics of the eusocial mole rat, whose hive-queens suppress the sexual maturation of their 'sisters' with the emission of pheromones (Dennett 1995: 484).
3. An examples of radical, non-situated difference might be the 'border incidents' in which something is said which transgresses linguistic norms. The whole point and importance of such 'events' is that they *cannot* be decoded (see Bennington 1994: 1–7).
4. As averred in Derrida (1988).
5. See Derrida (1982).
6. In Lacanian terminology 'the Other' denotes the field of signifying exchanges which position the subject. These signifiers need not be linguistic; in an observation applicable to Vaughan, Lacan writes 'The tattoo … has the function of being for the Other, of situating the subject in it, marking his place in the field of the group's relations …' (Lacan 1977: 206).
7. In Derrida's work 'auto-affection' is the 'phantasm' of self-givenness and the 'exclusion of difference' implicit in a self-sufficient subjectivity (Gasché 1986: 231–2).

References

Ballard, J.G. (1985) *Myths of the Near Future*, London: Triad/Panther.

—— (1995) *Crash*, London: Vintage.

Barthes, Roland (1987) 'The Metaphor of the Eye'. *Story of the Eye*, Harmondsworth: Penguin, 119–127.

Bataille, Georges (1987) *Story of the Eye*, Harmondsworth: Penguin.

Baudrillard, Jean (1988) *Jean Baudrillard: Selected Writings*, Mark Poster (ed.), Cambridge: Polity Press.

—— (1993) *Symbolic Exchange and Death*, tr. Iain Hamilton Grant, London: Sage.

—— (1994) 'Crash'. *Simulacra and Simulations*, tr. Sheila Faria Glaser, Anne Arbor: University of Michigan Press, 111–9.

Benningston, Geoffrey (1994) *Legislations: The Politics of Deconstruction*. London: Verso.

Butterfield, Bradley (1999) 'Ethical Value and Negative Aesthetics: Reconsidering the Baudrillard-Ballard Connection'. *PMLA 14/1*, 64–77.

Churchland, Paul M. (1995) *The Engine of Reason, the Seat of the Soul: A Philosophical Journey into the Brain.* Cambridge Mass.: MIT Press.

—— (1998) 'Conceptual Similarity Across Sensory and Neural Diversity: The Fodor/LePore Challenge Answered', *Journal of Philosophy, XCV, No.1*, pp. 5–32.

Dennett, Daniel (1955) *Darwin's Dangerous Idea: Evolution and the Meanings of Life*, London: Penguin.

Derrida, Jacques (1978) 'Structure, Sign, and Play in the Discourse of the Human Sciences'. *Writing and Difference*, tr. Alan Bass, London: Routledge & Kegan Paul, 278–294.

—— (1982) 'White Mythology: Metaphor in the Text of Philosophy. *Margins of Philosophy*, tr. Alan Bass. Brighton: Harvester, 207–272.

—— (1988) *Limited Inc*, tr. Samuel Weber, Evanston Ill.: Northwestern University Press.

Doane, Mary Anne (1989) 'Cyborgs, Origins and Subjectivity'. *Coming to Terms*, Elizabeth Weed (ed.), London: Routledge, 209–214.

Foster, Dennis (1993) 'J.G. Ballard's Empire of the Senses'. *PMLA 108*, 519–32.

Gane, Mike (1991) *Baudrillard's Bestiary: Baudrillard and Culture*, London: Routledge.

Gasché, Rodolphe, (1986) *The Tain of the Mirror: Derrida and the Philosophy of Reflection*, Cambridge Mass.: Harvard University Press.

Gray, Chris Hables (1995) *The Cyborg Handbook*. London: Routledge.

Haraway, Donna (1989) 'A Manifesto for Cyborgs: Science, Technology, and Socialist Feminism in the 1980s'. *Coming to Terms*, Elizabeth Weed (ed.), London: Routledge, 173–204.

—— (1991) 'Situated Knowledges: The Science Question in Feminism and the Privilege of Partial Perspective'. *Simians, Cyborgs and Women: The Reinvention of Nature*, London: Free Association Press.

Lacan, Jacques (1977) *The Four Fundamental Concepts of Psycho-Analysis*, tr. Alan Sheridan, London: Penguin.

MacCannel, Juliet Flower (1986) *Figuring Lacan: Criticism and the Cultural Unconscious*, Beckenham: Croom Helm.

Marsden, Jill (1996) 'Virtual Sexes and Feminist Futures: The Philosophy of Cyberfeminism'. *Radical Philosophy 78*, 6–17.

Poster, Mark (1990) *The Mode of Information: Poststructuralism and Social Context*, Cambridge, Polity Press.

Žižek, Slavoj (1995) *Tarrying with the Negative: Kant, Hegel and the Critique of Ideology*, Durham, North Carolina: Duke University Press.

9 Spirit in Crashes: Animist Machines and the Powers of Number

Iain Grant

Anthropologists since the late nineteenth century have agreed that there is a straight line linking magical to technological works: 'In magic, the social body comes alive. They become ... parts of a machine, spokes of a wheel' (Mauss 1972: 133). Magic and technology share 'a taste for the concrete' (Mauss 1972: 141) and aim to 'subject the forces of nature to the will of man' (Freud 1938: 127). Technology, however, in its own terms, is the more successful environmental manipulator: the sacred, extended time of chancy weather-influencing ritual becomes immediate success in the profane automation of onboard climate control. In accordance with the technological imperative of successful works, Jacques Ellul formulates a 'first law of technological development': the straight line linking magic to technology is 'irreversible' (Ellul 1964: 89); that is, it takes the one-way street to industrial modernity, on which there are no U-turns. While 'expansion' is the decisive factor in technical progress, 'there is no real progress in magic'; its real tendency is to regress (Ellul 1964: 26). During its expansion, moreover, technology becomes 'self-augmenting' (89), so that, for example, the invention of the long, straight road in turn necessitates the invention of the automobile in which we can travel, incrementally faster, into modernity.

All the more surprising, then, to find that in modernity, automobiles remain 'purely magical objects' (Barthes 1986: 88). No matter how far down the road modernity has travelled from its magical roots, no matter how fast we go, 'an evil demon is always there to make the beautiful machine break down' (Baudrillard 1993: 161), to make the car crash. But only primitives double things with demons, while modernity fates them to objectivism: 'animism spiritualizes the object, whereas industry objectifies the spirit' (Adorno & Horkheimer 1997: 28). Does demonic activity index an animism at modernity's core, or do these possessed, animated automobiles actually die when they crash? An anthropology of human crash-site rituals could answer the first of these questions, conjuring a proximate primitivism at the heart of modernity, and turning it, following Adorno & Horkheimer, into a critique of modernity's own, mythic content. But this would be a critique of false belief, a denunciation of the illusory 'omnipotence of thought' in late industrial society and its conceits of artificial life. By concentrating on belief, it could not answer the vital question 'do automobiles die?' To ask it requires not an anthropology of machine-animism, but an animistic anthropology of machines that follows the hypothesis of the Sorcerer's Apprentice: the subject's goal of total mastery only produces the total defection of the object. Having no subjective finality to lose, the question of machine death goes to the industrial heart of the challenge to human mastery, a challenge played out daily in the pile-ups, breakdowns and crashes that clog the earth's asphalt arteries.

1. Magic and Doubles

For as long as industrialization begets industrialization (Mead 1955: 237), we

> … assume that we are at one end of the scale of human progress, and the so-called savages are at the other end … on a rather low technological level. We are rational capitalists, primitive peoples prelogical … fetishists, animists, pre-animatists or what have you.
>
> (Evans-Pritchard 1965: 105)

The basis of Evans-Pritchard's mocking rehearsal of nineteenth century anthropology's social Darwinism consists in the isolation of discrete 'technological levels'; but what no longer applies to human, is now applied to technological history, producing a technological Darwinism. In quest of precursors, magic is cast in the role of technology's ground zero. According to Tylor, magic comprises the 'results of point-blank natural evidence and acts of straightforward purpose' (1871: 500), while for Mauss, it 'is the domain of pure production […] genealogical[ly] link[ed] with pharmacy, medicine, metallurgy, chemistry and industry' (1972: 141). Ellul gathers the industrial-technological roots of both ideas: 'material and magical technique … correspond perfectly', since both are fundamentally directed to enabling humanity to 'utilize … powers that are alien and hostile' (1964: 24–5).

The basis of magic's efficacy is the magician's soul, which he 'professes to send forth on distant journeys' (Tylor 1871: 438–9). The 'essential mobility' and easy separability (Mauss 1972: 34) of the magician's soul makes it his auto-motive double, an 'expression of his power and the way his actions work' (80). The double, able to 'cover vast distances in an instant' (Durkheim 1976: 50), fulfills 'the strategy of animism' (Freud 1938: 126) to become the travelling agent of all magical technique and the means of its efficacy. The double, in other words, creates the automobility of magic, while the multiple, as we shall see, creates the magic of the automobile.

If it is the animist double that makes magic work, then it is no surprise that technology, magic's industrial successor in the field of the practical, also operates on animistic principles, by magic, with no 'as if' about it. All the derision Marx heaps upon the 'alchemical fantasy' (1973: 842) of industry as an 'animated monster' (470), an 'automated system of machinery set in motion by an automaton … a moving power that moves itself' (692), dissipates into the confirmation of industrial animism when he insists that because 'nature builds no machines … no self-acting mules…. The[y] are … natural material transformed into organs of the human will over nature' (706). All the missionary zeal he expends in dispelling the religious 'mist' (which is surely industrial effluent, in any case) in which mere things become fetishes and 'appear as independent beings endowed with life' (Marx 1974: 77), merely acknowledges the reality of the fetish insofar as they are 'productions of the human brain' (ibid), an index of the industrial perfection that as perfectly accords with Freud's definition of animism as 'the omnipotence of thought' (1938: 137ff).

Not all doubles, however, work to humanity's advantage, as not only archaic, but also contemporary evidence tells us; witness the actions of shadows and doubles in the tales of Peter Schlemil or the Sandman, for instance. Nor are we always in control of our doubles: in sleep, for instance, when the double goes on a journey, there is no guarantee of its return. When the double does not return, it results in madness. For these reasons, the magician must exercise caution in image-making, since each image captures a soul. Moreover, hostile demons often possess the bodies of tribespeople, and must be driven out by the same means, by making an image or by discovering its name. Thus animists are extremely careful about 1s and 2s, but they have a horror of the larger numbers the double might become. Thus, certain demons have a questionable relation to original persons, in which case, sorcerers remain uncertain as to their 'number and names'. 'They usually form of body of troops, a host of anonymous beings (mobs …), often called by all kinds of collective names' (Mauss 1972: 106). Collective names are also applied to the 'souls of the dead – who are seldom identified – and the gods' (ibid). Tylor confirms this horror of large numbers, so that, when Labillardière, a French explorer, pressed the Tonga islanders for examples of the extent of their number system, he obtained numerals 'up to 1000 billion'. These were duly printed up,

> … but proved on later examination to be partly nonsense words and partly indelicate expressions, so that the supposed series of high numerals forms … a little vocabulary of Tongan indecency.
>
> (Tylor 1871: 241)

More usually, primitive numeration runs in variations on the '1, 2, many' theme, which Tylor exemplifies in the Botocudo, Tasmanian and New Hollander vocabularies (1871: 242ff). Large numbers possess only singular, i.e. collective and general names, that cannot be separated from, but must rather be reduced to another '1', called 'many', 'more than two' etc, due to a stringent observance of what Adorno calls the 'mimetic taboo' (1984: 62f, 392–3), to which we shall return. The taboo imposes a care of the 1, and a proscription on naming, representing or touching doubles in other than totally controlled, that is heavily ritualized, circumstances.

The reverse is true, however, for industrial, as opposed to animistic, production. Rather than dwelling on the 1 and its double, on arithmetic reproduction, industrial production lives on multiples, insofar as they multiply themselves. Thus Ellul's 'second law':

> Technological progress tends to act not according to an arithmetic, but according to a geometrical progression.
>
> (1964: 89)

Mass industrial production thus 'lives' by self-augmentation, by expansion at a geometrical rate. For example, which comes first: the automobile or the assembly line? With Ford, the mass-production of vehicles is also the vehicle of mass-production, so that the one ceaselessly augments the other. To this must also be added the production of mass-consumption, the production of the means of consumption (wage labour, but also roads, bridges, car-parks, the redesign of urban landscapes, and so on). The automobile, while iconic of mass-production, also drives mass-production beyond itself to become the auto-production of mass-production, or mass-production squared. As Ellul puts it, '[t]he problem of the industrial machine is a numerical one in nearly all its aspects' (1964: 18). For an industry to grow, it must demonstrate proper numerical powers, and become the exponent of its own expansion. Multiplication is the subject and the technique of mass-production. As McLuhan claims, it is not the sudden appearance of the car, but 'the increase in traffic [that] ended the static tribal state' (1967: 48).

2. The Infinite Transgression of the Mimetic Taboo

Crash upon crash, *n* times; newsprint upon screen print, print upon print, *n* times, repeated *n* times, singularly, doubly and in multiples. What is the subject of these piled-up pile-ups? Is it the crash motif that runs through them? Insistently highlighted by their banal and banalizing swathes of uniform colour, however, the crashes appear more an element of indifference than of insistence; faces, flowers or electric chairs would serve equally well. Try another route: what if, in these prints, the crash is being denatured and multiplied just as the mass-production of automobiles mass-produces the anonymous dead? The dead no longer make a journey to the necropolis, they die en route, and the necropolis is abolished, favouring the less durable, more compressible form of the newspaper obituary: one dead, two severely injured in crash ...; two dead ...; three severely injured ...; one dead ...; two dead ...; sixty dead in car crashes ...; and so on. Thus a 1912 tirade against autodeaths is primarily concerned with the statistics. In the first half of that year, notes Freiherr Michael von Pidoll, there were 438 car crashes 'in which 16 people died'. In a five-month period of that same year, the automobile took 7 children (in Sachs 1992: 29). Warhol is as modern as the newspapers, insofar as each is engaged in the serial transgression of the ancient taboo on image making, prompted by the fear that 'the magic of art' consists not in 'arous[ing] pleasure ..., but [in] conjur[ing] things' (Freud 1938: 144n), that the function of the image 'is to produce', rather than simply to reproduce, 'the person' (Mauss 1972: 68). Mass-produced images constitute a direct and unremitting challenge to the 'mimetic taboo' (Adorno 1984: 63) to halt them, testing the industrial magic of multiples against the animistic magic of doubles.

Warhol's prints fetishize the power of number, using a 'barbarically' accurate (Adorno 1984: 90) technique. It is only here that content becomes significant, since what gets industrially multiplied is not the automobile, but the automobile crash: the industrial crucifixion as an exponent of the self-augmentation of mass-production in the mass-production of death. Material technique, the perfected means for exercising rational and technological control, perfects itself even in the mass-production of our death. Perhaps the mimetic taboo is answered in the ritual destruction of human civilization at the pinnacle of its industrial modernity; just as it is enforced by the multiplication of destruction, its transubstantiation into rising numbers. Technological development is the only technical solution of finality.

3. The Automobile and Enlightenment

And yet modernity's other line of development, the straight road leading far from the Neolithic village, is also served by the automobile. 'The meaning of the automobile', wrote Julius Bierbaum in 1903, 'is freedom, self-possession, self-discipline and ease' (cited in Sachs 1992: 8). For Bierbaum, the 'auto' of 'automobile' is unequivocally the self that drives it: the self-directed mobility of the automotive subject, realizing the total freedom of the open road with an ease acquired through the discipline of this new means of exercising control over one's destiny, repeated daily. The automobile makes possible the breaking down of human destiny into simple destinations: 'Where do you want to go today?' Moreover, the limited number of automobiles initially available (as late as 1924, there were only 130,000 in circulation in Germany (Sachs 1992: 33)), due to their constituting a challenge to the mass-experience of railway travel, performed a relative individuation of the 'automobilist' with respect to the mass, a simultaneous liberation from the modernity of number and a return to the care of the 1 practised by cautious animists. The human will, driven by a motorized icon of progress, becomes capable of calculating its self-determination, conditioned only by space and time. Eventually, of course 'unlimited desire' for omnipresence rather than travel, as Wolfgang Sachs puts it, 'ran up against limited time' (1992: 166). As absolute freedom approaches, the horizon endlessly withdraws. Therefore, either the automobile, if it is to realize absolute freedom for us, must gain absolute speed, or, fearing like primitives the numeration of human freedom, quantized Enlightenment, technological progress must be reigned in, arrested. It is however a consequence of Ellul's second law that 'there is never any question of an arrest of the process'; although he adds, perhaps disingenuously, as we shall see, 'and even less of a backward movement' (1964: 89).

The straight road raises other fears, however. The straight road, linear space, has its corollary in linear time. Primitive time is notoriously cyclical, circulatory. No advance, no progress is possible in cyclical time. It is for this reason that 'there is no real progress in the realm of magic [...] no progress in space, no progress in time; indeed, the tendency of magic is to regress' (Ellul 1964: 26). While the transition from the cycle of magical time to the straight line of modern progress appears irreversibly multiplied by the automobile, the numerical tendency inherent in the multiplication of space and time lends this advance a disturbing reversibility, so that technology and magic exchange places once again.

Assume a journey, A to B, on a flat earth; the total possible distance constitutes the completion of the journey. But just as primitive time is cyclical, and primitive space is flat, so moderns inhabit a spherical earth and linear time; time and space have reversed their positions, prompting the terror that infinite speed will afford no gain, no real forward momentum, no progress, returning technology to magic. On a spherical earth, however, the total possible distance becomes a function of the number of times it is circuited, with the result that the straight road is an illusion that takes the strict sense out of time, every destination a stopover in an irrevocable destiny of reversal. The only solution of this finality would consist in forsaking space for the accumulation of time, defeating its linearity in 'revolutions per minute'; speed becomes the only solution to a lacking destination, a final end, a reason to drive, rather than driving being its own reason. If we experience the traversal of space in terms of linear time, however, rather than counting linear time by way of circuitous space, the forward direction of travel is formally maintained, albeit at the cost of the annihilation of content. Our freedom is merely a freedom to repeat identical content in irreversible time; the only remaining question is the rate of repetition, the revolutions of the earth. And while revolutions have always indexed modernity's progress, revolutions per minute cede control of that process to technological development, sacrificing freedom and autonomy, the care of the 1, for number as its historical finality.

It is for these reasons that Roman roads, with their straight lines, were never replicated. Roman engineers had no fear of the straight line since they were not yet confronted with the nightmare of a spherical earth that would place the end of their expansion back where they started, demanding that they begin all over again. If Enlightenment, tied irrevocably to the spherical earth, is not to be fated to a repetition of the same, but is instead to introduce and develop the difference that marks it off from its precursors, it then becomes vital that it quits the Roman roads that supply the illusion of the straight line whilst abolishing linear time. Enlightenment depends for its existence on a practical answer to the question, 'what difference does today introduce with respect to yesterday?' (Foucault 1986: 34). Thus Kant (1970: 53ff) defines Enlightenment not in terms of some positive end, as the completed maturation of the species, but negatively, in terms of 'exits' from immaturity. We no longer ask after destiny, or even destinations, but merely after the next exit. Freedom is thus realized in the subjective necessity of chance, rather than in the objective necessity of fatalist determinism; taking this exit, rather than another, is pure volition. Enlightenment modernity is no longer a straight road, but the endless ramification of exit ramps, diversions and slip-roads. With respect, however, to the quantizing methods of technological progress, the road now forks dramatically, preparing an ironic agonism between technology and freedom, insofar as the former was the first condition of the latter. The form this confrontation will ultimately take is the crash, the duel between the competing finalities of qualitative Enlightenment and quantitative technology; the question is, who's driving? Hence the perfect realization of the struggle – not of class, but of species – in Spielberg's *Duel* (1975): a driverless truck, the auto-mobile, self-moving embodiment of its own geometric expansion, shoving the driver in his Enlightenment automobile off the road. What is staked in this duel, however, is the unrepeatable singularity of biological death versus the endless capacity for industrial multiplication, and Warhol's prints are its scorecard.

Under self-augmenting technological expansion, space is multiplied by time and consumed as speed. Under this regime, however, the automobile is indifferent to autonomy, to freedom and self-realization, realizing its essence solely in the consumption of spacetime. A numerical factor, speed becomes the only measure available for the geometric development of automated freedom, or free automation. Thus Mumford:

> there is only one efficient speed: faster; only one attractive destination: farther away; only one desireable size: bigger; only one rational quantitative goal: more.
>
> (1970: 173)

Time must become simultaneity, and space omnipresence – against which indices, all time taken and space crossed count as loss. As already noted, the material content of modernity is its accelerating technological animus, which is indifferent to the differences introduced with respect to direction – 'exits from what?' What matters technologically is not the direction; formally, the material of technology is not space and time, but speed and number, ongoing marginal gains in efficiency and productivity. Its ideal is not to exit primitivism in terms of content, but to gain escape velocity with respect to its matter. All automobiles want to circuit the earth n times in one instant, and n^2 times the next. Machines do not want to linearize time, but to increase the circuits per second. Even the fabled production line is a means to multiply production rather than reach an end. Its logic is to increase the number of machines that complete the circuit: n on the first, and n^2 the second. Technology can live quite happily without destinations, and its only destiny is the fatalism of augmentation. Embodied in the automobile, speed approaches omnipresent simultaneity, continually cycling the globe. Technological development, once it motorizes the straight road from primitivism to modernity, dynamically recapitulates the cyclical time of the primitives, so that the automobile becomes not merely a time-saving but a time-travel device, ending before it began, gaining time in an absolute, unconditional sense.

The point is not merely that increased speed means an increased risk of death, a pitting of self against other in a struggle for authority and recognition. The only autonomy to which the automobile lays claim is that of movement, since space and time, the when and where, are of moment for it, only as markers of its efficiency. Rather, if the absolute speed that is necessarily implied by the geometric logic of technological development will be reached, then it already has. The one rational quantitative goal haunts every automobile as the spectre of attaining absolute speed, its ownmost potential; time travel is a necessary consequence of automobilist expansion.

4. Primitive Crashes, n Times

This is why the primitives have always been fending off crashes with magic: the cyclical involution of linear spacetime to speed means the immanent recapitulation of primitive life by the machines, the 'animated monster' (Marx 1973: 470) at the village gates. By the same token, moderns utilize animist magic to ward off crashes, in order to effect a reduction, if not an eradication of accidents, hoping to reduce number to rational control. The production of rational catastrophe is immediately followed by obliterating the crash site as an alibi for the forward motion of the automobile, as, for example, happened on the occasion of the worst road traffic accident in UK history.

When, in March 1997, 160 cars piled up in thick fog on a section of the M42, their molten engines reached such a temperature that the road surface melted in its turn. The 'liquifaction' of the crash was put to good use, however, so that by six o'clock the following morning, the vehicles had been removed and the road resurfaced.

But the reduction or eradication of the rational catastrophe, or the catastrophe of reason, might be better served by animist means. In 1935, J.C. Furnass suggested necromancy, summoning the doubles of the dead to return, as an animist alternative to the rational magic of disappearance:

> Minor details would include the raw ends of bones protruding through flesh in compound fractures and the dark red, oozing surfaces where clothes and skin were flayed off all at once. Ghosts could be put to a useful purpose, every bad stretch of the road in the US would greet the oncoming motorist with groans and screams and the educational spectacle of ten or a dozen corpses, all sizes, sexes and ages, lying horribly still on the bloody grass.
>
> (cited in Faith 1997: 19)

Just as the modern automobilist is haunted by demons and the Fates, so the first vehicles presaged the accident: 'spoked wheels first spread over temperate Europe, at least in any numbers, attached to the undercarriage of cult objects'. When a tribal leader dies, his 'parade wagons and chariots' are buried with him, 'or deposited in some bog as votive offerings' (Clark 1939: 213). According to Tylor, primitives' automobiles were sacrificed to their owners in order that the chieftain's double, as it appears in laymen's dreams and seers' visions, might complete its journey in the land of the dead with appropriate phantom means. Thus:

> Turanian tribes of North Asia avow that the motive of their funeral offerings of horses and sledges … is to provide the dead for his journey to the land of souls, and for his life there.
>
> (Tylor 1871: 488).

According to Tylor's animistic hypothesis, the wraiths and doubles of men, fully material, albeit composed of breaths, wander in dreams, illness and death, and to facilitate these journeys, require equally breathy vehicles, liberated to them by magic and sacrifice. It is thus hardly surprising that ancient representations of vehicles – and one might instance the 'four wheeled hearse depicted on a Halstatt urn from Hungary' – possess 'magico-religious associations' (Clark 1939: 212–3). Indeed, according to Mumford, the first vehicles were not transporters of goods or people, but of bodies (1967: 153).

Automobile deaths animate savage dreams as much as they do modern ones, although primitives dream of automobiles that can die: should death take the mobility from the auto, the auto can be captured by its double. This is an appropriate counter measure to the capture of the double of the accident victim, as Evans-Pritchard recounts. 'Primitives', he writes

Figure 9.1 The first vehicles. Horse-drawn hearse depicted on iron-age Hallstatt urn, Hungary.

> … are perfectly well aware that a buffalo killed the man, but they hold that he would not have been killed by it if he had not been bewitched. Why otherwise should he have been killed by it, why he and not someone else, why by that buffalo and not by another, why at that time and place and not at another? They are asking why, as we would put it, two independent chains of events crossed each other, bringing a certain man and a certain buffalo into a single point of time and space.
>
> (Evans-Pritchard 1965: 90)

Absolute rationalists, masters of magical technique, primitives refuse to acknowledge chance. As it is for us, accidental autocrash death constitutes a fatalist affront to our rational mastery, a mastery that, in accordance with the magical doctrine of 'sympathy and antipathy' (Mauss 1972: 70ff; Durkheim 1976: 355ff), can only be regained by utilizing the same techniques of control that proved fatal: a little necessity must be reintroduced. Consider, for example, the 'absurd death' that followed the 'significant life' of Albert Camus in a car crash on 4th January 1960:

> enquiries would show that Gallimard [Camus' driver] had been speeding, although some would always believe that the automobile, a Facel-Vega, was defective.
>
> (Showalter 1997)

By contrast, consider the explanations of the Diana crash: 'The demons that drove Diana's chauffeur' (*Sunday Times* 14.9.97). It matters little that the demons in question are chemical agents, rather, it is the displacement of the agent of the crash. What is vital here is that it was not Henri Paul, but a sequence of chemicals – Ecstasy, Prozac, Triapridol, marijuana, Zentel and alcohol – that drove Paul, Dodi and Diana to their deaths. Even by way of the expert scientific testimony of Dr Cyril Wecht, necessity finds its way into the accident: 'Having Henri Paul drive you around Paris is the equivalent of hiring a convicted child abuser as nursemaid for your kids' (*National Enquirer* 1.9.98). It was bound to happen. In each of these cases, what is never countenanced is the hideous prospect of the machine defecting from human mastery; the modernism of human error or defective machine does not therefore stand in contrast to the primitivism of demonic possession, despite appearances.

However, when crashes are involved, the investigations and explanations of the event must follow the strict rules of rational necessity, coinciding in almost every respect with the primitive eradication of the accident cited by Evans-Pritchard. All the more reason that the loss of the one gain Enlightenment modernity allows itself, the exit from primitive immaturity, not be reversed: too much magic, and we're back on the roundabout of cyclical time; too little, and the mere fact of the crash remains a stubborn and ineradicable affront to our rational mastery. Clinging to Enlightenment, searching for exits from the absolute speed that automobility has already attained, Durkheim's technique for managing the divorce between technology and magic deploys all the critical and rational resources of scientific modernity. He applies the spacetime of waking life to the dynamics of dreams as presented on behalf of the primitives by Tylor and Mauss, in order to disprove the double, thus admirably fetishizing reason. 'Let us admit', he writes,

> that the idea of the soul can be reduced to that of a double [as Tylor suggests ...] roam[ing] about in space; how could a man on awakening believe that he had really been assisting at or taking part in events which he knows passed long before? How could he imagine that during his sleep he lived a life which he knows has long since gone by?
>
> (Durkheim 1976: 56–7)

The problem Durkheim rationally points up is the inconceivability of time travel given uniform linear time: the A to B of highway travel. And yet he is able to note that even in waking life, through the agency of magic, primitives successfully revolt against this linear time. Indeed, the ideal of linear development is so alien to the primitives that 'before they arrive at old age ... the possessors of powerful spirits [are ...] regularly put to death' in order 'to keep the spirit from being affected by the physical decadence of its momentary keepers'. And the means by which the linear time of biological degradation is countered? Transport: the powerful spirit is taken 'from the organism where it resides ... and transport[ed]' (Durkheim 1976: 61). Durkheim has radically mistaken the impoverished spacetime of waking life for the magical transports of the spirit world. It is not that the primitives see in the first hearses the analogue of terrestrial transport; rather, vehicles are only needed after death in order to accomplish the miracles of travel there afforded the spirit, and this is why the first vehicles are carriages of the dead. Indeed, this is recognized even today, where cars are advertised not by way of their physical being, but rather as 'purely magical objects' (Barthes 1986: 88), through their *spirito di Punto*.

Thus even now automobile crashes breathe life into doubles. After a 1995 car crash in which he believed his wife to have died, Alan Davies was shocked when she seemed to have returned, but refused to admit that this 'double' was his wife. So convinced was he that 'Christine Two' had replaced 'Christine One', that this 'loving and affectionate husband' could no longer bear to touch her. Like the taboo on images, this is a version of the mimetic taboo that applies to all doubles. Modernity, however, gives it a scientific explanation, refusing to admit the victim's theory, just as he refused to admit theirs. Expert witnesses at the hearing into the crash told how the victim had developed …

> 'Capgrass' syndrome – a rare mental disorder in which the sufferer is convinced that someone emotionally close to him has been replaced by an exact double, often with evil intentions.
>
> (*Guardian* 5.3.99)

The key to this episode is not whether Christine Davies is alive or dead, but rather the fact that both theories – the pathological and the magical – concede the existence of the double, but dispute its material status: either the double is in Mr Davies' head, or she's walking around in Christine One's clothes, driving her car. Either way, magic and medicine agree that if the double is exorcised – perhaps by capturing the demon-double in yet another image, another double, perhaps by therapy or pharmacology – Christine One might return. Just like John Carpenter's *Christine*, in which the car bearing that name is wrecked so often that it acquires the capacity to rebuild itself, perhaps Christine the car is immortal, whereas Christine One died in a crash.

5. Duel: the True Nature of Drives

By means of the automobile, the straight road of modernity carries us not forward to Enlightenment, but ever faster towards primitivism. Modernity has invented, according to Lewis Mumford,

> an automobile that had neither breaks nor steering wheel, but only an accelerator, so that our only form of control consist[s] in making the machine go faster. On a straight road …, as we increased our speed, [we feel] gloriously free; but as soon as we wanted to reduce our speed or change our direction, we should find that no provision had been made for that degree of human control – the only possibility was faster, faster!
>
> (1952: 105)

Mumford's scenario reminds us of the fragile biologism, cocooned within its protective shell, to which modernity has destined us. For all the detours we take, for all the differences we introduce, everything is cancelled in the death drive, a destiny which we call our own, but is merely on loan from steam engines. Freud, the thief of engine-death, fits out the organism in industrial modernity with an appropriated destiny: 'the aim of all life is death … [but] the organism wishes to die only in its own fashion' (1991: 311). By placing the burden of individuation on the hopeless generality of the 'organism', Freud concedes that the drive differentiates the latter from all other engines only by its capacity to die. The manner of death is therefore specific only to our species-being, so that the individuation promised in the death drive, the absolute consummation of one's self, is an empty lure. Where once there stood the rational animal, there now remains only the death machine. Freud accomplished in magic what modernity had not yet caught up with; by way of an engineering diagram, replete with pressure valves, thermostats and servomotors, he conjured spirit into an engine, the 'soul-apparatus' or *seelischer Apparat*. It is only now, say British Telecom's artificial life researchers, that we are in a position to materialize the omnipotence of Freudian thought. Thus, given 'Soul Catcher 2025', a chip to record every waking thought and sensation in a lifetime, 'death has had its chips' (*Daily Telegraph* 18.7.97). Multiply downloadable, it promises a solution to demographic escalation while at the same time cancelling death. If Freud made us engines, he did so at the cost of the invention of death, since the primitives knew that the transport of spirits promised the eternity of the closed cycle. 'Death', as Freud noted, 'is a late acquisition' (1991: 319). Soul Catcher, by contrast, cancels death by making us engines, embodying primitive transport in the technological magic of multiples.

What, then, is the agent of 'animism' and what the 'patient'? Which is the master of industrialized magic and which its slave? Which is the sorcerer and which the apprentice? If the sorcerer is the one with the freely mobile double, then how powerful is the multiple magic of the automobile? Before we return to the death drive proper to animal engines, we need to look at the motive for Freud's magical capture of the drives.

'One of the merits of motivation research', writes McLuhan, 'has been the revelation of man's sex relation to the motor car' (1967: 56). With the characteristic idiocy of statistical rationalism, sex is therefore used to sell automobiles – not merely by draping them with the wholly extraneous fleshy trim of human bodies; rather, it is the automobile itself that is the agent of the seduction. 'Please remember it's only a car', ran a recent advertising campaign, showing a satin-swathed woman caressing her mechanical bridegroom in the disarray of their post-coital bed. McLuhan unwittingly suggests a reason for this: 'man becomes the sex organs of the machine world' (1967: 56). It could be, then, that the advert works like ancient animism, capturing the libido of the desiring subject in the image of the motor car by way of the lure of its perfected companion. On the other hand, if we read literally, like 'barbarians' (Adorno 1984: 90), then McLuhan is reversed, and it is the machine that becomes the sex organs of the biological world.

At stake is the ownership of sex, after organisms become the only engines on the face of the earth that die, putting them at a terrible reproductive disadvantage. Perhaps the machines are simply trying to humiliate us: after 'the mechanical penetration of the unconscious', writes Ellul, 'the breakdown of the automobile has become symbolic of sexual dysfunction' (1964: 404; trans. modified). The passage from animist primitivism to automobile modernity entails the transfer of potency from thought to reproduction, and as the machines, mass-produced, self-moving systems, multiply at a geometric rate, the omnipotence of thought (animism), materialized (industrial mass-production), robs us even of the capacity to reproduce. If man is the sex organs of the machine world, this is only because they are redundant in automated systems of mass-production.

The theft of reproduction counters the theft of the drives. What can death engines know of drives in any case, when biological finality is linear and irreversible, like its projects, while the object and end of the drive is infinite speed, omnipresence and simultaneity? With our future and our history in the balance, the automobile challenges us to a death drive, a duel. In the generalized account of the dynamics of human history, mastery and servitude are its prime movers. To remain the master, the master must recognize himself as master through the existence of the slave. Should the slave defect, then the master is challenged to stake his existence as master, his life, on the reappropriation of the slave as slave. Realizing this power, however, the slave acquires mastery over that of the master, but has himself nothing to lose but his chains. However, at the point of this realization, the slave-become-master faces the challenge of the master-become-slave, and must therefore stake his death in turn.

While this schema is premised upon the prospect of the immanent potential for the reversal of mastery and servitude, this reversal is pinioned around the moment of death. Between the self and its automobile, however, death is always inexchangeable: the driver cannot pass death on to the automobile, since cars do not die; the automobile drive is not diverted by deaths, little or large, its own or others, since the object of the drive is speed. In the crash, therefore, only the driver is lost. Even highway fatalities are suitable objects for geometric gain, and therefore only partial drives along the infinite interstate of absolute automobilism. Technology 'is always innocent of the imminent catastrophe' (Ellul 1964: 415).

The better hypothesis is the Sorcerer's Apprentice, where mastery is staked not on death, but on the return of the master who cancels the animist programme before it takes over. This is a duel that favours the automobile, insofar as sheet steel can always be recycled, while flesh and bone, skin and cortex, go up in smoke. The scrap merchant is not the Burke and Hare of 'the corpses of machines' (Marx 1974: 197), but the traffic police in the land of the dead. Automobiles are no longer sacrificed in order to accomplish animist transports, but consume crash-deaths as partial drives under the guise of serving only the living, an automated Eros, omnipresent and simultaneous, that answers the mimetic taboo with its infinite transgression.

References

Adorno, T.W. (1984) *Aesthetic Theory*. C. Lenhardt, trans. London: Routledge and Kegan Paul.

Adorno, T.W. & Max Horkheimer (1997) *Dialectic of Enlightenment*. John Cumming, trans. London: Verso.

Barthes, Roland (1988) *Mythologies*. Annette Lavers, trans. London: Paladin.

Baudrillard, Jean (1993) *Symbolic Exchange and Death*. Iain Hamilton Grant, trans. London: Sage.

Clark, Grahame (1939) *Archaeology and Society*. London: Methuen.

Durkheim, Emile (1976) *The Elementary Forms of Religious Life*. Joseph Ward Swain, trans. London: George Allen and Unwin.

Ellul, Jacques (1964) *The Technological Society*. John Wilkinson, trans. New York: Random House.

Evans-Pritchard, E.E. (1965) *Theories of Primitive Religion*. Oxford: Oxford University Press.

Faith, Nicholas (1997) *Crash*. London: Macmillan.

Foucault, Michel (1986) *The Foucault Reader*. Paul Rabinow, ed. Harmondsworth: Penguin.

Freud, Sigmund (1938) *Totem and Taboo*. A. A. Brill, trans. Harmondsworth: Penguin.

—— (1991) Pelican Freud Library vol.11: *On Metapsychology*. James Strachey, trans. Harmondsworth: Penguin.

Kant, Immanuel (1970) *Political Writings*. Hans Reiss, ed. and trans. Cambridge: Cambridge University Press.
Marx, Karl (1973) *Grundrisse*. Martin Nicolaus, trans. Harmondsworth: Penguin.
—— (1974) *Capital* volume 1. Samuel Moore and Edward Aveling, trans. London: Lawrence and Wishart.
Mauss, Marcel (1972) *General Theory of Magic*. Robert Brain, trans. London: Routledge and Kegan Paul.
McLuhan, Marshall (1967) *Understanding Media*. London: Sphere.
Mead, Margaret (1955) *Cultural Patterns and Technological Change*. New York: UNESCO.
Mumford, Lewis (1952) *Art and Technics*. London: Oxford University Press.
—— (1967) *The Myth of the Machine: Technics and Human Development*. London: Secker and Warburg.
Sachs, Wolfgang (1992) *For Love of the Automobile: Looking Back at the History of our Desires*. Don Renau, trans. Berkeley: University of California Press.
Showalter, Elaine (1997) 'Significant Life, Absurd Death' in *Times Higher Education Supplement* 12.10.97: 10.
Tylor, E.B. (1871) *Primitive Culture* (2 vols). Vol.1. London: John Murray.

10 Racing Fatalities: White Highway, Black Wreckage

Harjit Kaur Khaira & Gerry Carlin

Figure 10.1 'Indian Chiefs', by permission of the Hulton Getty picture library

Norman Mailer's essay 'The White Negro', first published in 1957, opens with a bleak account of the anxious historical opacity that had been produced by the technologies of death in the first half of the twentieth century. 'Probably, we will never be able to determine the psychic havoc of the concentration camps and the atom bomb upon the unconscious mind of almost everyone alive in these years', Mailer writes, arguing that the possibility of being 'doomed to die as a cipher in some vast statistical operation' has produced a new and logical if pathological sensibility. If the subject was to endure under the equal threats of death or numbing conformity ensured by modern state technocracies, then a radical acceptance of these conditions was the only response:

> ... the decision is to encourage the psychopath in oneself, to explore that domain of experience where security is boredom and therefore sickness, and one exists in the present, that enormous present which is without past or future, memory or planned intention....

Mailer's template for this brutal existentialism was the American negro, who, in 'living on the margin between totalitarianism and democracy for two centuries', had internalised such imperatives. What the white world was developing was 'a black man's code to fit their facts'; the new 'hipster' must absorb 'the existential synapses of the Negro' in order to become 'for practical purposes ... a white Negro'. In the face of hostile technology, the dissenting West must become black (Mailer 1963: 242–5).

To become black existentially (however problematic) is to become minoritarian historically. As Gilles Deleuze and Félix Guattari write: 'There is no history but of the majority, or of minorities as defined in relation to the majority', and they promote the minoritarian move to set oneself 'outside history' as a subversive 'nomadism', a variable and 'micropolitical' strategy which escapes history's demarcated terrains and fields of command (Deleuze and Guattari 1988: 292). But what if there is no outside, only implication and impact? What if racialised time-space is always a policed subtopian territory? What if the racialised body is *always* in history, but never actually perceived as *of* it?

Modernity has been defined as the simultaneity of uneven time-spaces, or 'the coexistence of realities from radically different moments of history' (Jameson 1991: 307), but there are also violent fractures within what are apparently the most integrated time-space territories and zones, fractures which demarcate and prescribe anterior and exterior positions to racialised bodies. However, a powerful qualifying force which such 'raced' fractures turn back upon 'white' theory, history, technology and mythology, is a *desublimation* – or brutalisation – of its terms and strategies. In desublimated terms, becoming black and historically minoritarian is to intensify subjection *to* history by occupying doubly dehistoricised terrain, for white mythology has always proceeded through a simultaneous denial of shared historical time and the conquest of all outside it. Colonialism has consistently translated geographical space, and ethnic difference, into temporal distance and historical exclusion – a protracted 'denial of coevalness' and intensification of otherness.[1] To inhabit Mailer's 'enormous present', or Deleuze and Guattari's micropolitical spaces, perhaps assumes a subtlety that evaporates in the heat of colonial discourses which have chronically configured the racialised body as always subject to, or in violent collision with the technologies of white history. Under the rule of technology the postcolonised body and environment remain pre-colonial, elsewhere, and detechnologised. In such conditions being 'doomed to die as a cipher in some vast statistical operation' means merely to be one of the more than 3,300 bodies around the Union Carbide Corporation plant in Bhopal in 1984 after the worst industrial accident in history ... or after an inevitable collision between zones.

Shortly after Mailer's essay appeared the postcolonial world was beckoned onto a stage where a new politics, supposedly driven by 'new subjects of history' (Jameson 1984), might play itself out. In 1967, Stokely Carmichael, architect of 'Black Power' and the perceived militant alternative to Martin Luther King's detechnologised Gandhian advocacy of peaceful resistance, spoke at a conference in London. Despite the backdrop of the Vietnam War, in that Summer of Love the conference leaned 'Towards a Demystification of Violence' through personal transcendence, pacifism, and the politics of institutional reform. But Carmichael spoke from different territory:

> What we're talking about around the US today, and I believe around the Third World, is the system of international white supremacy coupled with international capitalism. And we're out to smash that system ... or we're going to be smashed.
>
> (Carmichael 1968: 150)

Carmichael's revolutionary rhetoric, and his endorsement of 'counter-violence', terrorism and sabotage (citing Che Guevara on the efficacy of oppression and hatred in turning the postcolonial proletariat into 'effective, violent, selected and cold killing machines') almost caused a fight when protest erupted from the floor (Carmichael 1968: 162). Black Power seemed to want to revisit postcolonial time on colonial terms, in order to smash neo-colonial persistence (or be smashed, again).Typically, Carmichael was too late – or not 'in time'. He was attempting to utilise a revolutionary time to which he had never had access, and technologies which had never been his. As the symbolic victim of colonial history, his rhetoric was testament to a regression which was also a usurpation of white forms, and a contamination of the new reformism's version of the racialised body. Perversely, the time-space of technological violence had to be kept white, and had to have already passed Carmichael by. Black interventions *in* history appear as illegitimate reversals, denials or insufferable desublimations *of* history.

The delay and desublimation that the black body is subject to, and the violence that accompanies it on its entry into white history, is apparent in the future too. Consider the fate of Dr Miles Dyson, the black computer scientist in James Cameron's film *Terminator 2: Judgement Day* (1991). Although he doesn't know it, Dyson is working on a computer chip and mechanical arm which are the remnants of the first Terminator cyborg sent from the future (*The Terminator*, James Cameron, 1984). From this technology he is destined to develop a microprocessor which will, as the loops of *Terminator* history tell us, lead to the development of Skynet, a supercomputer which will become 'self-aware' and hostile on August 29th 1997 – Judgement Day (ironically, a technological apocalypse which coincides, almost to the day, with the high-speed collision which terminated Diana Spencer). What is fated is a nuclear war and a violent ascendancy of the machine, and a diversion of history must be perpetrated by those who can foresee its outcome: John and Sarah Connor – the future rebel leader and his mother – and a reprogrammed Terminator cyborg who, in contrast to the first film, has been sent from the future to guard the young John Connor against attack from a more sophisticated hostile model.

Without the benefit of future knowledge, Miles Dyson is unwittingly destined to be the innocent, but implicitly irresponsible orchestrator of the technologised end of history, and he becomes the legitimate target of Sarah Conner's bid to protect her son and the human history he represents. Dyson ends up wounded and prone, while the reprogrammed Terminator educates him and his terrified wife to the ways that his research will pervert the future of humankind; as Sarah Connor narrates:

> Dyson listened while the Terminator laid it all down. Skynet, Judgement Day, the history of things to come. It's not everyday that you find out you're responsible for 3 billion deaths. He took it pretty well….

In this postmodern catastrophe scenario Dyson, with his suburban home and non-dysfunctional family (he has a beautiful wife and young son, while John Connor has been in a foster home and his mother has been liberated from a unit for the criminally insane in an uncanny reversal of racialised urban/suburban danger scenarios) and his irresponsible lack of paranoia about the technology he is developing, is the epitome of an outmoded normality. As he laments, 'You're judging me on things I haven't even done yet!', but his wounded body is already marked for sacrifice.

In a film full of car, truck and bike chases, Dyson is the only major character who is never shown mobile. During the fateful group's journey to Dyson's offices at Cyberdyne we get only a shot of a darkly moving road with Sarah's voice-over:

> The future, always clear to me, had become like a black highway at night. We were in uncharted territory now, making up history as we went along.

The shocked and wounded black man in the car is the most spectacularly dangerous man on earth. History's highway has become black.

At the Cyberdyne complex the now enlightened Dyson, the Connors and the Terminator meet resistance from a massive police SWAT team. The group have planted explosives in the offices, and are attempting to make an exit when Dyson is riddled with bullets. The others make a break, while Dyson, gasping machinically in the spasms of death, holds a weight over the detonator switch, giving his colleagues and the police enough time to escape before he stops breathing, his arm falls, and he is blown apart along with his own doomsday inventions. While Dyson is the intellectual driving force behind the technology of the future in *Terminator 2*, he is unaware of both the origin and the consequences of his research project. Despite his intelligence, Dyson cannot move within the loops of history in the ways that white and cyborg bodies can; he is marooned inside a belated, doomed narrative, and in order for history to take its sublime course he must ultimately be removed from it (apart from the minor characters who are killed outright, Dyson, the product of an untimely miscegenation, is the only one who cannot recover from his wounds). The impact of history finally blows him apart, while the Terminator smoothly martyrs itself in a leather jacket. In the film's closing moments the dark highway shot with voice-over recurs: 'The unknown future rolls toward us. I face it for the first time with a sense of hope'. The black body has gone, its role as crash-test dummy completed, and history's highway is white again: it is chronological and open, the perverse loops and switchbacks in its timelines avoided by choosing an alternative highway after the black body has irresponsibly accelerated, suffered, and crashed into a technological dead-end.[2]

The meeting of the black body and modern technology causes unease and catastrophe, but the metaphor of mobility is also crucial here. After the American Civil War, a diaspora of the black population from the Southern 'slave' states to what would become the Northern ghettos began, and in the twentieth century these movements gathered pace. In 1900 only 10 percent of the black population lived in the North; by 1970 it was 50 percent (Lemann 1991: 6). Such migrations repeat the histories of displacement which shape diasporic cultural experience – histories which suggest that raced diasporic identities are appropriately traced not by appeals to roots and origins (European genealogies) but to 'routes' and movements (see Gilroy 1993). In America, migrations from country to city would reinscribe fundamental tropes of mobility and urbanity in minority discourses, and in black popular culture the 'signs of the city' would become the mark of the move away from the agrarian South and out of historical subjection. As Malcolm X states:

> Like hundreds of thousands of country-bred Negroes who had come to the Northern black ghetto before me, and have come since, I'd also acquired all the other fashionable ghetto adornments – the zoot suits and conk … liquor, cigarettes, then reefers – all to erase my embarrassing background.
>
> (Malcolm X 1968: 140)

A dissident Northern urbanity replaces a subject Southern ruralism, but the trope of black mobility is always social, political, temporal and technological (on black urbanity see Jeffries 1992). Predictably, the signs of black mobility are often read as deviant and threatening by the white majority, and they testify to incursions into coevalness – political emancipatory time and integration ('equality'), economic non-dependency and technological modernisation – which are focused powerfully in the fact and form of the car. Black American popular music has helped to centre the trope of technological mobility in the modern psyche,[3] but the racially marked driver is always deviant on the white highway.

By the riotous year of 1968, the Black Panther Party, founded in late 1966 in Oakland, California, had established itself as a force in the continuing fight for Civil Rights in America. Unlike the cultural nationalist and separatist groups of the time, the Panthers defined their fight as 'a class struggle and not a race struggle' (Seale 1970: 93), and it was in terms of equal rights, self-determination and *survival* that the Black Panther Party For Self Defense defined its objectives. From the beginning, the Panthers saw the urban street as a prime racialised site of danger, provocation and police harassment for the black community – one of the earliest Panther acts was to force the Oakland City Council to put up traffic lights at a hazardous intersection where black children had been killed – and black mobility sums up their programme well. In 1963 Martin Luther King's celebrated 'dream' had insisted that,

> We can never be satisfied as long as our bodies, heavy with the fatigue of travel, cannot gain lodgings in the motels of the highways and the hotels of the cities. We cannot be satisfied as long as the negro's basic mobility is from a smaller ghetto to a larger one.
>
> (MacArthur 1993: 333)

Echoing this, the Black Panther Party Platform and Program desired an end to subjection and immobility by insisting on no more than the Constitutional right to ensure it: 'The Second Amendment to the Constitution of the United States gives a right to bear arms. We therefore believe that all black people should arm themselves for self-defense' (Seale 1970: 88). The bearing of arms is a major source of the Panthers' notoriety (J. Edgar Hoover, Director of the FBI in 1968, called the Panthers 'the greatest threat to the internal security of the country') and the ultimate corruption and demise of their aims is often perceived as a result of the 'militarisation' of their project (cited in Caute 1988: 128. See also Durden-Smith 1976). But again the desublimation of technology – of the Constitution, of rights, of weaponry – is apparent here. When the black body adopts state and machinic extensions, white history sees only usurpation as technology reveals its usually imperceptible uses: force and subjection. In a twist to J.G. Ballard's stated intentions in the introduction to his novel *Crash*, technology when racialised becomes pornographic.[4]

This was shown on 6th April 1968, two days after the assassination of Martin Luther King. Eldridge Cleaver, a key intellectual figure and activist in the Panthers, was driving a car with out-of-state plates – an ostentatious sign of mobility which was known to draw police attention, but as Cleaver had a range of good ID cards (including a press card issued by the United Nations) and the car was a gift from a white supporter (a fact which, when communicated to the police, never failed to perplex them), Cleaver started 'using this car more frequently' to make a point (Cleaver 1971: 106). On that night the car formed part of a convoy of Panther vehicles. Cleaver had stopped, and was in the middle of having a discreet piss, when the police pulled up and ordered him to raise his hands. When he failed to do this immediately, the police opened fire; a shoot-out and chase ensued, and Cleaver found himself in a basement taking cover with 17 year old Bobby Hutton, another Party member. The police continued pumping bullets and tear gas through the thin walls of the basement for about half an hour. Cleaver was wounded in the leg and foot, and both he and Hutton were choking. Cleaver thought he was badly hit but couldn't locate the wound in the dark, and Hutton stripped him trying to locate it. In Mario Van Peebles' 1995 film *Panther*, Cleaver removes his clothes before emerging from the basement because he knows that the police would balk at shooting a *naked* black man for 'concealing a weapon', but whether as a survival tactic or an attempt to locate a wound, Cleaver finally surrendered to the police naked after he and Hutton had thrown out their guns. While under arrest, the police told both prisoners to run towards a squad car in the middle of the street; the naked and wounded Cleaver couldn't run, but, choking on tear gas as he was, Bobby Hutton did, and the police killed him with five bullets. Cleaver remains convinced that only a gathering from the black neighbourhood, drawn by the gunfire, saved him from a similarly staged fate (Cleaver 1971: 107–13).

As the Panthers discovered, the clothed and mobile black body is shot (it can be construed as illegal, 'pornographic'); only the naked, reduced black body, wounded and stationary, can be tolerated.

On 3rd March 1991 a similar chain of events would begin to unroll when a speeding car containing three black men was stopped on California Highway 210. At least 21 Los Angeles police officers were at the scene when, according to witnesses, a tall black man got out of the car, grabbed his behind and laughed. The police suspected that 25 year old Rodney King was on drugs, and subdued him with 'Fifty-six crushing blows, several stun-gun blasts, and random savage kicks and pushes'. King was hospitalised, and left with 'a split inner lip, a partially paralyzed face, nine skull fractures, a broken cheek bone, a shattered eye socket, and a broken leg' (Baker 1993: 42).

What brought this brutal collision into public view was a bystander who videotaped the whole event and delivered the tape not to the police, but to a local television station. At first, this seemed like good news for the people who wanted technological proof of unprovoked police violence (see Crenshaw and Peller 1993: 65). But when it came to disciplining the officers, the jury – 10 white, one Asian and one Hispanic juror – found them not guilty; indeed, the attorneys for the LAPD presented *King* as a bodily threat that couldn't go 'uncorrected'. The verdict sparked three days of bloody multicultural rebellion, reminiscent of Watts in 1965, when a black youth was arrested for drunken driving and beaten, provoking reactions which, after 4 days, turned Los Angeles into an official Disaster Area.

> 'For the jurors King was a dangerous person. Why?' asks Thomas Dumm:
>
> 'Because his movement was an indicator of his control. More specifically, King was mobile … His presence on the freeways of Los Angeles, moreover, was a sign of the free circulation available to even the poorer residents of Los Angeles ….'
>
> (Dumm 1993: 185)

What King's experience suggests is that the black body in possession of technology unleashes the machinic violence of the state, and that when representations are filtered through state technocratic surveillance the field of evidence is always racialised. Despite the brutality that the video depicts being meted out upon a black body, the jury's verdict attests to Judith Butler's claims that 'The visual field is not neutral to the question of race', and King was beaten 'in exchange for the blows he never delivered, but which he is, by virtue of his blackness, always about to deliver' (Butler 1993: 17, 19).

In conversation with the anthropologist Margaret Mead in 1970, black writer James Baldwin showed a prescient scepticism about her plea that evidence of the history of white racial violence needed to be 'faced' by America, as if 'what really happened' had been recorded by 'a camera there running on its own steam with no human being to press the button on or off what would have been on the film is what really happened'. Baldwin mistrusts such evidence, insisting that we must 'use the past to create the present', acknowledging, as the Rodney King events proved, that technology doesn't deliver the real, but merely inserts representations into fields of cultural interpretation. As Baldwin insists, 'my life was defined by the time I was five by the history written on my brow' (Baldwin and Mead 1972: 210, 212). The black body is in collision with technologies of signification as soon as it enters white territory, and on the white highway, technologised rather than subject to technology, it is perceived as a potentially violent anachronism. The blows Rodney King received seemed to be given in direct proportion to the speed his car travelled and his refusal to pull over. The black body is always speeding, jaywalking or trespassing on the white highway, and it has to be smashed back into its own detechnologised timescapes.

Police interruption of the (auto)mobile black body is frequent, and abuse of the law has often caused riots. In September and October 1985, riots in Brixton, Handsworth, Tottenham and other inner-city areas left thousands of shops looted, cars robbed and burned, and 5 people dead. The riots were, at least in part, a response to the 'sus' laws – the laws which allowed the police to stop and search a 'suspected' person (actually derived from the Vagrancy Act of 1824) – which were often used against, and resented by, young blacks in Britain. At the time of the 1985 riots, it was a racist 'visual field' colliding with auto-mobile black bodies which lit the fuse:

> In Handsworth another car stop and search and a beating led to the riot .... In Tottenham a car stop led to an arrest, which in turn led to a house search leading to the collapse and death of another black mother. Only days before the Tottenham riot, police set up a check point to search cars leaving the Broadwater Farm estate for drugs – white drivers were waved through.
>
> (Workers Against Racism 1985: 7)

A cursory glance at the newspapers shows that the highway continues to be a prime site of racialised surveillance and brutality. A black Birmingham man whose car was stopped 34 times in 2 years had his bid to sue the police for harassment turned down in February 1999, and a month later had been stopped a further 3 times. The same month, in Jasper, Arkansas, three white men went on trial charged with chaining a black man, James Byrd, to the back of a truck and 'dragging him three miles until his head was separated from his torso'.[5] Any who subvert ordained highway and vehicle use (New Age travellers, road protesters) are subject to vicious marginalisation and criminalisation,[6] but occasionally the white highway can become a place where responses are inverted – as in June 1994 when spectators apparently cheered the fugitive in a Los Angeles car chase, complete with a fleet of TV news helicopters, which formed the prelude to the arrest of the black American football star O.J. Simpson for failing to appear for an arraignment on charges of murder. Perhaps, as the star made his break for freedom in a white Bronco (which stayed within the media-friendly speed limits), his supporters took their cue for scepticism from the debacle of the Rodney King events nearly 3 years earlier. With a stationary audience on the freeway perhaps Simpson knew that he wouldn't be subject to the speed-by anonymity which usually accompanies freeway arrests. Perhaps he also knew that since the King incidents the freeway might be a place of relative safety *because* of the intensive surveillance. Whatever the motives, there is a real sense in which Simpson was consumed as a media product, providing a multi-media and auto-mobile public with a spirit of community through this event, allowing them to participate in and debate a hyper-real version of the generic 'Live TV' police chase. However, when this same public was asked for an opinion about Simpson's guilt, the results were clearly segregated: a poll suggested that 77 percent of whites thought that Simpson should stand trial, while only 33 percent of blacks thought likewise. On the white freeway, 'To the extent that O.J. was seen as a black man with a gun he symbolized a danger of the inner city which needed to be isolated and contained', for while auto-mobility means freedom for part of the population, 'for people of colour the freeway can be a place of danger rather than a place of safety' (Fotsch 1999: 130, 114, 129).

Of course, an opposed but structurally dependent aesthetics of technology and collision comprise the general mythology of 'white' modernity. Thus the death of Diana Spencer in a speeding car can be regarded as a singularly contemporary tragedy, a transcendent disembodiment, a sublimely high-tech 'white death'. J.G. Ballard suggested that it was,

> A classical death, if there is one. The fact that she died in a car crash *probably* is a validating – in imaginative terms – signature. To die in a car crash is a unique twentieth-century finale. It's part of the twentieth-century milieu.[7]

But transcendence is earthed when the ethnicity of her consort is taken into account – as graffiti at the crash site (the parapet of the Place de L'Alma's underpass) read, 'It was not an accident because the "imperial family" will not permit to half-breed children. However, they are the most beautiful' (Lichfield 1998: 13). As this anonymous opinion obliquely acknowledges, black passengers, whatever 'beauty' their presence promises, desublimate the most romantic journeys. But a sublime relation towards impact and dislocation is, as Ballard hints, the *signature* of contemporaneity. Take for example Salvador Dali and Luis Buñuel's short film *Un Chien Andalou* (1929), which was embraced by the surrealist *avant-garde* as something of a summation of a modern aesthetics of shock. The opening shots infamously present an impassive woman whose eye is sliced by a razor, and the laws of time and space are similarly violated by the technology of editing as anomalous zones are juxtaposed and dissolve, flow, or erupt into one another. In one shot an androgynous figure stands in a street, clutching a box which contains a severed hand, and is watched from above by the protagonists:

> She looks down at the street again, where the young girl, all alone now, stands as if rooted to the spot, incapable of moving, as cars drive past her at great speed. Suddenly one of the cars runs her over and leaves her lying in the street, horribly mangled.
>
> The man, with the determination of someone who feels sure of his rights, goes over to the young woman and, after staring at her lustfully with rolling eyes, grabs her breasts through her dress.
>
> (Buñuel and Dali 1994: 5)

The passionate 'drives' and the violence of technology fuse here, as desublimated energies circulate between the characters. But what is remarkable about the dynamics of *Un Chien Andalou* is the *lack* of shock its characters exhibit in the face of the film's dislocations, discontinuities, collisions and fusions. The signs of modernity manifest themselves as a sublime indifference in the face of the crash, the anomalous conjunction, the violent dislocation and mutilation. From this point, perhaps, the modern body *becomes* technologised, or, in the words of Jean Baudrillard from an essay on Ballard's *Crash*, the body begins to be delivered to 'symbolic wounds' that penetrate it and disperse it within a technological vista; technology becomes 'the mortal deconstruction of the body' – not a suffering body, but a body which has opened itself to systems of symbolic exchange which dissolve it (as in a filmic special effect) into merely another (banal) sign in the technology of modernity (Baudrillard 1994: 59).

From *Un Chien Andalou* to *Crash* the white body and its drives participate in a deconstructive collision with modern technology; but such collisions produce deconstructions which are also kinships, revelations of intimacy, identifications and mutual convergences in postmodern time. The racialised body, however, is laden with 'symbolic wounds' which tend to infect the marks of sublime intimacy with subtopian effects, historical disjunctions and 'uneven' patterns of relationship.

Consider, for example, another 'surrealist' and another version of the aesthetics of collision. Mexican painter Frida Kahlo was born in 1907, her father was a German-Hungarian Jew and her mother was of both Spanish and Mexican Indian descent. As an aspiring medical student in 1925, a bus Kahlo was travelling on was involved in a crash in which her spinal column broken in 3 places, she received multiple fractures, her foot was dislocated and crushed, and a handrail which entered her left side exited through her vagina, leaving her partially crippled, in pain, and under treatment for the rest of her life. Modern cultural migrations, collisions and technological interventions literally shape Kahlo, and her paintings are marked by 'native' bodies and costumes montaged into different cultural histories and environments – and by a glut of self-portraits. But Kahlo's obsessive self-portraiture *implicates* the artist in the crashes and fusions of the contemporary in ways that the sublime distance of European surrealism avoids, and the selves within these representations are often abject – bleeding, fractured, miscarrying, animalised and pierced by arrows, growing into the soil, or torn apart and bound by surgical braces, medicalised, colonised, eroticised and prostheticised. Kahlo's paintings desublimate the violent modernist sublime by endlessly placing bodies which are unstable but imperfectly technologised, only partly transformed, into its crash sites. Rather than a moment in an exchange, Kahlo's body presents a series of woundings which won't stop, or heal.

The example of Kahlo is important here, for the presentation and reception of her work has repeatedly extracted it from its specific contexts by presenting her as a tragic figure (a 'Mexican Ophelia') a 'native' surrealist artist 'free from foreign influence', and a woman who has provided a body of work whose chronotopes remain 'outside time'.[8] But Kahlo's modernism is precisely *in* time, to the extent that it suggests that the racially marked body cannot dispassionately absorb, be transcended or surpassed by the shocks of the new. Neither can this body be smoothly deconstructed by technology. Rather, it is variously temporalised and stigmatised, and, as in Kahlo's work, pierced, torn, disabled, and subject *to* technologies in ways that tend to strand it between cultures and time-spaces. The wounded body exists symbolically, but the racialised wounded body exists chronically, partially deconstructed and deterritorialised but often frozen at points of collision, invasion, violence and injury. Such a system of representation desublimates, historicises and brutalises modernism in the same way that the raced body conjures the pornography of technology to appear. Such bodies, as Paul Gilroy suggests, invoke 'enduring memories' of enforced mobilities (colonisation, conquest, slavery, migration and technological subjections which impel alternative understandings of modernity and postmodernity into view, 'other' time-spaces which demand their own 'periodisation and syncopated temporalities' (Gilroy 1996: 20–21). In a sublimely deconstructive technologised system in which depth is conjured away, the introduction of the racialised body disturbs the surface by making symbolic exchange uneven. It gives 'another side' to the story, and, in a depthless condition, where history desires to become a lost referent, 'another side' is precisely what cannot be tolerated.

Notes

1. Fabian (1983). By 'denial of coevalness' Fabian means 'a persistent and systematic tendency to place the referent(s) of anthropology in a Time other than the present of the producer of anthropological discourse' (31).
2. Something similar happens in Ridley Scott's *Blade Runner* (1982), where a polluted near-future Los Angeles now teems with oriental markets and 'raced' people who can't afford to leave an industrially ravaged Earth for healthier climes. It is among these second-class 'hordes' that the 'replicants' are pursued, maverick cyborgs who are on the run through this seedy but high-tech environment because of their wish to 'be human'. Again, a racialised zone acts as the site of technological nightmare scenarios.
3. Chuck Berry's 'Maybellene', for example, was one the first 'black' records to gain desegregated airplay in America, and it opens like this: 'As I was motorvatin' over the hill/I saw Maybellene in a Coupe-de-ville/Cadillac rollin' on the open road/Tryin' to outrun my V-8 Ford' (Chess Records, 1955). In 1972 the first question a *Rolling Stone* interviewer asked Berry, appropriately enough, was 'What model was the first car you ever had?' (Editors of Rolling Stone 1981: 226). Popular music continues to be an environment where postcolonial mobility, identity and displacement are interrogated; see for example Lipsitz 1994.
4. In the unpaginated 1995 introduction to *Crash* (Ballard 1995) Ballard suggests that it is 'the first pornographic novel based on technology. In a sense, pornography is the most political form of fiction, dealing with how we use and exploit each other, in the most urgent and ruthless way'.

5. See Gibbs (1999) and Young (1999). Murderous uses of automobility such as James Byrd suffered have historical precedents; see the record of an earlier, almost identical death drive in Gilmore 1993: 31. As we write London is experiencing a spate of nail bombings which have targeted minority groups.
6. See McKay (1996) for a treatment of British 'road' life and protest, and its persecution under the 1994 Criminal Justice and Public Order Act.
7. Cited in Sinclair 1999: 117. As Ballard notes elsewhere, 'apart from our own deaths, the car crash is probably the most dramatic event in our lives, and in many cases the two will coincide' (Ballard 1993: 111). On the sublimity of 'white death' see Dyer 1997: chapter 6.
8. Kahlo's biographer Hayden Herrera calls her a 'Mexican Ophelia' (Herrera 1989: xiii). André Breton asserted her freedom from 'foreign influence' in his introduction to her 1938 exhibition in New York. For a full discussion of this exhibition and the 'version' of Kahlo it presented see Gambrell 1997: chapter 2. John Berger's review of a recent exhibition (Berger 1998: 10) announced of Kahlo's work that 'Its time is outside time'. For a discussion of mythic, tragic and 'ahistorical' versions of Kahlo, see Khaira 1998.

References

Baker, Houston A. (1993) 'Scene … Not Heard', in Gooding-Williams (1993) 38—48.

Baldwin, James and Margaret Mead (1972) *A Rap on Race.* London: Corgi.

Ballard, J.G. (1993) *The Atrocity Exhibition.* London: Flamingo.

Ballard, J.G. (1995) *Crash.* London: Vintage.

Baudrillard, Jean (1994) *Simulacra and Simulation.* Translated by Sheila Faria Glaser. Ann Arbor: University of Michigan Press.

Berger, John (1998) 'Painted on the Body' *The Guardian.* 12th May 1998.

Buñuel, Luis and Salvador Dali (1994) *Un Chien Andalou.* London and Boston: Faber and Faber.

Butler, Judith 'Endangered/Endangering: Schematic Racism and White Paranoia', in Gooding-Williams (1993) 15–22.

Carmichael, Stokely (1968) 'Black Power', in *The Dialectics of Liberation.* Edited by David Cooper. Harmondsworth: Penguin.

Caute, David (1988) *Sixty-Eight: The Year of the Barricades.* London: Paladin.

Cleaver, Eldridge (1971) *Post-Prison Writings and Speeches.* London: Panther Books.

Crenshaw, Kimberlé and Gary Peller (1993) 'Reel Time/Real Justice', in Gooding-Williams (1993) 56–70.

Deleuze, Gilles and Félix Guattari (1988) *A Thousand Plateaus: Capitalism and Schizophrenia.* Translated by Brian Massumi. London: Athlone Press.

Dumm, Thomas L. (1993) 'The New Enclosures: Racism in the Normalized Community', in Gooding-Williams (1993) 178–195.

Durden-Smith, Jo (1976) *Who Killed George Jackson?* New York: Knopf.

Dyer, Richard (1997) *White.* London and New York: Routledge.

Editors of Rolling Stone (1981) *The Rolling Stone Interviews 1967–80.* New York: St Martin's Press.

Fabian, Johannes (1983) *Time and the Other: How Anthropology Makes its Object.* New York and Oxford: Columbia University Press

Fotsch, Paul M. (1999) 'Contesting Urban Freeway Stories: Racial Politics and the O.J. Chase' *Cultural Studies* 13 (1) 110–137

Gambrell, Alice (1997) *Women Intellectuals, Modernism, and Difference: Transatlantic Culture, 1919–1945.* Cambridge and New York: Cambridge University Press.

Gibbs, Geoffrey (1999), 'Black Motorist Stopped 34 Times Sues Police' *The Guardian*. 19th January 1999, and 'Black Motorist Stopped 3 Times Since Harassment Case' *The Guardian*. March 23rd 1999. Taken from the *Guardian Unlimited* internet archive (http: //www.guardianunlimited.co.uk, 20th April 1999)

Gilmore, Ruth Wilson (1993) 'Terror Austerity Race Gender Excess Theater', in Gooding-Williams (1993) 23–37.

Gilroy, Paul (1993) *The Black Atlantic: Modernity and Double Consciousness*. London and New York: Verso.

Gilroy, Paul (1996) 'Route Work: The Black Atlantic and the Politics of Exile', in *The Post-Colonial Question: Common Skies, Divided Horizons*. Edited by Iain Chambers and Lidia Curti. London and New York: Routledge 17–29.

Gooding-Williams, Robert ed. (1993) *Reading Rodney King: Reading Urban Uprising*. New York and London: Routledge.

Herrera, Hayden (1989) *Frida: A Biography of Frida Kahlo*. London: Bloomsbury.

Jameson, Fredric (1984) 'Periodizing the 60s', in *The 60s, Without Apology*. Edited by Sohnya Sayres, Anders Stephanson, Stanley Aronowitz and Fredric Jameson. Minneapolis: University of Minnesota Press. 180–209.

Jameson, Fredric (1991) *Postmodernism, or, the Cultural Logic of Late Capitalism*. London and New York: Verso.

Jeffries, John (1992) 'Towards a Redefinition of the Urban: The Collision of Culture', in *Black Popular Culture*. Edited by Gina Dent. Seattle: Bay Press 153–63.

Khaira, Harjit Kaur (1998) 'Post-Colonial Theory: A Discussion of Directions and Tensions with Special Reference to the Work of Frida Kahlo' *Kunapipi: Journal of Post-Colonial Writing*. 20 (2) 41–51.

Lemann, Nicholas (1991) *The Promised Land: The Great Black Migration and How It Changed America*. New York: Knopf.

Lichfield, John (1998) 'Diana's death: the plot thickens' *The Independent on Sunday*. 1st March 1998.

Lipsitz, George (1994) *Dangerous Crossroads: Popular Music, Postmodernism and the Poetics of Place*. London and New York: Verso.

MacArthur, Brian ed. (1993) *The Penguin Book of Twentieth-Century Speeches*. Harmondsworth: Penguin.

Mailer, Norman (1963) 'The White Negro', reprinted in *Advertisements For Myself*. London: Corgi Books.

Malcolm X (1968) with the assistance of Alex Haley *The Autobiography of Malcolm X*. Harmondsworth: Penguin.

McKay, George (1996) *Senseless Acts of Beauty: Cultures of Resistance Since the Sixties*. London and New York: Verso.

Seale, Bobby (1970) *Seize the Time: The Story of the Black Panther Party*. London: Arrow Books.

Sinclair, Iain (1999) *Crash: David Cronenberg's Post-Mortem on J.G. Ballard's 'Trajectory of Fate'*. London: BFI Publishing.

Workers Against Racism (1985) *The Roots of Racism* London: Junius

Young, Hugo (1999) 'Racial Justice Should Be More Than a Branch of Political Correctness' *The Guardian*. February 23rd, 1999. Taken from the *Guardian Unlimited* internet archive (http: //www.guardianunlimited.co.uk, 20th April 1999).

11 Negative Dialectics of the Desert Crash in *The English Patient*

Anne Beezer

> All pilots who fall into the desert ... none of them come back with identification.

The opening sequences of *The English Patient* (Minghella 1996) reveal the contrasting figures of a fragile bi-plane over-flying the contours of an undulating (and potentially enveloping) desert landscape. It is into this landscape that the plane will crash, obliterating the eponymous (and anonymous) pilot, and the film's narrative works retrospectively to try an unravel the seeming meaningless of this crash. This process of unravelling the event of a plane crashing into a desert is also the project of this essay.

Theodore Adorno's negative dialectical method, together with feminist theorisations of corporeality, will be used to argue that the conjuncture of the figures, plane and desert, work in the film to construct a binary in which a masculinist conception of disembodied technological mastery is opposed to a feminine and ethnic other who is variously represented – as the desert(ed) landscape of the Western imaginary, and as the out-of-time *jouissance* of the characters, Hana and Kip. We may see the event of the crash as bringing this binary into crisis, a crisis which remains unresolved and unresolvable in the film since the only solution offered is the dissolution of the self as represented by the burnt and indistinguishable figure of the pilot.

In *Negative Dialectics*, Adorno contrasts the imperialising mastery of the concept with the uncertain illumination that derives from the fragment; and in what follows a critique of key aspects of the Western imaginary will deploy this contrast between concept and fragment, firstly as a way of interrogating conceptualisations of deserts and subsequently as a means of undermining the binary between the technological, masculine ego, as represented by the over-flight of the plane, and the ethnic and feminised others that are given 'the burden of embodiment' in the film, *The English Patient*.

Thinking the desert

> Caresses have no meaning, except from a woman who is herself of the desert.

Baudrillard's 'feminist provocations', as he writes his epiphany to desert landscapes, are part of a well-established Western imaginary of the landscape of the desert

(Goshorn 1994: 257–291). Deserts, as Ella Shohat notes, have frequently figured in what she describes as 'Orientalist films' where they form the uninhabited ground across which the Western male figure embarks on a simultaneous voyage of conquest and self-discovery (Shohat 1993: 52). Shohat refers to the complex transgressions of sex and gender systems that such films unfold. Pointing to the homoerotic subtext in *Lawrence of Arabia*, Marjorie Garber argues, like Shohat, that in David Lean's film, Lawrence's 'cultural appropriation' of the 'chic of Araby' is at the same time an exercise in 'gender cross-dressing' (Garber 1992: 305). As portrayed by Peter O'Toole, Lawrence's persona shifts from that of the heroic male to the much more feminised and eroticised white-veiled bride of Feisal. The 'Orient', but more particularly the Orient portrayed as an empty desert(ed) place, provides a space for cultural reinvention. Landscapes, and especially desert landscapes, are often inscribed as empty spaces in the Western imagination. This writing on the text of the empty desert is not confined to popular representations of deserts in such films as *Lawrence of Arabia* (Lean 1962), *The Sheltering Sky* (Bertolucci 1990), or, more recently, *The English Patient*, but is a trope which can be traced back to Biblical sources, as John Durham Peters' critique of nomadism reveals.

Durham Peters notes that 'stories of pilgrimage, displacement, and dispersion are central to Western tradition' (Durham Peters 1999: 17). These stories often juxtapose the charged symbol of the tent as a temporary resting place with that of the wilderness conceived as a place without order, framework or outline – a non-place or desert. In Judaic, Islamic and Christian traditions, the importance of the desert attributes to its antinomial status as the 'other' of civilization.

That the desert as a space for spiritual rebuilding has had such a long and significant role in the cultural imaginaries of various peoples and religious traditions, might suggest that to affiliate to anything specifically 'Western' is yet another act of cultural appropriation. However, the desert, as a site conceived as a place on to which to project one's other self which is in need of spiritual re-awakening, takes on a quite different political resonance when it, along with its associated metaphors of the tent and the nomad, is constructed as the space inhabited by 'others' whose sole function is the reinvigoration of the jaded Western self. As Durham Peters acknowledges, in such a scenario:

> The centre ... feeds at a prissy distance on the wild glamour of minorities while neither alleviating their hardships nor recognizing their autonomy.
>
> (Durham Peters 1999: 35)

For Durham Peters, this projection of self on to the fantastic other, in accordance with the Hegelian and Lacanian conceptions of self/other relations, is something which will 'never be extirpated from the crooked wood of humanity' (Durham Peters 1999: 38).

In *The English Patient*, *Voyager* (Schlondorff 1992), *The Flight of the Phoenix* (Aldrich 1966), and *The Sheltering Sky*, it is in fact a masculine-coded self whose flight from embodiment is brought into crisis (and as figured in the first three films by the event of the plane crash) and projected onto nomadic figures who become eroticised and exoticised as protean forms of human embodiment, as moving and silent figures embedded in the ground of the desert. These figures, it could be argued, are often constructed in such films as a version of human cultural habitation who live in harmony with nature and who have, therefore, remained uncontaminated by the 'dialectic of enlightenment'.

My critique will be informed by the recent return to Theodor Adorno's critique of the dialectic of the enlightenment as evidenced in the work of Peter Dews (1987), Max Pensky (1997), Asha Varadharajan (1995) and Maggie O'Neill (1999). This return has taken the form of a dialogue, retrospectively constructed between Adorno's theorisation of negative dialectics and poststructuralist conceptions of the self as fragmentary, and 'foundationally' shaped by the illusionary wholeness acquired during the mirror phase of psychic development. Noting how Adorno's critique of the dialectic of the enlightenment is engaged in a similar critical trajectory to that of poststructuralist theorising, in that both perceive the philosophical attempt to provide a mediating strategy between self and other to be a dangerous and/or impossible political project, Max Pensky argues that:

> The closest affinity between Adorno and poststructuralism can thus be seen as their parallel efforts to recover an ethics of alterity by way of an immanent overcoming of the tradition of philosophical idealism.
>
> (Pensky: 6)

However, Peter Dews has argued that while Adorno and poststructuralist theorising, particularly as evidenced in the work of Jaques Derrida, may be united in their 'parallel efforts to recover an ethics of alterity', the points of divergence between them are of greater political significance than their points of convergence (Dews: 15).

Adorno's project in *Negative Dialectics* was the critique of the identity-thinking that he argued characterised philosophical idealism. As Dews notes, Adorno worked to lay bare the illusion that

> the moment of non-identity in thought and experience, the necessity of thinking or experiencing something, can itself be reduced to a set of conceptual determinations.
>
> (Dews: 38)

Adorno's critical project in *Negative Dialectics* was to release the object from the all-consuming domination of the conceptual subject. It is this domination that he characterised 'the dialectics of enlightenment', since idealist philosophy was but a sublimated expression of the desire to conquer and absorb all that is contingent or 'other' within 'the unity of self-preserving thought' (Dews: 38).

Dews contrasts Adorno's efforts to construct 'an ethics of alterity' by liberating the object from this conceptual imprisonment with Derrida's critique of philosophical idealism which, he argues, in contrast to Adorno's efforts 'to move "downstream" towards an account of subjectivity as emerging from and entwined with the natural and historical world', moves 'upstream in a quest for the ground of transcendental consciousness itself' (Dews: 19). Derrida's philosophy of difference is a movement upstream because it posits, according to Dews, difference as a primordial state of non-self-presence such that meaning is defined as an inevitable process of repression rather than a contingent, fragmentary or partial relationship between the subject and its others. To follow, therefore, a Derridean logic in a critique of *The English Patient* would involve a dissolution of the subject the Western imaginary, but would categorically prevent any release of its objects from their imprisonment in this conceptual imaginary.

Thinking the desert in *The English Patient*

There is nothing contingent about the desert location that is the setting for the film of *The English Patient*. According to Jaqui Sadashige, the original inspiration of Michael Ondaatje, on whose book the film was based, had been the image of 'a plane crashing in the desert' (Sadashige 1998: 243). The desert of the novel, the Sahara, was transposed in the filming to Southern Tunisia; but the aerial shots of the desert with which the film begins, confirms this desert not as one version of the range of desert terrains that can be found globally, but as conforming to the essence of 'desertness' that has so preoccupied Western filmmakers. This is a 'rolling desert' with fine, enveloping sands and sand dunes that ripple as if following the contours of the female form. This desert is also empty of human habitation; there are no marks on the sand. (However, as Jaqui Sadashige recounts, the lack of tracks in the sand was the result of artifice and human labour as, for each new shot, the sands had to be swept clean of all traces of trucks, cinema equipment and actors.) In its emptiness, it is both seductive and awe-inspiring – a geography of desire.

Reviewers of the film of *The English Patient* had a less sublime reading of this emptiness than do reviewers of the book. Cynthia Fuchs' dismissive review of the film starts with the aphorism 'Sweeping, sad and full of sand' (Fuchs 1999), whilst Jennie Yabroff notes that after the opening credits, 'we switch to a view of desert sands, and a two-person plane flying low. Bang! Bang! The plane is shot out of the sky' (Yabroff 1999). Reviewing the book, Annick Hillger deploys Deleuze and Guattari's idea of nomadology to reclaim the emptiness of the desert in *The English Patient* as a place where identities become cast off from fixed lines of affiliation or belonging. Hillger quotes Deleuze's view that 'we are deserts.... The desert is our only identity, our single chance for the combinations that inhabit us' (Hillger 1998: 30), to contextualise and underscore Ondaatje's articulation of Almasy's (the 'English Patient' of both the book and the film) retrospection that, in the manner of a postmodern Odysseus, 'All pilots who fall into the desert ... none of them come back with identification' (Hillger 1998: 30).

This postmodern consciousness ventriloquised by the character of Almasy, which uses the desert as both ground and metaphor for the dissolution of fixed identities, juxtaposes planes and deserts, or flight and the fixity of landscapes. Just as Jean Baudrillard contrasts his travelling and, therefore, boundless self to the feminised fixity of the American deserts he crosses (Baudrillard 1986: 71), so the figure of the plane flying over the desert suggests a flight of the ego in a fruitless search for some kind of mooring. The desert, foreknown to be an empty space, is a place which is used to question Western identities, a place where pilots fall from certainty into oblivion. In a later section I will return to this juxtaposition of plane and desert as a means of critiquing the concept of the self as defined by (a fragile) technological mastery over more embodied others.

What is interesting in the context of an examination of the cultural construction of deserts is the amnesiac qualities they inspire in literary, cultural and cinematic narratives based on them. Even more interesting is that this amnesia is both anticipated and known, constructing a kind of conceptual closure around the landscape of the desert. The desert appears in these formulations as a landscape that is known in advance as one that will inspire the self to dwell on its own rootlessness and dissolution. To return to Adorno's theorisation of negative dialectics the non-identitarian object of the desert, and its possible inhabitants, is engulfed in an act of conceptual closure.

Thinking the desert in fragments

The lead male character in the film of *The English Patient* is Count Laszlo De Almasy who, along with companions Peter Madox and Geoffrey Clinton (whose wife Katherine will become the object of Almasy's passion), is engaged in exploring the Gilf Kebir region of the Sahara desert. These men are mapmakers who use fragile bi-planes to over-fly these desert terrae incognitae. In the film screenplay, Almasy is introduced as an Hungarian explorer who is helped by 'an ancient Arab who draws in the sand, talking in an arcane dialect, scratching out a map' (Minghella 1997: 21). As in Bertolluci's film *The Sheltering Sky*, the Arab inhabitants of the desert in *The English Patient* remain anonymous, veiled figures who appear like ghosts from the enfolding dunes of the desert landscape. They are voiceless companions or saviours (it as an Arab who emerges from the darkness to offer aid to Almasy after his plane has been shot down in flames in the desert) who do not and cannot interrupt the silence that hangs across such a landscape. The desert and its nomadic peoples are mute; it is only the explorers who break this silence. If Baudrillard's revelling in the silence of the desert is an example of a post-modern (self) consciousness and *The English Patient*'s mute nomads are in the service of the explorer's libidinal economy, the effect on the other seems all but identical. As Asha Varadharajan notes, if a colonial policy was to exterminate the other or to represent the other as chaos and absence, then

> the postmodern delight in the simulacrum has a certain irony in this context. For the colonized, who have never had the luxury of being, figurality denotes not the play of the signifier but the trap of a specular economy that confirms, precisely, their inessentiality.
>
> (Varadharajan 1995: 15)

We might argue that the desert in the film, *The English Patient* is not an object that offers any resistance to the longings and desires projected on to it by the explorer, Almasy, and his associates; it is a geography of desire wherein the dangers that it presents form part of a libidinal economy bent on dissolution of the self, a dissolution of the self that is figured in the crashing of the plane.

Varadharajan poses the question, prompted by an attention to the negative dialectical method of critique, of how we might 'rethink the object' – in this case, that of the desert and its inhabitants, in a way that does not restore it to a category that is just the 'limit-text' of the conceptualising subject – its critical negativity. Reading through Adorno's extended debate with Walter Benjamin's strategy of reinvesting the object with historical contingency, Varadharajan notes how Adorno's method is to see the 'object's challenge to the dominion of conceptuality (as) represented stylistically in the form of fragments, aphorisms, and essays'. Following Adorno's method to approach the object as 'a fragment … (which) … is not an illustration of an idea … (but) instead, a constellation of particulars, a momentary illumination of the object's history of suffering …' (Varadharajan 1995: 76), other fragments of deserts might be a way to glimpse the 'object's history' and to reconfigure the desert in *The English Patient* within another 'constellation of particulars'.

Other deserts: fragments; traces and ruins

Two factual programmes screened on terrestrial television in the 1990s were Jeremy Clarkson's *Motorworld* (BBC Worldwide 1996) and Benedict Allen's *Edge of Blue Heaven* (BBC 1998).The only thing to connect these programmes is the fact that they both feature desert landscapes. It could be argued that Clarkson and Allen both represent antithetical cultural formations and ideologies, in that the former celebrates machinic culture as evidenced in the power, speed and 'performance' of cars, whereas Allen rejects this culture by travelling across the Mongolian desert using camels as his main means of transportation. In the Dubai episode of *Motorworld*, the desert featured is a playground for rich Arabs to race their four-wheel drive cars up and down the dunes, part of a 'high octane travelogue' as it is described on the back cover of the BBC video compilation of the series. On the front cover of the video is a monumental Dodge truck, which Clarkson visits while in Dubai. This truck is a kind of desert hotel and toy for its rich Arab owner; and the incongruity of truck and desert is underscored in Clarkson's commentary.

In contrast to Clarkson's high-budget production, Allen crosses the Gobi desert as a one-man production team, resting camera and sound equipment on his arm to record his travels, or staging his travelling from a fixed position camera. Whereas *Motorworld* celebrates machines and speed, Allen fears for the future of the Gobi desert and its peoples as the demise of the Soviet bloc opens it up to tourism and development. His journey is at the same time a lamentation and a valedictory for a fast-disappearing wilderness. Of course, Allen is not alone or without support since he is helped by Mongolian guides whose main means of transport to and from the isolated parts of the Gobi desert that Allen's journey takes him to, are four-wheel drive trucks. Camels for the Mongolians featured in the film are property to be used in a variety of ways, not least as an exchange value within a market economy.

Such incongruities and juxtapositions of desert and trucks, monumental or utilitarian, suggest another and more fragmentary narrative of the desert than that found in *The English Patient*. The question that is raised by these fragments is how to understand them, how to make them into useful illuminations and how, finally, to let them shuttle across more typical representations of the desert in a way that lights up another story. Again, we might use Adorno's method of allowing his gaze to fall on the exception rather than the rule where 'the exception ... becomes a fugitive glimpse of the rule's most profound truth' (Varadharajan 1995: 88). Both Clarkson's celebration of the incongruity of a monumental truck imposing itself in a desert landscape and Allen's fears for the survival of a post-Soviet Bloc Gobi desert inhabited by Mongolian peoples, imply if not an originary desert landscape, nevertheless a desert which is despoliated by the intrusion of cars and trucks. As both Vradharajan and Lisa Bloom have observed, the colonialist's fantasy is that 'he is occupying uninscribed territory' (Bloom 1993: 3). A post-colonial fantasy may be to inscribe territories with scripts that confirm the longings and projections of the Western self seeking an escape from the machinic culture of urbanised societies.

The deserts of Dubai and Mongolia are places of human habitation, places where work, play and movement are part of the fabric of everyday existence. These are not enclosed spaces but are closely if complexly connected to globalised economic and political forces. When we see four-wheel drive trucks in deserts, the chains of signification do not run in ways which are entirely predictable. The Gobi desert ceases to be a place of paradisal projection which might be used in the service of the jaded Western self. The desert as a landscape which celebrates or simply utilises machinic culture is an object which escapes easy categorisation; it does contain, however, the traces and fragments that connect in complex ways with larger global realities. Such an object demands that we think about otherness in ways which are not completely clear, closed or easily reconcilable with *us* or *our* world.

Planes and deserts (Bang! Bang! The plane is shot out of the sky)

Thus far, this critique of the representation of deserts in *The English Patient* has deployed Adorno's negative dialectical method as a way of rethinking the relationship between self and other, or conceptual categorisation and its object, in ways that have only fleetingly acknowledged that 'self' and 'others' are not disembodied figures but are, rather, historically constituted according to 'race' and gender. The analysis of another figure in the film, that of the plane in relation to the desert, brings into focus the ways in which *The English Patient* constructs a series of oppositions between the masculine self of Almasy and ethnic and gendered others. The event of the crash in the film, as the plane is consumed by flames and the desert landscape, will be argued to represent a crisis of this selfhood, a transfiguration of one form of disembodied self into the fragments and burnt remains of another, disfigured self, a self-referencing journey that precludes any acknowledgment of difference as signalling a totality which can and must include distance. What follows is an analysis of the film which uses the trope of the plane crashing into the desert as a means of rethinking the event as representing a crisis in conceptions of the masculine, European self as disembodied.

Feminists have sought to rescue the idea of embodiment from philosophical traditions which consign it to inert matter while elevating the mind and reason to a seigneurial position in which the body becomes, as Elizabeth Grosz notes, 'a source of interference in, and a danger to, the operations of reason' (Grosz 1993: 5). All too often this mind/body dualism works in tandem with others in which reasoning capacity is coded white and male while consigning brute embodiment to ethnic and gendered others. Such a dualism, when given political form, as in various colonial practices, can have devastating effects, reducing the other, for example, to a mere epidermal schema, as Frantz Fanon has observed (Fanon 1986). In less philosophically rigorous ways, this dualism is played out across a range of texts which put into play the overseeing eye/I and imagined geographies that are surveyed from this elevated position. This incorporeal self projects onto others a sense of location and connection, reproducing the colonial strategy of nostalgically claiming 'a space and a subject outside Western modernity, apart from all chronology and totalization' (Kaplan 1996: 88). Such is the dualism played out in *The English Patient* – as a series of oppositions between: plane and desert; insubstantiality and embodiment; self-referentiality and intercorporeality.

After the credits, the opening shot in *The English Patient* is of a tiny and fragile bi-plane over-flying the desert. In it are Almasy and (as we later discover) the dead Katherine Clifton. The plane is shot down by Germans and after the ensuing crash and conflagration, Almasy's burnt body is rescued by nomadic Bedouins. It is this event which transforms the charismatic Hungarian count into the disfigured and anonymous 'English patient'. As in the films *Voyager* and *The Flight of the Phoenix*, the crashing of a plane in the desert represents both catastrophe and crisis – of transfiguration, renewal or rebirth. In *Voyager*, the plane crashing in the desert is the event which propels the main character, Walter Faber (played by Sam Shepard) into a voyage of emotional and libidinal discovery; in *The Flight of the Phoenix* the technology of a model (or toy) plane is the means by which the male survivors of the crashed (adult) plane are rescued. These two figures, that of the plane and the desert, bring into crisis the relationship between the boundless ego whose flight over the grounding desert is at the same time an escape from the complexities of intercorporeal embodiment.

Overseeing or over-flying is a kind of privileged non-position defined against that which is stationary, embedded or embodied. This sense of mastery afforded by flight has characterised other forms of male exploration as Lisa Bloom's critique of American Polar expeditions reveals. When the polar caps could be over-flown, explorers were able to escape environmental hazards. The machine ensured their safety so they 'could adventure without distraction' thus ensuring that the 'polar ice (could) no longer open up beneath (them) and swallow (them) into the black waters of the polar sea' (Bloom 1993: 80). This also is the fallible masculine logic of discovery which is brought into crisis when Almasy's plane crashes in *The English Patient*. As he is carried away from the site of the crash, our point of view is that of Almasy's, the screenplay pointing out that 'his view of the world is through slats of palm. He glimpses camels, fierce low sun, the men who carry him' (Minghella 1997: 6). These men, as noted earlier, are simply men who are defined by their capacity to carry the English patient: they are mute forms of embodiment who transport a white man who can do nothing other than see. It is as if Almasy, the pilot of an over-flying and overseeing mechanical apparatus, has himself been reduced to the level of a vision machine, his embodiment the responsibility of those who transport him.

Embodiment and otherness in *The English Patient*

Almasy, as played by Ralph Fiennes, is an enigmatic figure, alone and disconnected, angular and awkward. His only connection is with the ethereal Katherine, and their doomed and adulterous love affair forms the bedrock of the film's narrative. While their love affair is transgressive, they remain isolated from all other forms of connection, unlike other characters in the film, such as Hana, the English Patient's nurse and Kip, an Indian bomb disposal engineer. The other transgressive relationship in both book and film is that between Hana and Kip, and critics of the book have focused on the character of Kip who carries the heavy 'burden of representation' of otherness. As Sadashige argues, 'he is made heroic because we can imagine all of Asia through the gestures of this one man' (Sadashige 1998: 247). The translation of book to film, apart from making Hana and Kip's relationship subservient to the narrative of Almasy and Katherine's grand passion, articulates their difference in ways that construct other dualisms.

In contrast to the casting of Ralph Fiennes and Kristin Scott Thomas as Almasy and Katherine, whose 'architectural' looks are used to project them as ethereal remnants of a Western civilisation that has lost its way (Katherine's message for Almasy as she lies dying in the Cave of the Swimmers is that 'we are the real countries, not the boundaries drawn on maps with the names of powerful men'), Hana and Kip, as played by Juliette Binoche and Naveen Andrews, participate in a world which, albeit temporarily, is one of child-like beauty and wonder. Hana's rounded face is filled with delight as she hopscotches by the light of oil-filled snail shells to the stable where Kip is waiting for her. In another scene, again cinematically conveyed as a crepuscular world of light and shadow, Kip arranges a hoist so that Hana can swing past the frescoed walls of a nearby church. In these scenes we are presented with a space where white and brown bodies can play, can carve out a time from 'external' realities of international conflict, racial bigotry, disillusion and death. Hana and Kip's private world is a sensuous and shadowy one, existing on the margins of that other world where passion leads to betrayal and ultimately death. In this world they take delight in their bodies as they touch and connect with environments which offer them a playground for the senses. Unlike the Bedouin Arabs, Hana and Kip are not mute but they are made to represent forms of human embodiment which have a sensuous connection with their environment in contrast to the self-referential world of Almasy and Katherine.

The dualism that results from the contrast between the destruction of Almasy and Katherine and Hana and Kip's marginal world is one that Grosz argues must be critiqued since it is 'a corporeality (that is) associated with one sex (or race), which then takes on the burden of the other's corporeality for it' (Grosz 1994: 22). Here, in relation to representations of embodiment in *The English Patient*, there is a rearticulation of the conceptual closure that defines the desert landscape as an already-known empty space. Hana and Kip's corporeality is transcribed into an ethnic and feminised otherness (Kip without his turban has long hair which falls to his shoulders) in a familiar post-colonial gesture that leaves the white asceticised self as a disembodied nomad searching empty landscapes for that sense of embodied connection which has been lost.

In the film of *The English Patient*, the conceptual closure of this dualism admits of no idea of difference which is not at the same time annihilation. Katherine dies in the Cave of the Swimmers and Almasy becomes a voice housed in an utterly disfigured body. The flight of the European and disconnected self is interrupted by the event of the crash; it can admit of no intercorporeality that falls outside of the laws of possession (as in Almasy's passion for Katherine). The ending of the film, where Hana parts from Kim and leaves the dead Almasy, differs in important ways from the ending of the novel. In the film we presume that Hana walks away to a post-war life which leaves behind all connection to her experiences in Italy, as lover of Kip and nurse to 'the English Patient'. The book ends by offering an alternative sense of connection which is both embodied but distant. As Raymond Aaron Younis proposes, this ending 'affirms a mysterious connection across space and time between Kip and Hana' (Younis 1998: 7), since Ondaatje leaves us with a view of the connection of Hana and Kip which is not dependent upon possession or proximity:

> And so Hana moves and her face turns and in regret she lowers her hair. Her shoulder touches the edge of a cupboard and a glass dislodges. Kirpal's left hand swoops down and catches the dropped fork an inch from the floor and gently passes it into the fingers of his daughter, a wrinkle at the edge of his eyes behind his spectacles.
>
> (Ondaatje 1988: 301)

The idea of such a connection as 'mysterious' remains only if we conceive the self as an enclosed ego which confronts the other as an object to be mastered in a gesture of self-fulfilment. As Horkheimer observed such an 'abstract ego (is) emptied of all substance except its attempt to transform everything into a means for its own preservation' (Varadharajan 1995: 52). In *The English Patient*, 'preservation' of the ego is at the cost of the dissolution of the body as the over-flying plane is interred in the folds of the desert.

An alternative conception deriving from Adorno's attempt to create 'an ethics of alterity' would view the connection between Hana and Kip as a model of the relations between self and other which acknowledges that 'embodiment, corporeality insist on alterity ... alterity is the very possibility and process of embodiment' (Grosz 1994: 209). This is a conception of intercorporeality as a connection that can at the same time be distant, and it is one which would require us to think of the self in relation to others that offers a different scenario to that of planes crashing into deserts. It also reminds that the masculinist myth of the disembodied and over-flying ego, as figured by the plane, must inevitably crash into the embodiment of the desert.

References

Baudrillard, Jean (1986) *America*. London: Verso.

Bloom, Lisa (1993) *Gender on Ice, American Ideologies of Polar Expeditions*. Minneapolis: University of Minnesota Press.

Dews, Peter (1987) *Logics of Disintegration, Post-Structuralist Thought and the Claims of Critical Theory*. London: Verso.

Durham Peters, John (1999) 'Exile, Nomadism and Diaspora: the stakes of mobility in the western canon' in Hamid Naficy, ed., *Home, Exile, Homeland, Film, Media and the Politics of Place*. London: Routledge.

Fanon, Frantz (1986) *Black Skin, White Masks*. London: Pluto Press.

Fuchs, Cynthia, *Man to Man, The English Patient Is A Bit Too Epic*, www.addict.con/issues/2.12...ews/In_The_Frame/English_Patient/

Garber, Marjorie (1992) *Vested interets: cross-dressing and cultural anxiety*. London: Routledge.

Gershorn, A. Keith (1994) 'Valorizing 'the Feminine' While Rejecting Feminism? – Baudrillard's Feminist Provocations' in Douglas Kellner ed., *Baudrillard: A Critical Reader*. Oxford: Blackwell.

Grosz, Elizabeth (1994) *Volatile Bodies, Towards a Corporeal Feminism*. Indianapolis: Indiana University Press.

Hillger, Annick (1998) '*And this is the world of nomads in any case*': The Odyssey as Intertext in Michael Ondaatje's The English Patient, *Journal of Commonwealth Literature* (33) 1: 23–33.

Kaplan, Caren (1996) *Questions of Travel, Postmodern Discourses of Displacement*. Durham NC: Duke University Press.

Minghella, Anthony (1997) *The English Patient, A Screenplay*. London: Methuen.

Ondaatje, Michael (1988) *The English Patient*. London: Picador.

O'Neill, Maggie, ed. (1999) *Adorno, Culture and Feminism*. London: Sage.

Pensky, Max, ed. (1997) *The Actuality of Adorno, Critical Essays on Adorno and the Postmodern*. New York: State University of New York Press.

Sadashige, Jaqui (1998) 'Sweeping the Sands, Geographies of Desire in the English Patient', *Literature/Film Quarterly*, (26) 4: 242–54.

Shohat, Ella (1993) 'Gender and Culture of Empire' in H. Naficy and T.H. Gabriel eds., *Otherness and the Media: the ethnography of the imagined and the imaged*. London: Harwood.

Varadharajan, Asha (1995) *Exotic Parodies, Subjectivity in Adorno, Said and Spivak*. Minneapolis: University of Minnesota Press.

Yabroff, Jennie, *The English Patient Vs Romeo and Juliet: Modernized Classic Beats Period Love Story Hands Down*, www.addict.com/htm/lofi/Columns/Through_A_Glass_Darkly/212/

12 The Iconic Body and the Crash

Jean Grimshaw

The Accident

Early in September 1997, the media were saturated with images of a wrecked Mercedes in the tunnel under the Pont d'Alma in Paris. Diana, Princess of Wales, was dead, and millions of people around the world were shocked and grieving. Such was the emotional impact of this crash that most people remember where they were when they heard the news, just as most people remember where they were when they heard that President Kennedy was dead.

The crash was a tragic accident, attributed, amongst other things, to a drunken driver. It could have been avoided. Individual car crashes always seem to us to require reasons: drunk driving, negligence, speeding, unsafe vehicles. And in one sense most car crashes *are* 'accidents' in that unless they are stunts or designed to test car safety, it is rare for them to happen as a direct result of human intention; even if a course of action or a failure to act leads to a crash, the crash is not normally the *goal* of that action. But in another sense, car crashes and the inevitable deaths that ensue are not accidents. They are a structural consequence of the relation between fragile human bodies and lethal chunks of metal travelling at high speed. They are a necessary consequence of the development of the internal combustion engine and the organisation of much of society around it.

Baudrillard (1993) suggests that to modern bourgeois thought death is a 'scandal'. It can no longer be fitted into some traditional vision and iconography within which it made sense; the problem of death has become insoluble in that it has no meaning any more. We are held captive by the idea of a 'normal' or 'natural' death, at the proper term, after a 'just' lifespan. Death has become, Baudrillard writes, the final object in the absurd collection of objects and signs from which we assemble our own private universe.

> The property system is so absurd that it leads people to demand their death as their own good.... A comfortable, personalised 'designer' death, a 'natural' death; this is the inalienable right constituting the perfected form of bourgeois individual law.
>
> (1993: 176)

In addition death is a constant challenge to ideas of reason and the technical mastery of nature. Natural catastrophes strike a blow to ideas of sovereign rationality and the mastery of nature, but the 'accident' presents a particular paradox, a kind of flaw in our world view. The accident possesses, Baudrillard argues, 'the fatality of necessity at the same time as the uncertainty of freedom' (1993: 160). The very concept of the 'accident' is given its meaning by the ideas of reason and mastery; within a world view premised on these ideas 'accidents' must inevitably happen. Yet the accident also possesses the 'uncertainty' of freedom, since no *particular* accident appears inevitable; it always seems that it could have been avoided if a different course of action had been taken. 'Accidents' are inevitable, yet due to chance; they are built into our world view, yet also absurd. Just as we embark on the endless and ultimately futile process of trying to postpone death, so we embark on the equally endless and futile process of trying to avoid accidents, the ultimate offence to ideas of human rationality and control.

'Natural' death, death which is supposed to come at the 'proper' term, has itself, Baudrillard suggests, been confined to the margins of social life. It no longer has any collective or symbolic meaning for us. The dead have nothing to exchange; they have simply passed away and become alibis for the living and their superiority over the dead. Death has become flat and one-dimensional, something in which the group no longer has any collective role to play. But whilst we may want to deny or control it, Baudrillard also argues that we live off the production of death. The institution of 'security' converts accident, disease and pollution into profit, and in our obsessional cultivation of security, we anticipate death in life.

A paradigm of this obsession with security is the question of car safety. We test and build cars that are supposed to be 'safer' than those that went before, and we install seat belts and airbags to shield us from the impact of the crash and preserve our lives. Yet the 'safe' car, Baudrillard suggests, can be compared to a sarcophagus; the driver no longer runs the risk of death because in a sense he is already dead, that is, insulated from the hazards of life to the point of being entombed in metal.

On the one hand, we see accidents as absurd; someone or something must always have been responsible, hence our obsession with safety and security. We cannot accept that accidents are a structural feature of the way we live and a consequence of our world view. Yet on the other hand, it is only violent, accidental or chance death that has any meaning for us; other deaths are often almost ridiculous and socially insignificant. A death that escapes 'natural reason', however, may become the business of the group and demand a collective and symbolic response. Hence, Baudrillard suggests, we may derive an intense and profoundly collective satisfaction from the automobile death. In the fatal car accident, the artificiality of death fascinates us; it can be compared to the significance of the sacrifice in other cultures. Other kinds of accidents, such as workplace accidents, may not have this resonance; they have no symbolic yield.

In the case of Diana, there was indeed a huge collective and symbolic response. But there are interesting questions about this response which Baudrillard's view of the car crash does not address. First, Baudrillard asks why it is that so few fatal car crashes have this symbolic resonance. The vast majority generate no more of a collective or symbolic response than 'virtual' deaths in a car on computer screens. We have developed a terrifying collective immunity to statistics about car crashes, such as the number of people who are killed and injured every year. Despite all the efforts of road safety campaigns, deaths on the road – unlike deaths in natural disasters such as floods or fire, deaths in rail or air crashes, or death inflicted by other forms of human agency – have become routinised, a 'normal' part of daily life. It is hard to imagine a huge motorway pile up involving multiple deaths receiving a proportionately similar amount of media coverage to that which was devoted to the Paddington rail disaster in October 1999. To individuals, car crashes may be a tragedy. Generally, however, apart from a voyeuristic frisson while passing the scene of a crash, car crashes figure in the popular imagination simply as RTAs (Road Traffic Accidents), bureaucratically reported and recorded by the police, and often little more than an annoying obstacle in getting to work by car, or a series of fleeting images of wrecked cars on TV which seem indistinguishable from each other and generate little public response. Far from demanding a collective and symbolic response, and despite the fact that the number of people killed in rail or air crashes is tiny compared with the number killed on the roads, the public memory and emotional impact of most car crashes remains marginal, ephemeral and unspecific. How are we to account for this?

The second question arises as follows. Baudrillard does not explain why he identifies the car crash in particular as that which may provoke a collective and symbolic response. But if it is the case that most car crashes do not generate this kind of response, then we need to ask why not, as well as what is different about the ones which do. Diana's crash was not an RTA. The images of the wrecked Mercedes were absolutely specific, and the public reaction emotional and intense. Plainly, her fame and constant media visibility ensured that her death would also be highly visible. I want, however, to suggest that the responses to Diana's death were over-determined. The horror created by her crash owed at least some of its emotional impact to the fact that it was a *car* crash rather than some other kind of accident or disaster. Understanding the particular qualities of this horror entails exploring what it is about our relation to the car which normally leads to the repression of such horror in the popular imagination.

The Relation to the Car

No kind of object in regular use in human life is ever merely functional, since all objects that humans use are invested with some kind of symbolic significance. This is true of the many forms of human transport, but the kinds of meaning and symbolism invested in different forms of transport are not identical.

An increasing number of us own and drive a car. A car is frequently an object of personal desire invested with particular meanings, and the sort of car we choose often functions as an indicator of our personality, lifestyle or social status. When I bought a Vauxhall Cavalier, people made jokes to the point of tedium about whether I was thinking of becoming a travelling salesman. The sort of person who would covet or own a Porsche would not normally be interested in buying a Cavalier. But whilst aeroplanes or yachts, for example, can similarly be objects of desire and indicators of social status, their ownership does not have the common kinds of daily significance that may adhere to ownership of a car, since few can afford them.

The car has become essential to the sense that many of us have of our own mobility, and the meanings this may give to our lives. The car allows me to think of myself as the sort of person who can be in ten different widely scattered places in just one day, and who can hold together these fragments of a life in a way that can be seen as coherent. Driving is also frequently a locus for perceptions of personal pride and skill. Few people would be prepared to consider or admit that they were 'bad' drivers, and many are quickly ready to condemn the lack of skill or driving habits of others. Driving is a focus, too, for intense emotions and stress, whether the frustrations of being trapped in gridlocked traffic, or the phenomenon of so-called 'road rage', when drivers behave towards other drivers in outrageously aggressive ways.

Cars are also a focus for acts of daring, criminality and foolhardiness. Car theft, driving cars recklessly without regard for bureaucratic niceties like insurance, and leaving them wrecked or burned out, has become one of the major criminal activities of adolescents and young men. The Australian sociologist R.W. Connell (1983) has argued that 'masculinity' for many young men is wrapped up with a feeling of a right to occupy space in public places and crowd others out, both by bodily stance, gesture and movement, and by using the voice loudly and aggressively. Cars and motor bikes, he suggests, provide for some young men a way of amplifying their occupation of space and putting their impress upon it; the car is both faster and noisier than the speed or noise of the human body. The daring act of appropriation and the intimate bodily immersion of oneself in the car can make it feel doubly like an extension of oneself. The accelerator can seem like an extra pair of legs which can go extremely fast, the roar of a revving engine like a shout of 'I am here!'

Cars have also been the focus of romance and dreams of sex. Chuck Berry's lyrics of teenage dreams and aspirations in the 1950s featured 'Riding along in my automobile/ my baby beside me at the wheel'. For young people who had nowhere else to go, the back seat of the car was where the first scenarios of fumbling teenage sex often took place. And it was the car, above all, which provided the means for a young man to impress a girl and show her a good time. For the older and more staid, the car was more likely to provide a vision of freedom and escape, out for a 'spin' in the country on afternoons at the weekend. Such dreams have become somewhat tarnished by the realities of gridlocked roads, pollution, and the overcrowding of once remote destinations, but they are still the staple of car advertising. The most common car advertisements either feature cars in isolated outdoor settings, away from human habitation and, most importantly, away from all other cars, or in 'chic' and expensive settings where the car becomes a metaphor for human sexual desire.

The Body of the Car

The kinds of investment in the car outlined in the previous section frequently involve bodily skills and desires. But cars themselves also have 'bodies'. Just as the 'bodyshop' is where cars are repaired and resprayed, so Anita Roddick's The Body Shop offers biochemical means to the same end for human bodies, means for concealing their flaws and imperfections. And just as people may tend their own bodies with cosmetics, creams and moisturisers, so they may tend the bodies of their cars. One can shampoo one's car just as one can shampoo one's hair. People wash, wax and polish the 'bodies' of their cars, and often suffer anger or even grief when these bodies are damaged or wrecked.

Rather like human bodies, cars too have body shapes which go in and out of fashion. The curved and quite fleshy shape of Monroe's body was replaced by the stick thin-ness of Twiggy, and then by the toned and lean shape epitomised by Jane Fonda. The dramatic fins and length of the fashionable American car of the 1950s gave way to the neater angular shapes of the 1960s and 1970s, and these in turn to the curved 'aerodynamic' shapes that are more fashionable today. The bodies of cars can also vary in ways analogous to human bodies; the Mini is snappy and petite, the Rolls Royce or the Daimler statuesque.

What is the relation between these two orders of bodies, the human and the car? The movie *Crash* (Cronenberg 1996) focuses on this relation. In it, the camera dwells pornographically on close-ups of scars and other, normally repulsive, injuries on the bodies of its human characters, turning fretworks of scar tissues into objects of erotic attraction. But the movie also treats car bodies according to the same pornographic regimen, under which they too become foci of erotic attention. Car bodies are also shown in close-up, their dents and 'injuries' lingered over just like the scars on injured human bodies. The characters in the movie are irresistibly drawn to stroke, touch and feel the 'body' of the car, and to photograph its injuries with the voyeuristic scrutiny of the pornographer.

The car thus becomes an extension of the human body, and a metaphor for it. Our investments in car bodies are the same as those we have in our own bodies, prompting a lived fantasy of repair and control to assume precedence over the actuality of fatal injuries and accidents. Accordingly, in Cronenberg's movie, the crash is no longer an accident, but is designed down to the last detail. The crash and the potential injury that may ensue, instead of being that to which we are fatally and accidentally prone, becomes something which can be controlled, orchestrated and invested with erotic attraction and obsessive fascination. This fascination results partly from the inversion of the normal that turns that which is 'accidental' into that which is intentional, but also partly from the substitutability of our own fragile bodies for the most robust, repairable, mechanical ones with which we are daily surrounded. Under these circumstances, if death does intervene upon this fantasy, it no longer functions as biological decrepitude ('natural' death) but assumes a fantastic or virtual form. It is arguably this virtual death that Baudrillard suggests has supplanted its older more 'natural' form. With it, however, goes the real body. In other words, when death is excised from the social imaginary, the body follows soon afterwards, unable, either physically or in the imagination, to bear the burden of the virtual immortality to which a society premised on the denial of death condemns it.

Virtual Death

It is interesting that computer and video games based on fast response and co-ordination which involve vehicles mostly involve the car. One is assumed to be at the steering wheel of the car seeing the road ahead from the position of the driver. In computer and video games death is of little consequence; death happens over and over again but the player recuperates.

A casual wander through any toy, games or video store will reveal the ways in which contemporary popular culture is saturated with death. Toys include guns and other electronic contraptions which bear resemblance to guns, and countless models of 'action' heroes whose main function is either to deal out or to avoid death. It is hard to find a computer or video game which does not routinely aim at 'zapping' or obliterating opponents, or which does not dice with death in some form as the outcome of the game. But 'death' in these forms is a kind of virtual death, two-dimensional and without consequences.

The 'Action' category in video stores is normally a euphemism for militaristic fantasy, or for films where a significant proportion of the characters will meet a violent death. Such death, unlike that of computer games, may be graphically or realistically depicted. But it is reversible. Characters in a film or a video do not die permanently; they not only retain their hold on the filmic imagination, but the video can be rewound and rewatched. One can die many times, yet be reborn. The impact of these deaths is momentary; graphic filmic representation, whilst aiming at a degree of realism, becomes 'virtual' through the possibility of endless repetition. Even TV programmes like 'Casualty' which specialise in the graphic representation of dead or dying bodies, of operations and of blood and guts, become absorbed by filmic conventions of death without consequences, geared to play on our emotional susceptibilities in a evanescent kind of way.

The main feature of what I have called 'virtual' death is that it is disembodied. It is not tactile, it does not bleed or leak or seep or smell and it is 'clean'. It is two-dimensional; it happens on a screen and one cannot walk around it. It is not 'real', and even if realistically depicted it may just be a game or a fantasy or a story. Death in car crashes seems to have become like this; in most cases it has little hold on our imaginations and we do not dwell on the bodily details and consequences of the crash.

The nearest we are likely to get to these bodily consequences is seeing test dummies in films about car safety. But the imaginative transposition between the dummy and human body is hard to make; there is no blood, for example. The imagined bodies of those who have suffered 'virtual' death make little or no impact on our imagination, and death in cars normally makes little more impact on us than virtual death.

In addition, it is arguable that the absence of the 'real' body in 'virtual' death can be seen as related to the general disappearance of dead bodies and the 'look of death' from everyday life. We rarely see dead bodies nowadays in the course of our everyday living, and we have lost the tradition, once prevalent, of accurate portraiture or photography of the recently dead. Dying and dead bodies are technically and hygienically removed not merely from our sight but from the rest of our senses as well. Pictures of 'real' death, once relatively common, now circulate only in limited contexts; they are normally the property of police, legal or medical authorities. The management of dead bodies is the business of increasingly professionalised institutions such as hospitals, mortuaries, funeral directors and crematoria, who usually allow sight of dead bodies, if at all, only under carefully controlled conditions in which visible signs of damage to the corpse will be removed from our sight as far as possible.

The Body and the 'Repression' of Death

Norbert Elias (1985) suggests that it might be fruitful to compare the contemporary insistence on removing dead bodies from our sight, and our defensive and embarrassed reactions to death, to Victorian attitudes to sex. We are, it might be claimed, 'prudes' about death now rather than about sex. Baudrillard (1993) has proposed that it is now the representation of the dead which has become pornographic; the exposure of dead bodies is seen as indecent, much as the exposure of bodily sex or organs once was.

Post Foucault, 'repressive hypotheses' should no doubt be treated with some suspicion. The twentieth century has witnessed mass death on an unprecedented scale, and, as I have argued above, popular culture is in some ways saturated with death and images of death. But I think it is nevertheless arguable that there are ways in which it is useful to speak of a contemporary cultural repression of death.

Elias suggests that dying has become 'a blank area on the social map'. For many people, at least those in relatively affluent western societies, life has in some ways become more secure, and it seems that death can be postponed. Many people die in hospital or hospices, no longer part of normal family or social life. This makes it easier for us to repress the idea of our own death, to regard it as something capable of being postponed.

This repression of the idea of death is reinforced by contemporary forms of fetishisation of the body. The cult of exercise and fitness generates an endless proliferation of institutions, strategies and techniques which seem to promise a new and changed body, customised according to one's own specifications. The 'makeover' in fashion promises a new image or presence; creams, treatments and surgery promise rejuvenation and the postponement of processes of ageing. These things all speak to us of control, autonomy, of what we can make of ourselves. But they also speak of the ways in which images of 'ideal' bodies are premised on other 'abject' bodies. The 'ideal' body is a normalized construction built on the exclusion of those characteristics of bodies which fail to live up to this fantasized perfection, and the quest for the perfect body, always doomed to failure, is responsible for a wide range of neuroses, obsession and disorders. Contemporary anxiety about the body perhaps focuses most acutely on the anathema of old age. Old age and weakened or debilitated bodies reveal the finally illusory nature of programmes of body control; hence in media imagery, whilst models may be airbrushed to achieve perfection, old age is mostly airbrushed right out. The sight of an old body, described in pejorative terms such as fat, flabby, wrinkled or sagging, is usually experienced as disgusting; representations of fat bodies or old bodies that do not intend to portray them as disgusting are often perceived as transgressive.

We fetishise young and perfect bodies, whilst condoning mass slaughter on the road. Crashes impact on bodies, mangle them and wreck them, turn into grotesque travesties of the perfect body. This also happens in rail or air crashes. But there is a particular kind of horror and paradox in the car crash. The car is human scale, and human bodies, no more than four or five of them, can fit neatly into it. They don't 'disappear' in the same way as they do in the immensity of an aeroplane fuselage or a railway carriage. The attachments of the car have a human scale, things we touch, press, stroke, hold, grasp and manipulate: knobs, wheels, columns, buttons which have the power to turn on us in an instant. The wheel I'm holding, the seat I'm sitting on, the knobs I'm turning can become the instruments of my death or disfigurement.

But the car, the potential instrument of my death, may also be experienced as a focus of personal pride, and as an extension of myself in terms of how essential it is to my projects. We may half live in our cars, and we like the illusion of being safe in the metal cocoon from which we are always separated by a mere whisker from death and tragedy. And that tragedy might suddenly be our own fault. Plane crashes and rail crashes can almost be seen as 'acts of God', and we don't feel that we might have been personally responsible. They are not routinised and they have names; Lockerbie, the Severn Tunnel Crash, the Clapham Junction or Paddington Disasters. We say 'Do you remember Lockerbie?' but not normally 'Do you remember that crash on the M6?' Recognition of the slaughter wrought by the car usually remains abstract, with little emotional impact. I think that this should be seen as a kind of cultural repression, a defence mechanism, because of the 'nearness' to us of the car, of what we have personally invested in our cars, and of the uncomfortable feeling that in the end we all share responsibility for death and tragedy on the roads, however much we feel safe in our cars or think that we are safe drivers. Car crashes lead to private horror and grief. Collectively, however, car death remains virtual, and the response is one of repression rather than of public emotion.

The Iconic Body and the Crash

But some crashes do not become obliterated in this way. Diana's crash is remembered as we might remember Lockerbie. What does it take to undo the cultural repression surrounding the car crash, and to allow its potential emotional impact to surface in a public and collective rather than a private context? What was the particular horror of Diana's crash, and of the fact that it was a car crash?

From the time of her engagement and marriage to Prince Charles in 1981 to her death in 1997, public and media interest in Diana, Princess of Wales, focused constantly and intensely on her body. The myth of the 'fairytale wedding' was shattered quite early on, and it became plain that the marriage, for Charles, was a cynically undertaken dynastic move in which Diana was brood mare for the continuation of the Windsor dynasty. In anachronistic and patriarchal mode, the Windsors required medical confirmation that Diana was a virgin and that she was capable of having children. They probably hoped that apart from that she would simply become a decorative and submissive accessory for the Prince of Wales. What they did not bargain for was the intense and unprecedented interest in Diana's body that was not at all focused on its reproductive capacities.

Diana's body can be seen as 'iconic'. What does it mean to say this? Simply as image, Diana's body became an icon of impossibly slender, beautiful and youthful high fashion. But the particular iconic power of Diana's body was not merely as image. It took many hours to transform Norma Jean Baker into 'Marilyn', but the processes happened behind the scenes, and what the public expected of Monroe was the final product and image. In the case of Diana, public interest focused almost as much on process as on the product. During the early years of her marriage, her painful thin-ness led to constant speculation about anorexia, and her later self-revelations revealed her ongoing bulimia. Her beautiful body, wracked by constant vomiting, became the most publicly visible symbol of many of the dominant contradictions and tensions in contemporary discourse about women's bodies.

But in her later years there was equal interest in the processes by which she came to transcend the bulimia and the emaciation. One of the most common images shot by the paparazzi was of Diana going to the gym, striding along in Lycra shorts. We knew about her colonic irrigation, and her constant deployment of 'alternative' bodily therapies in her quest for reworking her own life. She became an icon as victim of disorders such as bulimia from which so many women suffer. But towards the end of her life, tanned, toned and healthy looking, she also became an icon of woman as survivor, of woman as becoming 'her own woman', a survival understood as working on the body to produce changes in the soul. Her struggles became projected onto her struggles with her body. Diana's body was a paradigm not only of the 'ideal' body itself, but of the suffering it may undergo, and the struggles engaged upon in order to achieve it.

Her death at the age of 36 would have been shocking however it had occurred. But I think that there was a particular horror generated by the fact that it was a car crash, which was made all the more poignant by the former images we had of Diana in cars; those of her driving her red Mini during her engagement to Charles, seated decorously in 'safe' limousines during royal trips and visits, and driving herself to the gym in later years. Diana's death briefly undid the cultural repression of the dangerously symbiotic relationship between the human body and the car.

But it needed the iconic body of a star to undo this repression.

Diana's crash was absolutely specific; *that* car, *that* body and *that* drunken driver. It was not an RTA, and it does not merge into an abstract image of car crashes in general. But we knew little about what happened to Diana's body in that crash; bureaucratic police and medical experts removed the body from our sight and we were left to speculate. How damaged and broken was that famous body? How could such a thing happen to a body like that? There was no lying-in-state, and her face and body disappeared totally from our sight.

Our only route to speculation about Diana's body was the body of the Mercedes; this was all that we actually had to see. A kind of transposition took place between the body of the car and the body of the star. We imagine *that* piece of mangled metal in contact with *that* body, but the absence of visual evidence of what happened to Diana's body became sublimated into an interest in images of the wrecked car. The obsessive question about who was to blame for the accident can perhaps be seen as a diversionary move away from the question of whether in the end we are all to blame, since car crashes seem to be something for which we could be seen as holding a collective responsibility. We could have killed her ourselves; which of us can say that we have never driven carelessly or dangerously? We obviously cannot know what reactions there would have been had Diana died in some other way. But the intensity of the mourning following Diana's death suggests that it allowed the abnormal irruption of something else as well as grief at her death; a brief exposure of the horror of the car and its relation to the human body. This was made vivid by the unbearable idea of *that* iconic body broken, and *that* struggle brought to nothing in an instant, an idea which could only seethe in our imaginations, since Diana's body was removed from our sight. Her death briefly reinstated the real body in the car crash.

The ultimate power and paradox of the horror is that by dying, Diana defeated death and ageing. Death achieved in an instant what all those workouts and therapists could never have done; Diana will always remain young and beautiful. The iconic body, through the crash, becomes the only body that can live for ever, so that the mangled wreckage of the car comes to signify both the defeat of that body, and at the same time, its victory.

References

Aries, P. (1976)*Western Attitudes toward Death*. P.M. Ranum, trans. London: Marion Boyars.

Baudrillard, J. (1993) *Symbolic Exchange and Death*. I.H. Grant, trans. London: Sage.

Bauman, Z. (1992) *Mortality, Immortality and Other Life Strategies*. London: Sage.

Bordo, S. (1993) *Unbearable Weight: Feminism, Western Culture and the Body*. Berkeley: University of California Press.

Burchill, J. (1998) *Diana*. London: George Weidenfeld and Nicholson.

Campbell, B. (1998) *Diana, Princess of Wales: How Sexual Politics Shook the Monarchy*. London: The Women's Press.

Connell, R.W. (1983) 'Men's Bodies', in Connell, R.W. ed., *Which Way is Up?* Sydney: George Allen and Unwin.

Elias, N. (1985) *The Loneliness of the Dying*. E. Jephcott, trans. Oxford: Blackwell.

Faith, N. (1997) *Crash: the Limits of Car Safety*. London: Boxtree.

Gilbert, G. et al (eds) (1999) *Diana and Democracy. New Formations 36*. London, Lawrence and Wishart.

13 Of Hallowed Spacings: Diana's Crash as Heterotopia

By Carmen Alfonso and Nils Lindahl Elliot.

Photographs by Carmen Alfonso

... it is not possible to disregard the fatal intersection of time with space.

M. Foucault

As we write this essay, more than three years have passed since Diana, Princess of Wales, died in a fatal car crash. Since that time, many publications have appeared that have analysed various aspects of her life and her death. After years of debate, and indeed after years of obstruction on the part of some of the good residents of South Kensington, a memorial has finally been built that arguably echoes Diana's own life by eschewing the permanence of a garden or a monument in favour of a memorial 'walk'. This route enables her fans to continue the pilgrimage that began shortly after her death, and that every day leaves at least one or two bouquets of cut flowers wedged in the bars of the front gates of Kensington Palace.

Is there anything more to say after tons of newsprint and cut flowers have been recycled?

We believe that there is. This essay is about Diana's death as a 'crashing' of space and time, a crashing that is an instance, almost literally, of what Foucault (1986) once described as the fatal intersection of time with space, an intersection which, he argued, 'it is not possible to disregard', but which in our view has been overlooked by much of the literature on the life and times of Diana.

How to theorize the intersection of space and time in Diana's crash? In this essay we would like to do so by way of Foucault's concept of heterotopia. Foucault first spoke of heterotopia in the preface of *The Order of Things*: in this first usage, he regarded heterotopia as discourse, or rather, as utterance capable of shattering discursive order. After describing the celebrated Borges entry from a 'Chinese encyclopaedia', Foucault suggested that what made this entry both funny and unsettling was its *heteroclite* nature. Heteroclite, Foucault suggested, 'should be taken in its most literal, etymological sense: in such a state, things are "laid", "placed", "arranged" in sites so very different from one another that it is impossible to find a

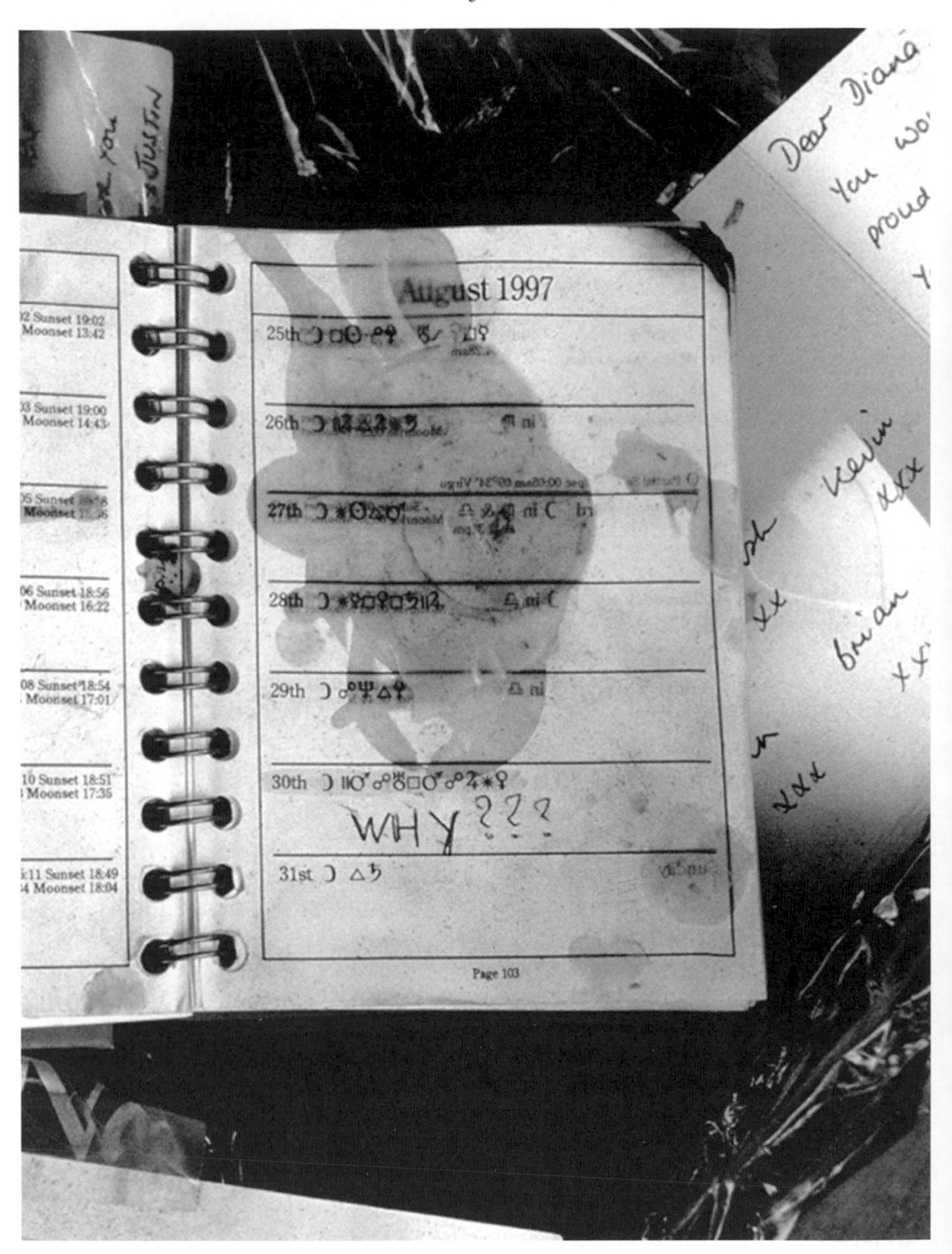
August 1997
25th
26th
27th
28th
29th
30th
WHY???
31st
Page 103
Dear Diana
You wo
proud
Kevin
xxx
brian
xx
xxx

place of residence for them, to define a *common locus* beneath them all' (1970: xvii–xviii). Directly after this definition, Foucault offered an account of the difference between utopia, and a term which seemed to appear out of nowhere: *heterotopia* (in fact the term had been used in medical contexts). He suggested that while utopias have no real location, they nevertheless 'afford consolation' insofar as they offer fantastic regions 'where life is easy'; in contrast, Foucault argued that heterotopias afford no such consolation insofar as they 'make it impossible to name this *and* that, because they shatter or tangle common names, because they destroy 'syntax' in advance … heterotopias (such as those found so often in Borges) desiccate speech, stop words in their tracks, contest the very possibility of grammar at its source; they dissolve our myths and sterilize the lyricism of our sentences' (xviii).

The year after *Les Mots et les Choses* appeared in France, Foucault returned to the concept in some lecture notes. These notes would only be published in 1984 in *Architecture-Mouvement-Continuité,* and then in English translation in *Diacritics* in 1986. Foucault gave the notes the title of *Des Espaces Autres* and this was translated as *Of Other Spaces* by *Diacritics*. In these notes Foucault seemed more concerned with developing a universal anthropology of a phenomenon with a 'real' geographical existence. According to this account, heterotopias are found in all cultures, and are 'real places – places that do exist and that are formed in the very founding of society – which are something like counter-sites, a kind of effectively enacted utopia in which the real sites, all the other real sites that can be found within the culture, are simultaneously represented, contested, and inverted. Places of this kind are outside of all places, even though it may be possible to indicate their location in reality' (1986: 24). Although Foucault provided a bewildering array of types and examples – the category included cinemas, cemeteries, brothels, gardens, ships, prisons, honeymoon trips and boarding schools – he suggested that what these all had in common was 'the curious property of being in relation with all the other sites, but in such a way as to suspect, neutralise or invert the set of relations that they happen to designate, mirror, or reflect' (24).

In his brief notes (just five or six pages long), Foucault proposed six 'principles' for the systematic description of 'heterotopology'. For reasons of space, we cannot describe each of these principles in detail. A very brief interpretation of the principles, which are themselves no more than sketches, is that heterotopias share the following characteristics: they occur in all cultures; they have precise, historically determined, but changing cultural functions; they juxtapose 'in a single real place' several sites 'that are themselves incompatible' (25); they have a temporal dimension insofar as they include 'slices of time' or 'heterochronies' which are themselves structured as 'absolute breaks in traditional time' (26); they are separated off from other places and spaces insofar as entry to heterotopias is a forced, or mediated process that entails the crossing of a discrete boundary; and finally, they 'have a function in relation to all the space that remains': '[e]ither their role is to create a space of illusion that exposes every real space, as the sites inside of which human life is partitioned, as still more illusory' or 'on the contrary, their role is to create a space that is other, another real space, as perfect, as meticulous, as well arranged as ours is messy, ill constructed, and jumbled' (27).

الى أجمل حبيبين....
ديانا ، ودودي
We miss you
From: H.D.R.W.N
KhaliD and Dr
EmaD, Dr. Ismail
DOHA_QATAR

As suggested earlier, Foucault's lecture notes were never reviewed for publication, and doubtless there was a good reason for this. However, the concept enjoyed something of a renaissance in Cultural Studies in the late 1980s and in the 1990s. As early as 1989 some scholars noted problems in the formulation of the concept. Benjamin Genocchio (1995) has summarized what he regards as the main problems: there is, firstly, a 'coherency problem'. Paraphrasing Noel Gray's critique, Genocchio suggests that Foucault (1984) failed to differentiate heterotopias sufficiently clearly. If heterotopias are both 'outside of' and 'inside of' society, then criteria have to be drawn up that clarify the nature of their difference. Secondly, there is what we can describe as the paradox of naming – a point made by Genocchio, and earlier by Steven Connor (1989). In Genocchio's words, 'in any attempt to mobilize the category of an outside or absolutely differentiated space, it follows logically that the simple naming or theoretical recognition of that difference always to some degree flattens or precludes, by definition, the very possibility of its arrival as such' (39). This critique holds for both accounts of heterotopia, but especially for the one that appeared in the preface of *The Order of Things*, insofar as this account emphasizes the otherness alluded to by Borges.

On the basis of these two 'problems', Genocchio criticizes any literal applications of the concept. 'Scouring the absolute limits of imagination', he says, 'the question then becomes: what cannot be designated a heterotopia? It follows that the bulk of these uncritical applications of the term as a discontinuous space of impartial/resistant use must be viewed as problematic' (39).

In our view, the second of these problems is the less substantial one. Just as it can be argued that any utterance begins to reify the world, so any scholar can be accused of normalizing so-called 'absolute' otherness. On the other hand, it is true that very little in the modern world seems *not* to be heterotopic in nature. In our theory, we thus make a distinction between the noun ('heterotopia', properly speaking), the adjective ('heterotopic'), and, departing quite substantially from Foucault insofar as we introduce what is in effect a heterotopic *subject*, the verb: *to heterotopicalize.* Heterotopic sites are sites which suggest some of the 'functions' mentioned by Foucault, and certain institutions or popular practices may *heterotopicalize* sites by transforming them into heterotopic spaces, or even 'actual' heterotopias. Of course, nothing makes a site *essentially* heterotopic; and with Hetherington (1998) we assume that the 'dissonance' or incompatibility suggested in the first instance by a 'heterotopia' may eventually become the 'normality' of a new order.

In our view, Diana's crash itself was not so much a heterotopia, as a *heterotopic* site. Although it did not have a discrete boundary, and it certainly was never 'designed' to bring together all possible sites relating to Diana, it can be described as exhibiting a number of heterotopic features. First, it did have a location in reality, even if it is now no more than so many infinitesimal droplets of blood and fragments of shattered glass lying next to pillar 13. Second, in the days that followed the first 'actual' collision, the crash became an extraordinary profusion of spaces, a new set, as it were, of juxtapositions. These were not collected from one single location (although we will argue below that this was true in some respects of the shrine outside of Kensington Palace) but from a multiplicity of *mass mediated* sites: Diana's crash, as represented in

news print and television, was transformed into a proliferation of mass mediated *narratives* which themselves seemed to incorporate all other narratives, and through these, all other sites: narratives about where Diana and Dodi had been, and where they *might* have been had the crash not occurred; about where the rest of the Royal family was before, during and after the crash; about the hospital, the investigation, official responses around the world … and of course the narratives which many people spun in response to *those* narratives: where were *you* when Diana crashed? The original site of Diana's crash, like the original site of all major crashes covered by the mass media, almost instantly seemed to become all other 'real' sites. It was *made* heterotopic – it was *heterotopicalized* by the mass mediated coverage to the extent that this coverage instantly linked it to what seemed like all other worlds.

Admittedly, this *topos* is somewhat different from the one that Foucault described. Although Foucault does suggest that the cinema is an example of heterotopia, his essay does not refer directly to the many changes in the experience of space that have been both produced, and reproduced by mass mediation – changes described by some in terms of globalisation, or in terms of 'space-time compression' (Harvey 1989) and 'mediazation' (Thompson 1990). Harvey (1989) dismisses the 'idealism' of the concept of heterotopia, and Lefebvre (1974) goes so far as to accuse Foucault of failing to theorize 'space itself'. Even so, we believe that the concept of heterotopia provides a way of explaining a fundamental dimension of these changes. During events like Diana's crash, the mass media *heterotopicalise* culture. In the days that followed Diana's death, it seemed that few people – few worlds – did not travel, in body or by image, to the Pont d'Alma, to Buckingham Palace, to the shrine outside Kensington Palace, to the Ritz Hotel. It would seem in this sense that the process of mass mediation has the capacity to assemble all places in a simulacrum of co-spatiality. From this perspective, we can suggest that so-called 'media events' are in fact signs of the heterotopicality of *modern culture* in the late twentieth century. The mass media in particular play a fundamental role in an epoch which, as Foucault explains, is one of 'simultaneity', 'of juxtaposition', 'the epoch of the near and far, of the side-by-side, of the dispersed' (1986: 22), one in which 'space takes for us the form of relations among sites' (1986: 23).

If we use the notion of simulacrum, it is because the way in which the juxtaposition of space occurs is complex and is as creative as it is reflective. Homi Bhabha (1998) notes how the mourning for Diana frequently took for granted a nearness to her: *we felt we knew Diana, she was part of the family, we lost a loved one*. He interprets this with reference to the work of Claude Lefort, who suggests that mass media representations constitute the paradigmatic example of new ideological formations insofar as they *collapse* social distances by creating a sense of *'entre-nous'*: in Lefort's words, an 'incantation of *familiarity*', a 'hallucination of *nearness* which abolishes a sense of distance, strangeness, imperceptibility, the signs of the outside, of adversity, of otherness' (1986: 228, emphases in the original). It can be argued that so many different spaces – so many different people – are brought together by mass mediation because an enormous social distance *remains*. Governmentality in modern democracies is about shaping, moulding, mobilising but also *limiting* this heterogeneity; and one manner of

WILLIAM
H.R.H PRINCE
When
Someone
You Love
GOD'S
OFFER
is expiring

doing so is by way of the sense of *entre-nous* that the mass media generate after major crashes, disasters, deaths and other phenomena. By means of a variety of procedures – informal talk between TV and radio presenters, 'fly-on-the-wall' and 'wall to wall' coverage of events, but at times simply by 'being there' – the mass media produce a sense of proximity where there is distance, 'sameness' where there is alterity. Coverage of Diana's death was an instance of this process; a member of the aristocracy suddenly became the princess that everyone felt they knew, that everyone seemed to be weeping for, in Tony Blair's now famous words, *the people's princess.*

We are not suggesting that Diana's crash, as a heterotopic space, became a simple space for containment: as Foucault explained, heterotopias are 'counter-spaces', spaces outside of all spaces, spaces which can provide the kernel for subversion. To be sure, most contemporary theorists have emphasized the 'marginal' dimension of Foucault's concept, despite the fact that his examples in *Des Espaces Autres,* unlike his broader work, do not seem to authorize the privileging of 'resistant' spaces. But certainly Diana's crash, as heterotopic space, can clearly be regarded as such a space. The first signs of this emerged when the spotlight of blame was switched on and focused in succession on the paparazzi, on the tabloids, and on the readers of the tabloids. Although the spotlight was ultimately allowed to rest on Henri Paul, many analyses quickly spiralled into far more complex and all-encompassing debates about the role of the media and even the monarchy in British society. This happened partly because Diana was arguably 'the celebrity of celebrities', and indeed, this is one reason why her death was the point of origin of new narratives that were instantly communicated by reporters covering the crash to publics around the globe. But it is also true that Diana the royal celebrity inhabited an ambiguous space, and this is one of the reasons why her death in a car crash had the potential for subversion. She was what with Edith and Victor Turner (1978) we might describe as a 'liminal' royal: at the time of her death she was a royal both literally and figuratively in transit. Her liminality had to do with the circumstances of her struggle, a struggle which was about retaining and enhancing her own form of royalism, about attempting to shift the Royal family from traditional conservatism to neo-conservatism, from traditional patriarchy to the kind of 'neo-feminism' advocated by the most progressive sectors of neo-conservatism: 'women *should* have a role'.

These changes were related to transformations in the social *visibility* of the Royal family. In order to maintain an appearance of social legitimacy, 'old' monarchy, as represented by 19th and early 20th century British monarchs, did not need to be *seen* to be virtuous. Its power rested partly on its capacity to generate and police boundaries which *prevented* visibility, and which thereby guaranteed virtuosity, or the presumption thereof. Here the rule was: less visibility equals more power. This is what the British press described in the aftermath of Diana's crash as the 'distant', 'remote' and 'outdated' monarchy. In contrast, Diana sought to acquire social legitimacy by shifting the boundaries in order to make public, or rather to *appear* to make public, more and more of the monarchy's everyday life. Here the admittedly hazardous rule was: the appearance of less distance is equal to more *entre-nous.* Diana, as a mass media-constructed, but also as a self-constructed icon, both produced and reproduced an era of unprecedented visual, verbal, and emotional awareness: both consciously and

unselfconsciously, she seemed to bring light – the light of flashing strobes – to the mustiest corners of the royal household. This left its members with a changed picture of themselves and the institution they claimed to represent.

As if to underscore the difference, Diana died precisely at a time when her relationship with Dodi Al Fayed seemed to be giving her *happiness*. But Dodi was Muslim and black; in a nation that would only begin to recognise 'institutional racism' in the last year of the millennium, this added to the liminality of Diana, to the ambiguity of the moment. Diana's power was, from this perspective, her capacity to create, apparently single-handedly but actually as the embodiment of a much broader social process, a moment of liminality for the Windsors themselves. The Windsor version of the Victorian myth of the virtuous family lay in tatters; in the wake of Diana's battle for the soul of the monarchy, what would emerge?

If Diana occupied an ambiguous space in relation to the monarchy, she was also ambiguous in relation to changes in party politics in Great Britain. She died a year after Tony Blair had been elected Prime Minister, and, like Tony Blair, she represented herself as a symbol of a *caring* Great Britain. But in the wake of the Ecclestone affair, her death, like tobacco stains in what then seemed like the freshest of political smiles, seemed like a portent that all goodness might well be dying, even in the society of *entre-nous*. In this sense Diana's death provided many with a metaphor with which to mark the death of 'old caringness', the welfare state. This was paradoxical because Diana was the embodiment of what New Labour was representing as the *alternative* to the welfare state: the ideal of a *charitable* society – a Victorian politics which the New Labour party especially was using to dismantle (and to this day continues to use to dismantle) what remained of the welfare state. Indeed, whereas New Labour had arguably been elected on the basis of promises to curb the neo-liberalism of what seemed like a century of Tory governments, for many constituencies, Diana's death came at a time when it seemed that the totalitarianism of market discourses would, if anything, be extended. Here we use the term 'totalitarianism' as Lefort does, not to refer to a form of dictatorship, but to 'a form of society', a form in which 'all activities are immediately linked to one another, deliberately presented as modalities of a single world', one in which 'a system of values predominates absolutely, such that every individual or collective undertaking must necessarily find in it a coefficient of reality' and this in such a way that the social form 'exercises a total physical and spiritual constraint on the behaviour of private individuals' (1986: 79). Diana seemed to be one of few voices that spoke out against the 'uncaringness' of the post-cold-war totalitarianism, even if she was, or would be transformed by Tony Blair into, its very ambassador.

From heterochrony to anachrony

Foucault's analysis of heterotopia privileges space. In our view, this is both the strength, and the major weakness of his articulation. Heterotopia, and by extension 'heterotopology' must be as much about space, as it is about time. A critique of historicism must now be critiqued for its 'spatialism'. To be sure, Foucault does begin to recognise the importance of time by coining, and briefly defining the concept of *heterochrony*:

> Heterotopias are most often linked to slices of time – which is to say that they open onto what might be termed, for the sake of symmetry, heterochronies. The heterotopia begins to function at full capacity when men [sic] arrive at a sort of absolute break with their traditional time.
>
> (1986: 26)

According to Foucault, there are heterotopias, as in the case of the museum, which are premised on a concept of indefinitely accumulating time, but there are also heterotopias such as the carnival or the fairground which are linked to time 'in its most fleeting, transitory, precarious aspect, to time in the mode of the festival. These heterotopias are not oriented toward the eternal, they are rather absolutely temporal [chroniques]' (1986: 26).

In certain cases the two forms co-exist in one place. This happened in both the media coverage of Diana's crash, and in the shrines to Diana that appeared most notably in front of Kensington Palace. Both the media coverage and shrines were museum-like. As with a museum, the mass media coverage of Diana's death was an instance of an extraordinary accumulation of time. This aspect can be thought of as a kind of biographical archive. Magazines, newspapers and television reports provided multiple periodizations of Diana's life. The different headlines gave her date of birth and death, with interior sections that provided accounts of the different stages of her life. The periodizations then reappeared in the shrines: press images of Diana when she was a child, when she was a young woman, when she married, when she had the romance with Dodi.

But both the media coverage and the shrines were also very much like the fairground: the representations, in the written and time-based press, but most obviously in their reincarnations in the shrines, were extraordinarily fleeting. The tons of print generated about Diana's death seemed to vanish into the rhythms of everyday life almost as soon as they were circulated. Less than a month after their publication, the newspapers had begun to yellow, the television programmes had been forgotten, the links in the websites had been lost, and the extraordinary accumulation of artifacts had long since been removed from Kensington Gardens. This despite the efforts of the shrinemakers to frame, encase, wrap, box, and cover their offerings, mass media and other, with plastic. In the end, it was not 'the elements' that should have worried the people; leading residents of Kensington opposed the creation of anything like a permanent memorial in the gardens, and all that could be achieved was a walkway. Perhaps this was appropriate inasmuch as it suggested that remembering Diana would, henceforth, be a matter of crossing space, and not creating it.

The co-existence of different temporal forms suggests the simultaneity of different cultural times, and we would argue that just as heterotopias bring together multiple spaces in one place, they also bring together *multiple times.* Just as heterotopias both are and are not of their social spaces, they are and are not of their times. As part of this process, we are particularly interested in the way that Diana's crash was both the result of, and itself generated practices which were *anachronistic.* An anachronism is generally defined as something which is 'out of place' – perhaps we should say out of time – from the perspective of chronology. In this sense anachrony is generally understood as an 'error' of chronology, as something which is outdated. We understand it as a

DIANA
HUNTED &
HOUNDED.
NOW FREE!
SPEECH
WAS

simultaneity of cultural times which can somehow be judged to be contradictory, 'incompatible', or simply different. This is not to imply that a culture *ought* to be of one time, or that one time *completely* dominates it as seems to be suggested by Lefort's definition of totalitarianism; on the contrary, it is to underline the temporal discontinuity that is as much a part of culture as is continuity.

Diana's crash, and the heterotopic sites it generated juxtaposed times partly because Diana herself was 'anachronistic'. Many would say that the idea of a monarchy in modern culture is anachronistic. Republicanism seems to 'go' with modernity in a way that royalism does not. But from a different perspective and for reasons we have already presented, we could equally argue that Diana was anachronistic with respect to the Royal family. Whatever the case, in this essay we are particularly interested in the anachronies associated with fatal crashes. A fatal crash immediately produces the most fundamental of anachronies, a juxtaposition between the times of life and the times of death, not just as Foucault puts it 'an absolute break with *traditional* time', but rather, an absolute break in *time*. There are many reasons for this; in modern culture, life does not 'go' with death. Although the last century has witnessed the emergence of 'crash detectives', whose role it is to bring death by crash back into the living death of numbers, this is by no means a pervasive discourse in the everyday life contexts of the vast majority of people. Even in many crashes where there is no fatality, everyday experience of crashes makes them *évènements* in the strongest sense of the word: they bring everyday life to an abrupt stop, they are cemeteries of everyday temporality.

This in turn suggests another anachronism: it is remarkable that crashes should remain such important events in a global car culture that is crashing every minute of the day (Faith 1997). Indeed in the early and not so early days of car culture, the car industry regarded car crashes as being so extraordinary that they did not exist: there were no crashes, there were *accidents.* Whereas in contemporary investigative discourse crash-investigators emphasise that a crash is never accidental, until recently crashes were regarded as being *purely* accidental. Car manufacturers did not make cars 'crash-worthy' because if one drove properly, one did – should – not crash.

At the beginning of the twenty-first century we seem to be moving to the other discursive extreme, as illustrated by Mercedes-Benz's concept of 'crash compatibility':

> Mercedes-Benz engineers understand that vehicles don't just crash into laboratory barriers and brick walls. In the real world, there are are [sic] both larger and smaller vehicles with vastly differing ways of managing impact energy. So our engineers design vehicles with a concept in mind called 'crash compatibility'.
>
> (Mercedes-Benz 1999)

This discourse opens up a panorama in which car crashes might either cease completely, or cease to be *évènements*, a fairground-world where people in cars deliberately bump into each other for the fun of it, or, more radically, a world in which such attractions cease to make sense: funny cars are funny because real cars aren't. This world would nonetheless still have to cope with a dilemma: cars are, in principle at least, meant to transport human bodies, and bodies, from the engineering perspective,

Diana 1961-1997
SUMMERTOWN STARS
FOOTBALL CLUB
A SHINING LIGHT ON EARTH,
A BRILLIANT STAR IN HEAVEN,
GOD BLESS YOU PRINCESS DIANA.
YOU WILL NEVER BE FORGOTTEN.

manage impact energy poorly. Diana, like all the victims of car crashes, was herself not 'crash compatible'. If it is true that she was not wearing her seatbelt, then perhaps Mercedes might argue that an emergency seatbelt retraction system might have saved her. But even this might not have prevented the *displacement* of Diana's internal organs, the collapsing of the distances *within Diana's own body*. In the last moment – in the first space – the body could not itself be engineered, could not itself resist the ultimate effect, the most lethal form, of *entre-nous*. Diana's body had become, perhaps like all bodies in the late twentieth century, a travelling anachronism.

The hereafter

It is tempting to speak of the space and time of the car crash – and in this case, what we might call a *media crash*, that is, a crash 'induced' by the mass media – in the strongest of causal terms. But a media crash also produces practices which cannot be analysed in terms of such crude models. We have already noted the heterotopic nature of the media coverage of the crash. But even as this heterotopic practice developed, another was in the making which was perhaps even more charged with anachronism. This was the shrine outside Kensington Palace. Initially we understand a shrine as a place or object hallowed by its associations. A place that acquires significance because of the material and symbolic links that it makes possible to establish. For a few people at first and many others later, the gardens of Kensington Palace became the place where they could most closely associate with Diana after her death. This was perhaps because the shrine was located, like Diana herself, in an ambiguous space: Kensington Palace was simultaneously of a place of belonging, and of disavowal.

But we also understand the modern shrine as an association hallowed by an extraordinary proliferation of spaces. In this sense the shrine was clearly heterotopic in Foucault's sense of the term: it provided a venue where a multiplicity of real sites could be simultaneously represented. The tributes left for Diana gave an insight into the worlds of the shrinemakers: teddy bears, Arsenal T-shirts, tourist guides of London, messages written in Welsh, American and Colombian flags, a prayer by St Francis of Assisi, framed paintings of Diana done in pencil and other materials, extraordinarily personal letters and handmade cards, baby shoes, saris, comic books, old dolls, crucifixes, plastic crowns, mobiles (one with shells in which each shell had a name written in it), and a printed leaflet that used the text of an advertisement title – 'God's offer is expiring'. Like Foucault's quote of Borges' reference to a 'Chinese encyclopaedia' in the preface to *The Order of Things*, the objects in this list constituted a surprising taxonomy of objects apparently incongruous not only with the site in which they were placed, but also with the occasion: the ritual of mourning a royal.

But the shrine also was the embodiment of explicit counter-space insofar as it was the site of political inversion and contestation. Many people left tributes which pinned the blame for Diana's death on the paparazzi, the press in general, the Royal family, or simply an undefined 'them'. Others left tributes with references the destructiveness of hunting, calls for the banning of land-mines, abolishing the Royal family, investing in AIDS research, and rejoining the path of God. Still others left messages, cards, images, and objects which turned the world upside-down by giving Diana her royal title back,

appointing her a queen and Dodi a king, returning Diana's crown and declaring her 'more royal than the royals'. Her life story was rewritten in equal measure as a fairy tale and as a tragedy. The outcome of this narrative was, until recently, never seriously in dispute: Diana died having found total happiness, a happiness that was pointedly contrasted with the pain she suffered while still Charles' partner.

These aspects clearly make the shrine 'heterotopic'. But this practice was *itself* heterotopicalised by the news media. Although the shrine took shape slowly at first and the media only mentioned it in passing, it gradually grew in size and importance, to the point where it became a subject of extensive news coverage in its own right. As it grew it generated a dialectic whereby its size prompted more news media coverage which in turn increased the number of tributes and this generated even more coverage. The mass media arguably contributed to a process that transformed the shrine into a 'full' heterotopia. Yet for its extraordinary magnitude, each offering, each tribute was couched in completely personal terms, in terms of *entre-nous*.

This is not to agree with analyses such as Ghosh's (1998) which oppose the 'immediacy' of the mass-observer as true 'participant' with 'vicarious' and 'mediated' mourning. Ghosh's formulation does not seem to have an awareness of critiques of realist conceptions of participant observation, let alone critiques of realist conceptions of authenticity. And although we agree with Couldry (1999) when he suggests that this and other shrines in London were a testament of a 'lack' or 'exclusion', we do not believe that the shrines were a form of communication that occurred *beyond* mass mediation. If we also use the work of Michel de Certeau (1984), it is to suggest that many if not most forms of communication in and via the 'shrine' were neither entirely 'induced by' nor 'beyond' mass mediation. They were *tactical* in the sense that de Certeau uses the term: they were practices that circulated in and amongst dominant categories, practices which were neither simply the product of, nor simply *not* the product of the work of the mass media.

This point can be illustrated with the many tributes that were assembled using images published by newspapers and magazines. The shrine outside Kensington Palace was an ensemble of ensembles which tended to represent either a particular moment in Diana's life (especially widespread were photographs that pictured her with Dodi) or a history echoing the periodization offered by the media, with key events added to, or deleted from the chronologies provided by the news media (for example, pictorial 'histories' of Diana which at times blithely excluded her marriage to Prince Charles). Insofar as the tributes used existing mass media representations, they were clearly in the aegis of media discourses. However, the tributes could not be *reduced* to the logics of the mass media insofar as the *second-hand* signs were used to create at least partially *new* signs, expressions which in many cases gave meanings to the 'old' signs in ways that contested or inverted the discourses of the first contexts.

The 'original' tributes left for Diana in Kensington Gardens were taken away years ago, and even the new tributes that appear with each anniversary are swept away by the park authorities. And it seems that with every year that passes, Diana's opponents find more and more subtle ways of undermining her 'image'. This seems to be in keeping with de Certeau's suggestion that the strategies (of the powerful) are *'the*

triumph of place over time', 'the mastery of time through the foundation of an autonomous place' (1984: 36, emphasis in the original); and that in contrast, the tactical practices (of the weak) are 'procedures that gain validity in relation to the pertinence they lend to time – to the circumstances which the precise instant of an intervention transforms into a favourable situation …' (1984: 38). From this perspective – and indeed from Foucault's – the keys are *space and place*; the shrinemakers engaged in an opportunistic practice which seized the space and place of the powerful, but only for a historical moment; in the end, the space was recuperated by powerful institutions.

And yet … can the space-time relation not be read in exactly the *opposite* way? As both *space* and *place*, the gardens in front of Kensington Palace *were* comprehensively reorganised and re-articulated by what seemed like a million flowers and cellophane wrappers. However, it was only *in time* that the ensemble of ensembles was removed by park authorities (the non-organic parts allegedly to be classified and stored as Diana *memorabilia* in some undisclosed location). Conversely, it was *in time* that the gardens came to be *overcoded* as the place where the shrine had been. From this perspective, the privileging of space over time seems inappropriate: as de Certeau himself suggests, any given practice is necessarily a space-time matrix constructed by trajectories that are ineluctably relative – relative to each other – but we would add, relative to the relativity of the relation between social space and time: metaphors of space and time, like practices in space and over time, cannot be but 'mixed'. It is tempting from this perspective to suggest that there are the spaces and *times* of the dominating, and the times and *spaces* of the dominated. It is in this sense more meaningful, if also more awkward, to say that there are the *circumscribing* spaces of the dominating, and the *circumscribed* spaces of the dominated, just as there is the *momentarized* time of the dominated, and the *momentarizing* time of the dominant. Any individual's trajectory –and not just the tactical – is constituted by, and indeed circulates 'in between' – these twin dialectics.

To be sure, even as the tributes remained only 'for a time', many of them made references to the eternal. Again, this was a heterotopic practice that mixed Foucault's temporal categories: it was as much about fleeting representation, as it was about the representation of perpetuity: wings, birds in flight, printed angels and blue skies were part of many tributes where references to heaven, the hereafter, eternal happiness, freedom at last, images of virgins (some of them black), wooden and metal crosses, incense and candles, prayers and religious songs. These and the shrine as a whole were considered to be so anachronistic (in the traditional sense of the term) that many observers spoke of a return to Roman Catholicism. In many cases the tributes clearly *were* an expression of a Roman Catholic iconicity and, more than a 'return', were a reminder if any was needed of the multiculturality of London. But our own interpretation is that in many other cases, the representations constituted a metaphysical turn which must be interpreted in relation to what we described earlier as the totalitarianism of the marketplace. For all their market metaphysics, for all their efforts to co-opt all worlds, both real and possible, modern institutions have no meaningful discourse about death. It seems that when a celebrity dies in a crash, the death and its 'accidental' nature opens up, if only for a fleeting moment, the portals to a 'beyond', a *beyond Modernity* which can only be represented by recourse to an iconography which may seem anachronistic to some observers, but which actually activates the signs of constellations whose subjects were and to this day continue to be far more familiar with the otherness of death. These constellations may be called Catholic or medieval, but they may also be the recognition of a fundamental otherness which the new totalitarianism may perhaps never colonise.

From this perspective, what was so easily written off as the 'sentimentality' of the 'lament' for Diana can be interpreted as an effort to say what, thanks to the 'mundanity' of their own transcendentalism, most dominant institutions of modern culture prohibit us from saying: that death marks a boundary beyond which there is something which cannot be expressed or simply contained even within the constantly shifting boundaries of heterotopic practice. To dismiss the iconography of the crash on the grounds of a media-generated soap opera is to forget that all *poiesis* has the capacity to evoke metaphysical flights. In this sense, even as we say from the perspective of de Certeau that there is no such thing as a dead metaphor – even the most 'common' of metaphors can give, and be given new *life* – Paul Ricoeur rightly speaks of a 'non-semantic' moment of *symbols*, a moment that 'resists any linguistic, semantic or logical transcription', one that 'hesitates on the dividing line between *bios* and *logos*' and thereby testifies to the 'primordial rootedness of Discourse in Life' (1976: 57–59, emphases in the original). From this perspective, the shrine was a reminder of anachronism, in our sense of the term: the quasi-Catholic, but not quasi-metaphysical representations were a tacit critique of one of the main superstitions associated with Modernity, a superstition according to which there is no life after death.

* * *

Diana was apparently not wearing her seatbelt (does a princess *ever* wear a seatbelt?) at the time of the crash, and presumably she hit the back of Trevor Reese-Jones' seat. But even if she *had* been wearing a seatbelt, and even if emergency seatbelt tensioning retractors had fired pyrotechnic charges, they might not have prevented that final, and arguably most severe of collisions: the one between Diana's heart and the walls of her thoracic cavity, the one that ruptured her left pulmonary vein and produced a cardiac arrest, the one that became itself a charge which, for a moment at least, took the slack out of the British monarchy and revealed the dangers of the most extreme forms of co-spatiality and co-temporality.

Diana not only died in displacement, she was killed *by* displacement. Hers was the most modern of deaths, and it is appropriate that during the TV coverage of her funeral, the last images were of Diana's coffin being driven to eternity in a car that was covered in flowers.

References

Bhabha, H. (1998) 'Designer Creations' in M. Merck (ed.) *After Diana: Irreverent Elegies*, London: Verso, 103–110.

Connor, S. (1989) *Postmodernist Culture: an Introduction to Theories of the Contemporary*. Oxford: Blackwell.

Couldry, N. (1999) 'Remembering Diana: The Geography of Celebrity and the Politics of Lack', in *New Formations*, No. 36, 77–91.

Faith, N. (1997) *Crash: The Limits of Car Safety*. London: Boxtree.

Foucault, M. (1970) *The Order of Things*. London: Tavistock.

Foucault, M. (1986) 'Of Other Spaces', in *Diacritics*, Vol. 16, Spring, 22– 27.

Genocchio, B. (1995) 'Discourse, discontinuity, difference: the question of 'Other' spaces', in S. Watson and K. Gibson (eds.) *Postmodern Cities and Spaces*. Oxford: Blackwell, 35–46.

Ghosh, p. (1998) 'Mediate and Immediate Mourning', in M. Merck (ed.) *After Diana: Irreverent Elegies*, London: Verso, 41–48.

Grey, N. (1995) Unpublished manuscript cited by B. Genocchio (1995) in 'Discourse, discontinuity, difference: the question of 'Other' spaces', in S. Watson and K. Gibson (eds.) *Postmodern Cities and Spaces*. Oxford: Blackwell, 35–46.

Harvey, D. (1989) *The Condition of Postmodernity*. Oxford: Blackwell.

Hetherington, K. (1998) *Expressions of Identity*. London: Sage.

Lefort, C. (1986) 'Outline of the Genesis of Ideology in Modern Societies' in J.B. Thompson (ed.) Claude Lefort: *The Political Forms of Modern Society*. Cambridge: Polity Press.

Mercedes-Benz (1999) http: //www.usa.mercedes-benz.com/security/crash.html.

Ricoeur, P. (1976) *Interpretation Theory: Discourse and the Surplus of Meaning*. Fort Worth: Texas Christian University.

Thompson, J.B. (1990) *Ideology and Modern Culture*. Cambridge: Polity Press.

Turner, V. & Turner, E. (1978) *Image and Pilgrimage in Christian Culture*. New York: Columbia University Press.

14 Fuel, Metal, Air: The Appearances and Disappearances of Amelia Earhart

Story by Michelle Henning

Images/text by Rebecca Goddard

I follow
tar paint
earth and sun
and watch my hands guided by someone else's

It was a white, one story building which opened directly onto the sidewalk. Behind it, a cyclone fence surrounded a small patch of crab grass and a thirsty-looking orange tree. Part of the lawn was taken up by a wood and chicken wire contraption. Inside were two tortoises. They came with the lease.

My secretary Josie and I had been at the new premises a week. It was a hot July morning and I sat among the U-Haul boxes, willing my phone to ring. When it did, my hand was on the receiver quicker than a cat swats a fly, but I held it there a moment, let it ring a couple of times before picking it up. A bright, young-sounding woman's voice inquired if I was open for business.

'What kind of business?' As if I could afford to be picky.

'Some property of mine has been taken. I want it back'

I figured she was talking about blackmail. 'How much do they want?'

'Oh.' The voice sounded surprised. 'It's not what you think. He's looking for… well, a missing person, and he thinks I'm her, he thinks he can make me come clean'.

'You've spoken to him?'

'I've met him. His name is Gervais'.

'Who does he think you are?'

She paused, then said 'Amelia Earhart'

my road and sky are ghost-littered with wrecks
who are road signs
with what a sense of direction

the site of eight unmarked graves excavated near old Garapan cemetry Saipan on the 63 expedition

I laughed. Earhart disappeared back in '37. That's twenty eight years ago. When a person's been missing that long it's time to close the case. I told her to come on over, and hung up.

Earhart. At the time it was big news. I even had a connection with the case. In '37 I was in the California Highway Patrol. and I was called to a head-on collision on the highway outside Fresno. The guy who caused it was an Irishman from Chicago named Fred Noonan. Turns out he was Earhart's navigator. Some navigator: the guy had been driving in the wrong lane and reeked of whisky. So, I predicted it, and sure enough, Earhart crashed a couple of months later. I could have made big money if it hadn't been a sick thing to bet on.

I told Josie about the call. She was silent for a moment and then said, 'What do you know about her?'

'Amelia Earhart?'

'Uh huh'

'Well, she was married to a publisher promoter guy called Putnam. She crashed her plane during the last leg of her round the world flight in 1937. They searched the

could be explained by death drive;
always needing joy rides
but always finding death rides
I have a joy-death drive

photograph of campfire found in Japanese officers house 1944, said to have been taken on Mili Atoll, Marshall Islands, July 13th ,1937

Pacific but found nothing. In the end they figured she and her navigator drowned in the ocean.'

'What did you think about that Chamorro woman?'

'Chamorro?'

'Yeah, Saipanese. In the news four–five years ago. Says that when she was a little girl she was at Saipan harbor and saw two American fliers, man and a woman, off a plane that crashed. She said the man had hurt his head and Japanese soldiers took them away.'

'Japanese?'

'There was a Japanese Navy base there.'

Similar stories had circulated during the forties. They claimed Earhart was a government spy shot down and captured by the Japs. Basic anti-Jap propaganda. I figured Josie was testing me.

'It's an old conspiracy theory', I said, too slow to sound as dismissive as I intended.

She changed the subject. 'I'm gonna get those tortoises some leaves. If you don't need me…'

**that's like watching my fingers typing an obscenity
the thought shouted loud**

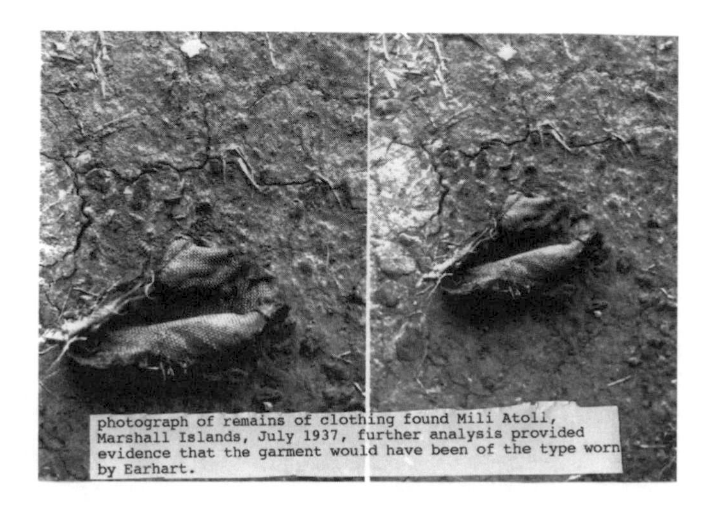

photograph of remains of clothing found Mili Atoli, Marshall Islands, July 1937, further analysis provided evidence that the garment would have been of the type worn by Earhart.

I shook my head. Josie planned conversation like a military strategist, always distrustful, always keeping me at arms length. She had her reasons. She'd spent the war in a 'relocation center' in Gila River, Arizona. Meanwhile, her cousin Iva was in Tokyo, being forced to broadcast propaganda to the US troops. When Iva got home she was tried for being Tokyo Rose, and jailed. Josie's family maintained that she wasn't the legendary seductress, but it made no difference. A Jap was a Jap.

Josie called herself Japanese American, and she was the best secretary I'd had, organized and immaculate. She wore pearl earrings and her hair was always polished and pulled smartly back. She could take a twelve hour bus journey and arrive looking like she'd just stepped out of the shower into freshly laundered clothes.

When the buzzer sounded, my appointment book was on the desk, the bourbon tucked away in its drawer, and the files arranged in the bookcase. Some flies had made the window sill their final resting place. I was folding them into my handkerchief when I realized that Josie was still out, and answered the door myself.

the thought the cause
that causes crashes
makes me want to go, vapourise with

I had expected a woman in her thirties. But Mrs Bolam was an impressive sixty something, dressed in a tobacco-brown slack suit that looked expensive but well-used. She was tall and slim, with a back as straight as a ruler. It crossed my mind that this Gervais had something. She did look like Earhart, or how you might imagine Earhart would have looked had she lived to collect her pension. The same high cheekbones and unruly hair I had seen in photographs. Mannish good looks, I thought. I recalled something else about Earhart. They called her Lady Lindy because she'd looked like a female version of Charles Lindbergh. I couldn't imagine this woman putting up with that kind of name-calling. She looked like someone toughened not by a hard life but by the strength of will it took to reject an easy one.

She took no notice of her surroundings but looked me over with eyes so clear and blue that I felt myself run a finger around the inside waistband of my pants to check my shirt was tucked in.

'You're older than I thought,' she said abruptly

'Touche' I said, but my left hand flew up to feel the thinning hair at the back of my head. 'Shall we skip the niceties and get straight to business?' I held out a chair for her.

'Gervais came to my house yesterday evening. He's an officer in the Air Force. Seemed like a very decent man, interested in the Amelia Earhart mystery'. She sat down tentatively on the arm of the chair. 'I knew her you see. We learned to fly around the same time'. She looked at me to gauge my reaction but I studiously displayed none. 'Anyhow, then he starts with this nonsense about me being Amelia. He actually thinks she survived and that I'm her. This morning I discovered something was missing.' She paused, and on cue I asked, 'something?'

'A photograph… in a brown manila envelope.'

'You want me to retrieve it.'

She nodded.

'What's it of?'

'It's of her,' she said, 'The envelope is marked A.E. '

'And that's all I've got to go on?'

'Yes' she said, fixing me with a hard stare as if to say any wisecracking I was about to do I might as well abandon. 'I'll pay you your normal hourly fee plus expenses.'

no weight,
just body in the sky, words in mid air
to feel weightless in vapour
she could predict them though

I took a pack of cigarettes from my jacket pocket and yanked one out with my teeth. She watched me in silence for a moment, and then her hand darted into her bag. 'He left this', she declared triumphantly, handing me a matchbook. On it was written Carlita's in looping tomato-red letters. I opened it, there were three pink tipped matches left. I tore one out and lit my cigarette. On the inside cover was scrawled the name 'Gardner' in ballpoint pen.

Josie was back by the time Mrs Bolam left. I had her look up Gervais in the phone book. She located a J. Gervais at 1640 Curson Avenue, between Sunset and Hollywood.

It was a white bungalow, with a sloping lawn of real, well-watered grass. I parked the Chevy on the opposite side of the street a few houses down. A large black four-door Oldsmobile was sat outside the house, its engine running. I poured myself a bourbon from the bottle I kept under the dash, lit a cigarette, and waited. After five minutes the front door opened and two Japanese men in dark suits came out of the house, shut the door behind themselves, walked down to the waiting car and drove off. I waited two more minutes for luck and then walked up to the house. The screen door was slightly open. I went through, and knocked on the inside door. When no-one replied, I pushed it gently. The lock had been broken, but there was no damage to the wood at all. A professional job.

The living room contained two leather armchairs, a large color TV in a dark wood cabinet and a HiFi. A nice set-up, if you've got that kind of money. Opposite the door was a walnut bureau, the contents of which had been emptied onto the polished wood floor. In the kitchen, cutlery was scattered over the linoleum, and in the bedroom, letters, books, cufflinks, were strewn across the otherwise neatly made bed. There was a ballpoint pen next to the telephone on the bedside cabinet. I got down onto my knees on the caramel colored carpet and felt under the bed. I pulled out what I was looking for, an ivory telephone pad. In it were jotted several names, some with phone numbers next to them, some underlined, some crossed out. I picked up the phone receiver, dialed my own office and read the list of names to Josie. Then I left the house closing the front door as well as I could.

Carlita's was a small bar on the edge of Watts. It was a colored joint. I didn't picture Gervais, a white military officer, hanging out here. I slipped my .38 into my

**he had planned some sudden deaths
except the chance**

Corroded Airplane parts recovered from Tanapag Harbor, Siapan, during the authors 1960 expedition.

pocket and braced myself for confrontation. I didn't have the effect I anticipated: the place went quiet, heads swivelled, but the conversation resumed again.

The barman was a skinny young Negro with a big ball of hair, wearing gold chains round his neck, and a bright green polyester shirt. He watched me warily, as if I'd come to deliver his draftcard.

'I'm looking for a man named Gervais,' I said.

'Never heard of him,' he said softly,

'What about a man named Gardner?'

'Him neither. You sure you don't want to speak to mister Jackson here?'

He motioned to a large, muscular man sat at the bar with skin the color of eggplant and big sad eyes so red-rimmed that it stung my own eyes just to look at him.

'The others all did. One of them was probably your man Gervais'.

'Most probably was', Jackson agreed. I ordered him a bourbon.

He took the drink and looked me over. 'Navy or Air Force? You don't look like a Marine.' Ex-marine. It figured. He looked fit.

'Neither .' I toyed with saying ex-cop, but thought better of it. 'I'm just conducting my own research. You say you spoke to Gervais ...'

of me and my doppelganger
ever meeting
and her image is still wet from the printer when I see

'Yeah, him and all the others', he said, 'Most of them Air Force and Navy, and one from a San Francisco radio station'. He thought for a moment 'You must be the sixth...',

Then he launched in to an account of how he fought in the battle of Saipan, when the US took Saipan from the Japs. Took a shell in the chest and still wondered how he survived it. He saw things in the Pacific that would keep him awake at night for the next twenty years, but the thing everyone was interested in was just a photograph he saw pinned to a wall in a house with a ribbon. Just before he got his chest blown off. Now everyone was asking him why he didn't pocket it. Only a few years ago had he realized the significance of that photo, after that Saipanese woman was in the Times, so he started mentioning it to people and pretty soon those white officers were wanting to hear his story so he met them here in this bar.

Those white officers. Five men investigating a crash that had happened before the war. It didn't make any sense to me. If I'd learned anything as a patrolman it was that the later you arrived at the scene of a crash the harder it was to piece together what had happened. In a crash you have basically two kinds of evidence. Here they had neither: no witnesses and no wreckage. But maybe they did have something...

'What was the photograph of?'

'It depicted Miss Amelia Earhart', he said in a tone of voice usually reserved for cross-examination in a witness box, 'standin' next to a Japanese soldier in a field.'

'What do you think happened to it?'

'Well sir, I guess it went the same way as a big chunk of me,' he said with a smile, and pulled up his shirt to reveal the leaf shaped crater that decorated his heavyweight torso.

I smiled back 'Nothing more you can tell me about Gervais?'

His mood changed in front of my eyes. I ordered us both another bourbon but he knocked his back in silence then said, 'He's the last one I spoke to – why do you want to know about him?'

The bourbon was making me feel mellow and warm. I liked this guy. I decided to come clean, 'I'm not interested in what happened to Amelia Earhart way back when, I'm mainly after this guy Gervais he has some stolen property.'

Radio direction finder recovered in September 1961 from Tanapag Harbor, Saipan. (Authors photograph)

myself
not searching for her as some are
I didn't mean to find her

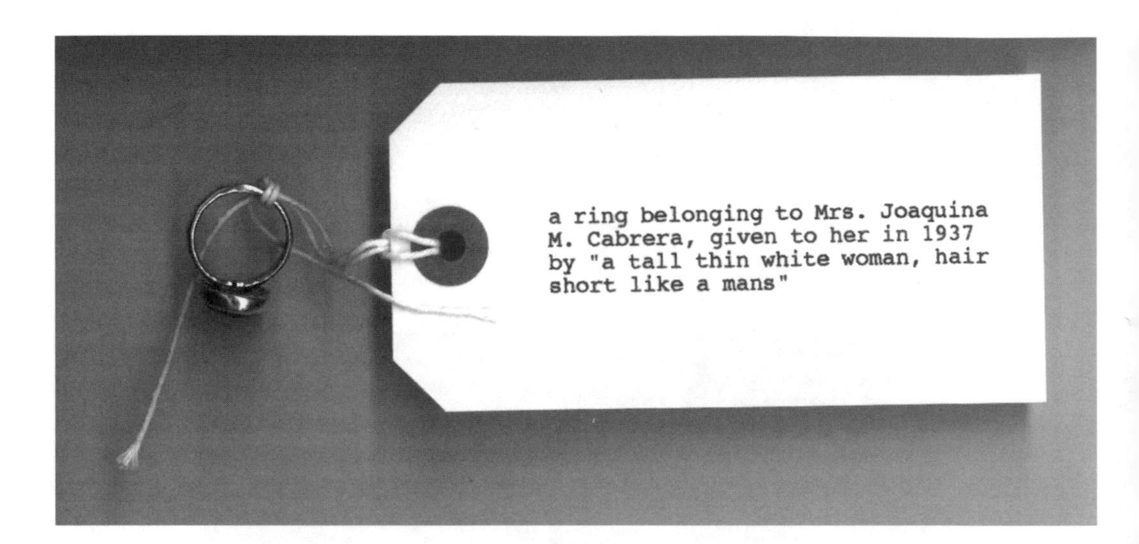

His face hardened, 'You're a cop.'

The bar fell suddenly quiet and I felt as if everyone was looking at my back, though I didn't feel like turning round to find out if I was right.

'No private investigator.'

I fumbled in my pocket for my card. It occurred to me too late that maybe I should be reaching into the other pocket where my .38 was nestling. Then my face exploded. My right eye was knocked back into its socket. The brass edge of the bar came up to meet my left ear, then a whack on the back socked the air out of my lungs.

I lay for a moment imagining myself in the big soft bed at Gervais's house and slowly opened my eyes hoping to see cream drapes and walnut dressing table. Instead, all I could make out was a mustard colored patch of ceiling. My left eye was blurred and my right eye refused to open at all. A pool of wet stuff had formed in the crevice between my nose and my upper lip. I tried to remember the name for that part of my anatomy but couldn't. I wondered idly if I had ever

but a chance find
a chance connection
shared by face and skin and the shape of our bones
she was lost without bones or earth bound things

known it. Then I saw a hand reaching down to pull me up. Jackson with his big sad eyes looked genuinely remorseful at the damage he'd inflicted.

'Cop or no cop. That's for not playing straight with me.'

When I walked in Josie stared at my swollen right eye but didn't comment. 'Two FBI men were here,' she said flatly. 'They wanted to know what you were doing at 1640 Curson avenue this afternoon.' She looked at me with vague concern but without curiosity. I wondered wnat it would take to surprise Josie.

They had been there to warn me off. Josie had palmed them off with some cock and bull story about a divorce case I'd been working on. I've been warned off cases by cops before, but this was my first brush with the FBI. All because of a photograph. It occurred to me that I was getting pulled in to something serious. Feds and Jap officials. It was pretty clear that this photograph could be embarrassing. We weren't at war with Japan till they attacked Pearl Harbor. So what were the government doing sending famous lady pilots for jaunts around the Pacific, getting lost over Pacific islands, where there just happened to be a Japanese Naval base? Or, alternatively, what was Japan doing capturing American civilians and possibly executing them before we were at war? With the situation in Vietnam, a little picture could do a lot of damage. Gervais was being hunted down, and not just by me.

Getting whacked earned me certain privileges. I got to inspect the sewing on Josie's blouse as she held an ice pack to my face and recited the details of the people listed on Gervais's phone pad. Two names interested me. Jackie Cochran, an extremely wealthy lady, famous pilot and one-time psychic, and Paul Mantz, stunt pilot extraordinaire who ran a company based at an airfield out in Orange County.

Josie had used family connections to find out more about Cochran. Her uncle had been Cochran's gardener. Back in the thirties they all had Jap gardeners. He remembered after Earhart's disappearance, the press swarmed like drones around Cochran's ranch in Indio as the queen bee used her psychic feelers to track Earhart and Noonan's movements in the Pacific . He gave Josie some newspaper cuttings showing that Earhart had joined Cochran in dabbling in telepathy and

but those things couldn't specify her sex
I think her hair grew long with her feet on the earth
and now there's sun on my dirty windscreen

clairvoyance. Even back then California was full of psychics, spiritualists and crystal-gazers who set themselves up in business pampering to the wives of tycoons and business magnates, jaded socialites whose lives were so empty they'd believe in anything, and even more so if they had to pay through the nose for it . But these women preferred to try it at home. Around Christmas '36 Earhart had phoned Western Air Express from Cochran's ranch, saying she'd had a vision in which a trapper had found the wreckage of an airplane belonging to them. Sure enough, some time later a trapper in Utah reported finding the wreck. Then a United Airlines flight went missing, and Earhart told them to look for the wreck at Saugas, where it was eventually found. Two weeks later another plane crashed and again Earhart told them where to search.

When Earhart disappeared, only a few months later, her husband Putnam called this Jackie Cochran and she came up with the goods, saying the plane had crashed into the ocean, that Noonan had smashed his head and blacked out and that Earhart was alive. Putnam pulled out all the stops, and Roosevelt himself

engineered around me like the rest of
my reliant machine
we're every moment entertaining imaginings

evidence of human settlement Mili Atoll, Marshall Islands, July 1937

authorized the Navy to comb the area. For two days the press camped out at her ranch , until finally Cochran made a statement that Earhart was dead, and she herself so traumatized that she vowed to never again publicly use her phony 'abilities'.

Old Putnam called off the search a year later, and had Earhart declared legally dead so he could get himself hitched again. A while later he had moved to an isolated lodge at Whitney Portal above the Owen's valley, and lived there until his death. The address rang a bell, though I couldn't recall why.

I was curious about Cochran, but not enough to want to test the security arrangements at her ranch in Indio. I had a hunch that Gervais wasn't going to turn up there, with a manila envelope stolen from another lady pilot in his hot little paw. I figured Cochran would think he was crazy, even by her loose standards. Paul Mantz looked a surer bet. Mantz had been Earhart's business partner but there were intimations of another kind of partnership between them too. Also, he was Earhart's technical advisor, yet she left for her world flight without waving goodbye, let alone consulting him. I figured he'd be sore about that. Of all people, Mantz would be most familiar with the detail surrounding Earhart's disappearance, and might be willing to talk to Gervais. He had a house out in Palm Springs and that was where I'd put Gervais.

of careless crashes
of dummy runs and trying outs
the in-jokes of technical diagrams

Earharts own collection of toy planes photographed with kind permission begun when she was a small girl. authors photograph. 1960

My head was feeling kind of furry. I took some leaves out to the tortoises and sat on the roof of their little hut. I lit a cigarette and studied the Carlita's matchbook. Gardner. Josie hadn't come up with anything on him. I thought about crashes. The weirdest time was a couple of years back when Cactus Jack Call died in a car crash, and then Patsy Cline, Cowboy Copas and Hawkshaw Hawkins were on their way to a concert in his memory when their plane crashed in Virginia and they were killed. Then a couple days later the singer, Jack Anglin, died in a car crash on his way to Patsy Cline's funeral. It was a clear sign that God didn't like country music.

The cigarette was making my head worse. I stubbed it out on the grass. I needed fresh air. I needed a trip to the desert.

A couple of hours later I was driving down the mountain from Idyllwild toward Palm Springs. I drove this way for sentimental reasons, I liked the contrast, the

of owners manuals
are all we need
once we've gone away

way you could be in pine forest one minute and turn a corner to see the desert spread out before you. I thought of George Palmer Putnam in his Whitney Portal Lodge, making a clean start with a new wife, looking down from his mountain with its icy streams and forest onto Owens Valley and beyond to the orange black rock of Death Valley. It came to me, suddenly, why I recognized the address. Years ago, when I was still on Highway Patrol, I heard of how the priest from Lone Pine had a stone lodge built on the mountainside. It took years to build, then, the day before he was due to move in, he drove his Packard straight into a rockface. The patrolman at the scene was so shook up he handed in his resignation. The lodge stood empty for years, I guess till old Putnam stumbled across it.

The warm mountain air smelt of pine and wild strawberries. Thin wispy clouds like sheeps wool caught on barbs released a few fat droplets of rain to clean the LA smog from my skin and clear my head. The pines became sparser and were replaced by stumpy cactuses and sage bushes, and a dusty soil dyed to soot by the shower.

I pulled over and got out for a stretch. The scent hit me as soon as I switched off the engine. It was a smell that could only exist in a moment after brief rainfall on hot soil, and only here where alpine meadows met the high desert. It made it hard to exhale. A couple of yards from the car was a large flat topped rock, and behind it the road curved steeply down the mountainside. Another more familiar smell attacked my lungs. The smell of oil and gasoline, of a recent narrow escape, as testified to by white paint marks on the rock and tread marks in the dirt. Someone took the corner too fast, and not long before I had pulled over . As I walked back to the Chevy it occurred to me that I'd have been sore if I'd scraped that boulder. I'd spent thirty bucks on a new paint job only a week ago.

It was almost dark by the time I arrived at Palm Springs. The wide palm-lined avenues were faintly lit by the picture windows of low lying modern houses. Come winter, the desert silence would be replaced with the swish of sprinklers on real grass, the purr of cadillacs and the hum of poolside conversation. Now, it was out of season and the town was quiet. Even so, nothing indicated that this was just another piece of desert. I always had the feeling that Palm Springs was even more a reaction against the desert than LA, its luxury tainted by its own fear that someday the desert would claim it back. Dust to dust.

away from home
past a runway to runaway

evidence of settlement, site of excavation old Garapan, Saipan, june 1944

Paul Mantz's place was dark. I left my car on the street and walked up the gravel track to the house. At the top of the track was a small light colored car. I shone my pen torch on it. It was a white '59 Austin Healy. A smart looking sports car with red leather seats. Some paint had been scraped off the right front fender. I put my hand on the hood and felt the warmth from the engine. Gervais. I must have been right behind him. I padded round the house, taking care not to tread on the gravel, until I found a glass sliding door. I slid it just open enough to step through sideways, and felt my feet sink into thick, soft carpet. I could just make out a big fireplace in the centre of the room, and a built-in bar. I was halfway across the room when a voice from behind me said 'Stop right there'.

Shit, he had been outside. I put my hand in my pocket to reach for my .38. Too late. I heard a shot and felt the impact just below my right knee. I dropped to the carpet and clutched at my shin, feeling for a wet patch. He switched on a light. It took a moment for my eyes to adjust. There was no blood. The bullet had passed through the leg of my pants and out the other side without even grazing my skin.

'Martini?' he asked casually. I looked up. A tall man was standing at the edge of the bar, looking at me quizzically but not unkindly. The pistol hung from his right hand.

'Gervais?'

He nodded. This wasn't at all how I'd pictured the guy. Too handsome, too together, too good a shot.

'Put the gun down. I'm kinda fond of these legs.'

**to come home (to my location, my connection)
my machine hears me**

Found on Marshall Islands,
later dismissed as a Red herring

He smiled and placed it on the counter. I'd definitely underestimated him. I had him as some snivelling, nervy type, with a wet handshake, ready to sell any half-cocked story to the press for a few bucks and a bit of notoriety. This guy was roughly the same age as me, though time had treated him better, well-dressed, tanned, and muscular in an easy kind of way, not pumped up. Above all he seemed sane.

I asked myself where I'd got my image of Gervais from, an image which had not been dislodged by the orderly, tasteful Hollywood home, or the handsome little British car parked outside. No, it was Mrs Bolam, and even then I guess I was reading into what she said, forming my picture from the clues she gave me. I had the geography right, here he was, exactly where I'd figured he would be, and yet it wasn't the man I'd imagined, but a man who at first glance looked very like myself.

'I thought you were Goerner,' he said, as he stood behind Mantz's bar and mixed two Martinis in highball glasses.

through an ear in the engine
and with hums
responds

I got up from the carpet, perched on the edge of a large orange leather sofa, and pulled a crumpled card from my inside pocket. 'Here'.

He glanced at it. 'Mrs Bolam sent you, I presume.' He passed me a Martini. He had mixed it good and strong. He sat on a barstool, a reassuring distance from his gun.

'Who's Goerner?' I asked.

He sighed, as if this character wasn't worth wasting words on. 'Radio guy, pudgy looking face, thinks he knows what happened to Amelia Earhart and Fred Noonan and is real interested in making sure no-one else gets a piece of the pie. He's got some big money behind him, and he is doing his best to wreck my investigations. He's pretty unscrupulous. At one point I had some funding to go to the Pacific, but after Goerner spoke to my backers they pulled out.'

'You were expecting him?'

'No not really'. He laughed.

I told him about the little visit the FBI had paid me. He grimaced. 'I hadn't figured on the government getting involved. Why'd you think they want the photo so badly? '

I offered him a cigarette. He took it, and smiled as I took out the Carlita's matchbook. I lit both cigarettes with the last match and put the empty cardboard folder back in my pocket.

'If its the photo I think it is', I paused. He nodded. I told him about my Pearl Harbor theory, and about the Japs in the Oldsmobile.

He asked about the state of his home, and seemed relieved when he realized they probably hadn't seen the phone pad. It occurred to both of us that both the FBI and the Japs could turn up here.

'Where's the photo?'

'Not here', he said. 'I met Mantz at Santa Ana and gave it to him. He gave me the keys to this place. We should be safe – there's an alarm which goes off when a car approaches the drive so we'll know if we have any unexpected visitors.'

We. Funny how I was on his side now. Maybe I should leave, since the photo wasn't there, but something made me want to stay, made me feel that we were investigating the same case. And what I'd been feeling earlier in Carlita's, about how pointless it was investigating a case that had long been closed, didn't hold

Corroded Airplane parts recovered from Tanapag Harbor, Siapan, during the authors 1960 expedition.

The controversial generator is at left.

U.S. Navy photograph.

but acts upon whim
not calculated decision
its memory box

any more. It all seemed very recent, as if Earhart had only just disappeared. Here I was, in the home of her long time technical advisor and possibly lover, and there were photographs of Earhart on every wall. I got up and studied one.

Gervais came up and stood beside me. He handed me another Martini. 'Good looking woman. Slept in that leather coat to make it look used, and always wore pants. In those days, she was pretty unusual. Mantz doesn't think much of her as a flier. Technically, that is. He has a huge admiration for her daredevil attitude though. Pretty much like his own. You know he's a stunt man now.'

He pointed to another photo, showing Mantz on a film set. 'He's working on another film right now. Flight of the Phoenix. They're filming out in the Nevada Desert. It's supposed to be the Sahara, but they figure Nevada will do.'

He laughed. I could tell Gervais was a precise man. For him as for me, the devil was in the details.

'Tell me about Mrs Bolam,' I said.

'Sure'. He pointed to the glass sliding door. 'Do you mind if we sit outside by the pool?'

We reclined in semi-darkness on white vinyl loungers. The garden smelled of rosemary, of creosote bushes and faintly of chlorine.

I told him what Mrs Bolam had told me.

'She's a smart lady,' he said, 'she told you the truth but only up to a point. I said I'd return the photo in exchange for some information she's holding back.. At first she was really helpful, got out lots of old photographs of Earhart.'

'Then a picture slipped out', I said. 'A picture she didn't want you to see.'

'Mm. Guess she forgot it was there. My first thought was to take it just so Goerner couldn't have it. You see, ostensibly, it proves his Saipan theory. Ostensibly, it's the one Jackson saw… you met Jackson?'

'Yeah,' I said, touching my bruised eye.

"Well', Gervais said, 'I think he saw what he says he saw, but this photo isn't it.'

I waited for him to explain. A cicada near me was suddenly silent. 'It's a photograph of a Japanese soldier standing with Earhart. The captor and the captured. Only it's not Saipan. It looks to me more like a patch of airfield I happen to know well, just outside Tucson, Arizona. Apparently, Earhart landed there on

telling tales after me
telling its tales
(use the cameras to catch our speed)

A copy of a photograph found by U.S.Forces in a Japanese officers house on Saipan in June 1944.

her way to Miami in '37 and had an engine fire on take-off which caused some delay. But I'm not sure that its even Earhart in the photo, it could be Bolam.'

'Bolam?'

'Yeah. You know Paul Mantz had already told me she bore a strong resemblance to Earhart. He'd met her once, a year before Earhart's disappearance. Amelia had just acquired the Lockheed Electra and he was teaching her to fly it. It's a heavy plane and takes some handling. One day this girl turns up with Earhart, very much like her, they could have been twins, Mantz said, and she sat in on the lessons, even having a go at the controls sometimes. Earhart was seeing a lot of Jackie Cochran, and apparently she turned up too for a try at the new plane.'

'You think the three of them were up to something?'

Well, I'm convinced the photo is a deliberate fake. And Mantz says something was definitely up with Earhart. She didn't really like socializing, she was only happy in the sky. She liked the danger and the isolation and she didn't like what

so work on some numbers
guess some figures
and fake some maths
our movement ceases

Ariel view of Western tip of Saipan Island showing airstrip closest to Garapan City.
authors photograph 1962

Putnam had turned her into. He thinks she wasn't in love with Putnam and wanted a way out, though maybe that's sour grapes. Looks like they had one thing in common: a talent for faking evidence. Putnam once planted an Eskimo skull in Death Valley during an archaeological dig. It certainly caused some confusion.'

'So you don't think Earhart is alive and well and living as Mrs Bolam?'

He shrugged, 'I think she and Cochran know something. They're very close. Cochran's had some recognition now but it was hard for lady pilots of that generation. In the war they were virtually grounded.' He paused, then said 'I went to see Cochran, before I came here.'

'What's her story?' I asked

my controls are left
now left without
for now all the hours are recorded

evidence found California during authors 1960 expedition

'Same old same old', Gervais replied. 'Earhart and Noonan die at sea though not instantaneously. Remember her psychic vision?'

'That phony stuff. I still don't understand why they 'd go to the trouble of faking this photo and then support the crashed at sea theory.'

'They didn't at first. At first Cochran said the plane had crashed near the Itasca, which was the US Coast Guard ship acting as radio contact for Amelia. She also claimed to 'see' a Japanese fishing boat in the area. She was laying the ground for the Japanese involvement theory.'

'What about the Japanese soldier in the photo?' I asked.

'You're going to love this,' he laughed. 'Cochran's gardener --Josie's uncle.'

I nearly dropped my Martini. 'How d'you know Josie?' I asked weakly.

by miles on the clock
which stays ticking
and then is stuck clicking

'I met her a while back. You know the theory that Earhart was Tokyo Rose?'

I didn't.

'I was following up this theory and met Josie because she's involved in campaigning for a Presidential pardon for Iva Toguri who was imprisoned for being Tokyo Rose. I figured Josie might know something about who Tokyo Rose actually was. It turns out there were several women broadcasting in English from Japan, but Tokyo Rose never actually existed.'

'Did Mrs Bolam know Josie too?'

'No, I guess that was a coincidence, that she came to you. She had no reason to think Josie would know me. Josie tipped me off. Came out to meet me this morning, and I showed her the picture. I had no idea it was her uncle until she said so. She's pretty concerned. Her uncle was treading on sensitive ground, dressing up like that. She knows I won't publish it. I think she figured if we met up I could explain the situation to you.'

wipe clean the dirty screen
and smell that fuel and metal and air
and let me look at your face

pieces of fuselage, Marshall Islands. (June 1944). authors photograph

Little Josie. So it wasn't happenstance that she had known so much about the Amelia Earhart mystery. Josie had been putting me here, setting up this encounter.

'So you see I was expecting you.'

I smiled sweetly. 'Yeah, thanks for the welcome party.'

We sat there for a long while, listening to the cicadas and staring out into the warm darkness beyond the pool. Finally I remembered the matchbook.

'You wrote Gardner on the matchbook you left at Bolam's . That refer to Josie's uncle?'

'No actually it doesn't,' he said. He leaned forward on his lounger and I could see his profile against the reflected light on the water. It struck me again how much he looked like me.

'It refers to another theory. Gardner is an uninhabited island in the Pacific. Belonged to the British during the war. Apparently some bones were found there in '39. Its the one thing I haven't followed up yet.' He paused. 'I don't like to think of her dying of starvation on an island like that.'

being such a good match
then go buy a ticket
and give me half.

powder compact later identified as that of "American woman flier". found in sand on beach Jaluit Atoll.

I thought of the tough and dignified Mrs Bolam and the leather clad grinning girl in the photos. I looked up at the wide open desert sky, and the thin pale moon like a dirty nail clipping. Me neither.

Postscript

The best known "conspiracy theory" book about Amelia Earhart is The Search for Amelia Earhart by the San Francisco radio broadcaster Fred Goerner, published in 1966. It concluded that Earhart and Noonan had crashed into the ocean, spent time on one of the Marshall island, and were picked up by a Japanese fishing vessel and taken to Saipan. Joseph Gervais was an Air Force pilot and accident investigator who initially argued that Earhart was a US government spy. In 1965 he met a woman named Irene Bolam and became convinced she was Earhart. His research was eventually partially published in 1970 by another pilot, Joe Klaas, in Amelia Earhart Lives. Mrs Bolam subsequently sued Gervais for harassment. The stuntman Paul Mantz was killed when the makeshift plane he was flying crashed during the filming of The Flight of the Phoenix on July 8th 1965. That same year the pilot Jackie Cochran was invested in the International Aerospace Hall of Fame. Her autobiography, The Stars at Noon (1955) detailed her and Earhart's clairvoyant visions. In the 1990s the organisation TIGHAR (The International Group for Historic Aircraft Recovery) recovered artifacts from Gardner island (now Nikumaroro) including aircraft parts and remnants of an woman's shoe. In 1997 a file of British colonial correspondence was found in the national archives of the Republic of Kiribati in Tarawa which confirmed that human remains and other artifacts had been found on the island in 1940. At the time, analysis of the bones had concluded that the individual was probably male, but in 1998 TIGHAR located the report and forensic anthropologists suggested that the skeleton was a white female, about 5 feet 7 inches tall. A TIGHAR press statement concluded 'We have probably the most dramatic archival and scientific evidence in 61 years to indicate that we may soon know what happened to Amelia Earhart."

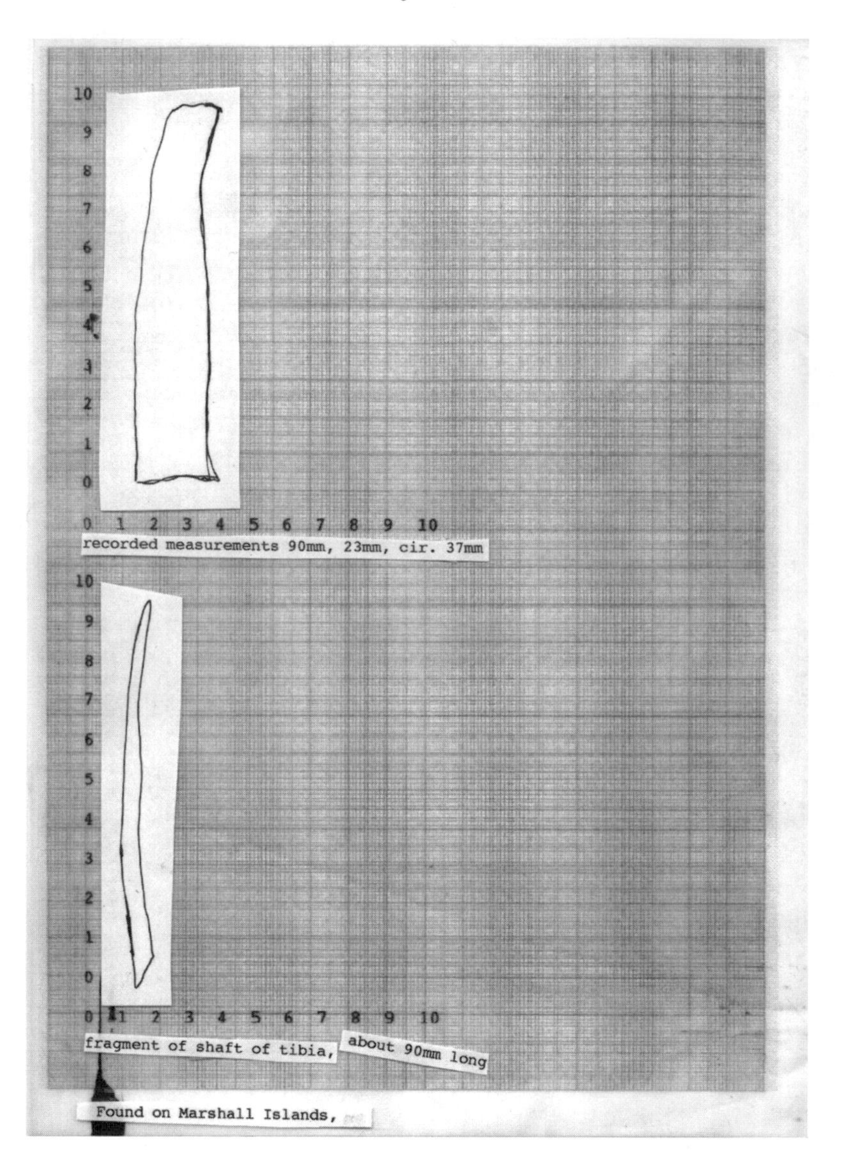
10
9
8
7
6
5
4
3
2
1
0
0 1 2 3 4 5 6 7 8 9 10
recorded measurements 90mm, 23mm, cir. 37mm
10
9
8
7
6
5
4
3
2
1
0
0 1 2 3 4 5 6 7 8 9 10
fragment of shaft of tibia,
about 90mm long
Found on Marshall Islands,